Damn you, John Christie!

The Public Life of Australia's Sherlock Holmes

John Lahey

W0007269

State Library of Victoria
Melbourne

State Library of Victoria
328 Swanston Street
Melbourne
Victoria 3000

First published 1993
© John Lahey 1993

Text design & typesetting by the State Library of Victoria
Original jacket illustrations by Mina Shafer copyright ©
Printed by Brown Prior Anderson Pty Ltd
5 Evans Street, Burwood 3125.

National Library of Australia Cataloguing–in–Publication data:

Lahey, John.
Damn you, John Christie! : the public life of Australia's Sherlock Holmes

Bibliography.
Includes index.
ISBN 0 7241 9943 8.

1. Christie, J.M. (John Mitchell), b.1845.
2. Detectives – Victoria – Biography.
3. Crime – Victoria – History.
I. State Library of Victoria.
II. Title.

363.25092

For Jenny Holinger

Contents

		Page
List of illustrations		ix
Acknowledgements		xi
Preface		xiii
Chapter 1	"Stand or I'll fire"	1
Chapter 2	Take that, you bully	11
Chapter 3	Fighting among themselves	25
Chapter 4	Life with the Duke	41
Chapter 5	Driving the boss mad	61
Chapter 6	Did he sleep with Mrs. Walker?	79
Chapter 7	Doing a dirty deal	93
Chapter 8	Hanging by a pigtail	103
Chapter 9	Playing the old banjo	117
Chapter 10	Otto Berliner strikes again	135
Chapter 11	The nursery of crime	145

Chapter 12   Drawing his trusty Colt   157

Chapter 13   Whisky on the rocks   171

Chapter 14   Bamboozling the lawyers   183

Chapter 15   Swindlers beware!   195

Chapter 16   The Sherlock Holmes   217
                  connection

Appendix   245

Conversion table   249

Notes   250

Bibliography   271

Index   277

List of Illustrations

Page

The young Detective Christie   *frontispiece*

Christie arresting Tom Delaney at Warrnambool   49

The Nirranda still raid   49

Christie's Melbourne   50

Melbourne in 1869   52

View of Melbourne, 1871   52

Foundation stone laying – Melbourne Town Hall   54

The Eastern Market   54

Bourke Street looking east   55

Bourke Street and the Post Office   55

Frederick Standish   56

Superintendent Charles Nicolson   57

Superintendent Power LePoer Bookey   57

Prince Alfred, Duke of Edinburgh   58

Christie disguised as a sailor   58

Melbourne's city blocks 1856 and 1993   59

The Theatre Royal, Bourke Street, 1860   60

Olinda Dowling – a Melbourne prostitute   60

Christie as a three year old in Scotland in 1848   125

Champion sculler of Victoria, 1876   125

Sir Harry Wollaston   126

Smugglers and their dodges   127

Hussey Malone Chomley   128

Tom O'Callaghan   129

Superintendent Frank Hare   130

Christie & the New Zealand police commissioner   130

The Customs House, Melbourne in the 1870s   131

Customs men arrest a Chinese smuggler 1895   131

Newspaper reaction to the Harry Weenan case   132

Duke and Duchess of York in Australia, 1901   132

Christie boxing Abe Hicken, 1876   205

Sherlock Holmes trounces a ruffian   205

Christie disguised as a 'Salvo'   206

Holmes as a 'simple minded clergyman'   206

Christie as a swagman   207

Holmes as a 'common loafer'   207

Holmes matches a slipper to a bloodmark   208

Christie in his Christy Minstrel outfit   209

As a tinker Christie infiltrates the Nirranda district   209

Watching a suspect house   210

A picture of Christie late in life   210

Christie's grave — Box Hill cemetery   211

Pro Rege   211

Christie's Christmas card   212

Acknowledgements

The State Library of Victoria readily granted the author permission to publish the Christie manuscripts and items from the Christie scrapbook. Special thanks are due for the kindness of staff of the library's manuscripts collection, which was led during this research by Desmond Cowley. The author also acknowledges a debt to the Public Record Office of Victoria, at Laverton, and particularly to Ian MacFarlane, who was so skilled in tracing documents; to the Police Historical Unit and its director, Gary Presland, for help and interest which did not flag; to Dr. Mimi Colligan for alerting the author to little-known material about Otto Berliner; to Lucy Sussex of the University of Melbourne, for imparting her knowledge of early Australian detective fiction; to Helen Doxford Harris for expert research; to Mary O'Callaghan and Anne Crooks, Delaney family descendants; to Ellena Biggs, who scanned some of the old newspapers of the Western District; to Lorenzo Iozzi of the Royal Historical Society of Victoria; to Darren Watson of Australian Archives; to the Police Media Unit, and to others who contributed bits here and there, all of it important.

Joanne Gourley stood apart as a tireless and excellent research assistant. It was she who perceptively traced a relationship between John Christie's writing style and that of other Australian authors influenced by the Sherlock Holmes phenomenon.

Preface

Scorning danger as he dropped through a roof; or donning disguise as he chased the lawless; or flourishing his Colt revolver in a tight spot, John Mitchell Christie cavorted through the latter half of 19th century Melbourne as a fearless, cunning, intelligent detective who always caught his prey. "Damn you, John Christie!" or similar words spilled from the lips of many a criminal who turned in surprise too late, and discovered he was trapped. Christie was almost too good to be true, for he was also a champion boxer and champion sculler; he raised large sums for charities; he twice was bodyguard to royalty; he had the manners of a gentleman and the toughness of an ox. We know all of this because Christie himself told us so in J.B.Castieau's book, *The Reminiscences of Detective-Inspector Christie* (George Robertson & Company Propty Ltd., Melbourne, 1913).

Three events in the 1980s have led to this new look at him. The first event was a decision by the Victoria Police to employ a public servant named Ted Collins to bring order to the voluminous, scattered and chaotic files which spanned its history from 1852. Working alone at first, and then with volunteers, Mr Collins, who is now dead, brought such order to the files that they are now lodged in 500 boxes at the Public Record Office, Laverton. They are in steady public demand and are easy to manipulate if you know what you are looking for. To untie the fading red tape and unfold the old paper is to peer at great treasure, rich beyond any expectation.

The second event leading to Christie was Superintendent Robert Haldane's doctoral thesis on the history of the Victoria Police, subsequently published as the book, *The People's Force* (Melbourne University Press, 1986). Given the complex topic, this is a work of stunning research, lucid detail and vivid reporting. *The People's Force*, which takes a sweeping look at history, made it possible for others to focus on mere aspects, and at the same time to be aware of a fuller background.

We come to the third event. It occurred in March 1991, when the anonymous owner of some of Christie's manuscripts put them up for auction in Melbourne. The State Library of Victoria already owned one of Christie's scrapbooks (three others apparently are lost) and it began hustling up money to bid. In the background was the Police Historical Unit, anxious to see the manuscripts find a suitable home, and ready to subsidise the library's offer. As things turned out, the Australian Customs Department, through its national history project, gave the library enough money to bid successfully.

Christie is historically important to customs, because he finished his career as a famous customs detective-inspector, full of honour. In fact, he spent the bulk of his career—perhaps the most exciting part of it—as a customs man. Anything he wrote about customs is additionally valuable because most of the department's colonial records in Victoria have vanished; but Christie endures. A relative-by-marriage of Christie, two generations on, still lives in Melbourne. She says her late husband could remember many Christie documents in the house when he was young. During the Depression of the 1930s, her husband's mother, tired of moving goods in moonlight flits, made a bonfire of everything that was not immediately needed. In this way, Christie's documents were destroyed.

The three events we have considered—the work of Ted Collins, the publication of Robert Haldane's book and the surprise appearance of Christie's adventures in his own hand-writing— gave a new generation the first chance in 77 years to re-evaluate him. The first task was to establish that this was indeed Christie's writing. There is no doubt of it. As he got older, the clear, confident, well-shaped words of his youth (preserved in the Ted Collins documents) became slightly scrawled; but his distinctive characteristics are obvious.

The second task was to establish that any police investigation which Christie wrote about had in fact taken place. Therefore, Christie's manuscripts were compared with the old police records which were now so freely available. This was wonderfully rewarding. In every case in which such a comparison was possible, Christie was correct. Yes, he did chase Chinaman Jack and Tommy the Dancer.

Yes, the courts did praise him; and his department did give him many rewards. Some of Christie's manuscripts tell the same stories as those in J.B.Castieau's 1913 book. Probably, Christie wrote them for Castieau as the raw material.

Nobody can possibly know how many cases Christie acted in. Certainly hundreds during his eight-and-a-half years in the detective force. There were hundreds more for the Victorian and Australian customs departments, which lack verifying documents such as the police papers. The research involved reading scores of 19th century newspapers, and occasionally they would yield a story that appeared in neither the manuscripts nor other records. The result of this is that I have drawn on all available resources to tell the Christie story in a fresh way, taking everything as fact. The story reads better that way. Nothing here is invented, although a few minor things, such as isolated newspaper reports, are beyond confirmation.

This book contains a lot of dialogue. None of it is spurious. It is scrupulously reproduced from Christie's writing or that of his contemporaries, and this too is presented as fact because it is more satisfactory to say, "*Stand or I'll fire!*" Christie said, than "*Stand or I'll fire!*" Christie allegedly said. The only thing I have altered is Christie's punctuation. He was an excellent speller, but he did not bother much about quotation marks, and seldom about commas. This deficiency makes him difficult to read at a glance. What about his literary style? Ah, this comes later and is the big surprise.

Finally: a few ugly things have come to light. No man is totally good.

John Lahey,
Melbourne,
January 1993

CHAPTER 1

"Stand or I'll fire!"

When Detective John Mitchell Christie received orders in 1893 to seize illicit stills in the Victorian bush, he went to his wardrobe for a disguise. He was always doing this. The man should have been on the stage. Disguised as a Salvation Army officer, he would try to sell you the *War Cry*; disguised as a negro minstrel, he played a banjo and sang requests. Acting as bodyguard to royalty, he dressed as a sailor from the royal yacht. In a thrilling career of chasing criminals, he had also posed as a parson, swagman, railway porter, ship's steward, horse cabbie, street sweeper, surveyor, opera lover, haughty foreigner and helpless drunk. Now he decided to be a tinker.

The thing about Christie was that he lived every part he played. It was not enough for him simply to dress as a tinker; he needed to act as one, so he went to a Melbourne tinsmith and spent three weeks learning enough of the trade to look competent. From his wardrobe he took old clothes and a blanket-swag, which he bundled up with some borrowed tools and some special boots. One of these boots had an iron heel, which made him limp. He sent the lot to a trusted farmer near Warrnambool in the Western District. Soon Christie quietly joined him and disguised himself. Inside his singlet he hid a revolver.

He intended to limp 20-odd miles to Nirranda, where he knew that moonshiners were operating stills. Before Christie set out, the farmer told him: "Your own mother would not know you," and added: "Remember, if you make the slightest false step, the gang will settle you quick, as they have frequently said if they catch any detectives near their drum they would make poteen out of them, the same as was done to Fitzpatrick in Ireland." Christie replied: "If they try that game on, I have a good revolver in my shirt, and some of them will lose the number of their mess."

1

Christie was camped that evening at a small lagoon which he named the Red Waterhole, when a mounted constable named Snowden rode up and questioned him. The two men knew each other slightly, but Snowden did not recognise Christie. Snowden said there had been some larcenies at Terang, and he would have to search Christie's swag and clothing. Fearing that the constable might feel his revolver if he kept his clothes on, Christie took off his vest and shirt and handed them over. The revolver remained under his singlet. Finding nothing, Constable Snowden went away.

Christie knew this district well, for he had once walked it as a swagman from Cape Otway to Warrnambool, secretly preparing detailed maps of where he believed stills were hidden. It was an Irish district, close-knit. Christie appeared to be a tattered old man living on damper and scraps, but he ate well, for food was buried for him at certain spots in a zinc-lined case.

His main quarry on this present trip was Tom Delaney, a thick-set, muscular man, who was said to be producing 100 gallons of whisky a week. Delaney labelled the whisky 'Mountain Dew', and put the official government stamp on it, an act which probably annoyed customs as much as the distilling itself. Everyone knew 'Mountain Dew'. It was popular at district weddings; and at the Koroit races one day, it was the only drink on sale, and by the end of the second race everyone is said to have been "in a fighting mood".

Christie seems to have been obsessed with Delaney, whom he regarded as the leader of a gang of desperadoes and whom he had prosecuted two years earlier on a smuggling charge. Delaney had been caught carrying a small quantity of liquor away from a beach after the barque *Fiji* had been wrecked on rocks at Moonlight Head and had strewn its cargo over the shore. Christie called Delaney's men 'the Kelly gang', even though the great Ned had no connection with it and had been dead for 13 years. Christie kept referring to them as smugglers, although he was now tracking moonshiners.

Continuing his tramp towards Nirranda, Christie called at all the settlers' places along the way, asking if he could mend anything. Each settler referred him to another, a practice which made him seem well-known. "On getting to Maloney's," Christie wrote later, "I did

2

several small jobs for the missus such as soldering some tins and putting in a few rivets in a boiler, for which I charged her two shillings." He took a shilling of this in grub (food) and one shilling in cash. "I was now close to the smugglers' retreat, so I had to use great caution", he said.

Soon Christie reached the Delaney house, where Tom's wife greeted him cautiously. But she gave him a few small jobs, and paid him a shilling. As he was leaving, she hailed him and said: "If I thought I could trust you, I have another job wants doing." He replied: "You can depend on me, but what is up?" She said: "I have a pipe that wants mending, but that damned fellow Christie might be about, and if he came along we would have bad luck." When Christie asked why, she said: "Did you not see that he was down the forest about a month ago and seized Long Wilson's still and had him convicted for it?" Christie replied: "I was aware of it, but I have no truck with coves like Christie as he would as soon pot me as anyone else if he nicked me making a still or a worm for any of the boys." (The worm was a coiled tube connected to the head of a still. In this vapour was condensed.)

Mrs Delaney seemed satisfied, and said: "Tom is away from home, but I will get the worm and bring it to you to see if you can mend it." She made Christie sit in the kitchen as she left, and he tried as best he could to see which direction she took. Two little girls were with him. After about ten minutes, he told them he would put his billy on and make a drop of tea, as their mother might be some time if she had far to go. The younger one replied: "Oh! She won't be long. She has only gone across the creek to Sparks's to get it." The elder girl told her to shut up. "That was enough for me," wrote Christie, "I now knew where the still would be."

Mrs Delaney returned with the worm after about 15 minutes. A horse had trodden it out of shape. Christie said it could not be mended but his boss could make a new one out of copper for £5. She said: "It is all very well talking about getting a new one, but the job is to manage it without being caught by that old bugger Christie." Christie said: "If you give me the order, you can bet Christie won't drop on the worm, as I will put it in a bag of chaff and bring it down by the back track myself." He left, promising to deliver the worm by daylight on New Year's Eve.

When Christie got back to Melbourne, he arranged to seize the still in a few days time, and he sent coded messages to constables at Camperdown, who were to rendezvous with him on the night beforehand. Christie was not a police detective at this stage; he had left the police department and joined customs, where he eventually rose to the rank of detective inspector. The customs department hated illicit stills, for their owners could sell spirits at five shillings a gallon at a time when the taxed price was 16 shillings. This difference in price was not all excise, but it provides some idea of the amount of revenue the government lost. It ran into thousands of pounds.

Having made his arrangements, Christie left Melbourne by train with Inspector Tyrrell of the police, who was to act as his assistant. "We were both well-armed," Christie wrote, "as we were given to understand that we might expect a warm reception from the Delaneys." When the train reached Colac, Christie jumped into the guard's van with his swag, and disguised himself as an old sundowner with a bandaged eye. He got out at Camperdown station. Shouldering his swag, and limping along the platform, he adopted a stoop to make himself look shorter. The only notice he attracted was from two small boys, one of whom said: "That old man has a string halt" (a lameness peculiar to horses).

Christie accidentally bumped into Mounted Constable Snowden, who failed to see that this was the tinker from the Red Waterhole, and who said: "Where the devil are you going to? Can't you see?" Christie passed on without replying, and met Tyrrell and Mounted Constable Arthur at an arranged spot. Arthur was a staunch colleague, one of two men who had buried food for Christie in the zinc-lined case on the previous long walk. The other was the Warrnambool farmer.

Christie, Tyrell and Arthur went to the Camperdown police station and until they explained matters, Inspector Kilmartin thought Christie was a prisoner whom Arthur had just brought in. They heard Snowden coming, and Kilmartin, playing a joke, told Christie to sit on a form. When Snowden came in, Kilmartin told him to lock up that old man for insulting behavior. Snowden put his hand on

4

Christie's shoulder and said: "Come on, old man, into the logs" (an old expression for watchhouse). When Christie raised his head and began to smile, Snowden said: "Why, this is the cove that nearly knocked me over at the station." It dawned on him that he had been tricked for the third time.

The Red Waterhole was Christie's telegrammed code for the rendezvous he had arranged with the police for the following day. Christie, Tyrrell and Arthur spent the night at Cobden. They kept under cover all the next day, and at dusk a butcher's cart drove into the police station. Christie and Tyrrell lay down in it, hidden by corn sacks, and were driven about eight miles into the Heytesbury Forest to a place where Arthur joined them with their horses.

They rode through swamps up to their saddle pads, and over ranges, until they reached the Red Waterhole about 9 p m. This is where they were to meet Constables Snowden and Jones, who were riding from Tanmure. At the Red Waterhole, Constable Arthur imitated the mopoke's call, and received a reply almost immediately.

Christie wrote: "We had to act with great caution as if any of the settlers or cockatoos or wood-splitters saw us, a bush telegraph would be sent through the forest to warn the Kelly Gang." It is true that the bush people would not have hesitated in this, for the illicit whisky was their staple liquor. Even mounted constables were said to leave demijohns at arranged places in the bush, expecting to come back and find them filled. This whisky for the police was put through the still twice to make it stronger. It was not the populace who wanted the stills seized; it was the customs department, worried about revenue, and the police department, trying to enforce an unpopular law.

"After having a nip, we started on our difficult journey across mountains, gullies and creeks," wrote Christie. "The night was dark and made the journey dangerous. On getting to the river we found the bridge had been washed away by the floods which were then running a banker. We had to make a detour of three miles to get to another bridge higher up the creek, and we had the misfortune to find it also gone. Arthur suggested we should swim for it. As it was pitch dark and the current was running six miles an hour, I would not allow it, as it looked like courting death. The only other bridge was

5

five miles higher up, so we pushed on for it at extra speed as I had to be at Nirranda at 2 a.m., just before daylight.

"We were in luck's way as the other bridge was standing, so we crossed the old log structure (over) the devil's punchbowl, and the water was running level with the top. As we ascended the mountain after crossing, we heard a roar and crash. Arthur said: 'There goes the bridge,' which was a fact. The shaking our horses had given it started it, and the bridge was swept downstream."

By coming this way, the party had to pass up a dangerous gully close to the house of a noted sympathiser named Deasy, who had a yelping dog. They had to get rid of it. Constable Arthur went by himself on foot with a lump of meat, and soon returned, saying the dog would not bother them. "We made no inquiries as to how he had pacified the animal," said Christie. They quickened their pace, and after a rough journey got to where Christie had arranged to be at 2 a.m.

They boiled the billy and began to eat breakfast, and suddenly saw Deasy galloping up the road after them. He had heard the sounds of several horsemen passing through his yard and, suspecting what they were up to, he was riding furiously to give the alarm at Nirranda. Christie jumped on his horse and bailed him up.

"I had no right to do so," he wrote, "but I knew well that the game was up if we did not detain him." Christie commanded Deasy in the Queen's name to help him capture a still. Deasy said he would be damned if he would, not one little bit. Christie ordered him to remain with the party. Deasy agreed, and said: "I can't make out how you got past my place without my dog giving tongue, nor could I find the damned cur when I was saddling up."

"We now prepared for action, saw to our revolvers and started for the Delaneys," wrote Christie. "Just before daybreak we sighted Pat's house (he was Tom Delaney's brother). Deasy began to be very frightened and said, 'Oh! Murther, if they see me with yez boys they'll belave I'm an informer and it will be all up with old man Deasy, so for the love of old Ireland let me go back home'." Christie saw that Deasy could no longer do any harm, so he told him to go home, and threatened to arrest him if he went off the road or turned back.

Then the party "dashed for Pat's, bailed it up, ordered all the inmates into one room and put a constable in charge. We did the same at Jack Delaney's and his brother Tom's, but we only found a few appliances used in the manufacture of spirits, and all the casks and jars empty, in fact everything sold out for their Christmas customers. Mrs Tom Delaney told us if Tom had been at home he would have potted us with his government rifle.

"It was now daylight," wrote Christie, "and I collected my team together to make a dash for Sparks's place, which was a small selection across the creek. On arriving there, no-one was astir, so we surrounded the premises and called on the inmates to open the door. The two men and a woman were thunderstruck when I told them I was Detective Christie of the customs. We searched the two rooms, and in the back one we found a complete distillery and spirits."

Christie arrested Sparks, who was later fined £200, a huge sum for the times. He could not pay it, and went to gaol for a year. But the main quarry, Tom Delaney, had not been sighted, and there was no good evidence against him. Christie made up for this in 1894. For nights on end, sleeping in hollow trees or on the ground, Christie and Constable Arthur reconnoitred an area around a stream that became known as Whisky Creek. When they were certain they could catch moonshiners in the act, they arranged a night-time rendezvous with Constables Snowden and Jones, and the four of them crept through undergrowth on hands and knees towards a spot where they could hear men's voices.

The scrub was so thick that they could see nothing, and it took them an hour to get close enough to discern a hut made of saplings, open on one side. Then they saw everything clearly. By the light of a kerosene lamp and the glow from a fire, Tom Delaney and James Love were making whisky in a large still. Love came towards Christie and peered into the darkness without seeing him, and said: "Tom, there is someone about." Delaney said something about possums. Christie rushed them with his revolver drawn, shouting: "Stand or I'll fire. You are my prisoners."

The hut's walls were hessian bags, and Delaney ducked under them. Christie fired a shot in the air. Delaney shouted: "Come on!", and Christie thought he meant fight. He was hit by a piece of wood, and fired straight at Delaney, but he got away. Love and Delaney sped through the scrub on their hands and knees.

At daylight, Arthur and Jones tracked Love to his home, and brought him back. Other tracks led to Tom Delaney's, but he was not there. In a creek, however, the police found a cask with the initials JMC on it. Christie had made these marks the previous January when he found the cask at Delaney's house. Later, the initials were part of his court evidence.

James Love was a poor man struggling to keep a wife and five young children, and he had committed no previous offence. His lawyer tried to get Christie to say he did not want to press the charge except to secure the lowest penalty, which was a £50 fine or three months in gaol. Christie said: "I must leave that to the bench."

The police magistrate, Mr G.J.McCormick, told Love the government regarded moonshining so seriously that the penalty for it was the highest mentioned in any Victorian statute. It was impossible to estimate the amount by which such acts had defrauded the government year after year, he said. He gave Love the choice of a £250 fine (which he had no hope of paying) or a year in Geelong gaol.

Tom Delaney stayed at large for three weeks, and became something of a celebrity as he eluded police searchers. The big hunt did seem melodramatic. One newspaper reported that the police were wearing armour; and at this distance from the event, it is hard to know whether the report was meant as fact or satire. In either case, it reflected the public's view that the hunt was pompous. At one stage, the police stumbled into little-known Aboriginal caves, and found signs that someone had just been there. Quite casually, at 6.30 one morning, Delaney drove into Warrnambool and knocked on the door of Inspector Tom O'Callaghan, an old colleague of Christie's from the detective force. Delaney said he wanted to surrender, as he had heard there was a warrant out against him.

A crowd packed the court later that day to look at this elusive rascal who had been portrayed as a desperate man ready to use firearms if cornered, but when Delaney appeared he seemed sensible and inoffensive, smiling now and then at spectators whom he recognised. Once again, a lawyer used the family's poverty as a reason for seeking a lenient sentence; and Christie, when questioned, agreed that Delaney's family was suffering. "Judging from the appearance of the house," he said, "he is in poor circumstances."

The lawyer tried a different tack. He said 'Delaney's whisky' was known all over the district, and whenever people heard of whisky they associated it with Delaney; but the sins of others should not be visited upon him. Mr McCormick, PM, disagreed, saying the bench knew that Delaney had been distilling for years, and had been remarkably fortunate in remaining free while his employees and dupes got into trouble.

Because Delaney had been fined £25 for smuggling at the wreck of the *Fiji*, and because he was the principal in this latest case, the bench did not give him the option of a fine. Delaney got 18 months in gaol. Christie considered Delaney the last of the moonshine men in the Western District. After he was captured, the district went quiet. Again at this distance, Delaney seems a likeable man, who left behind him a legend of cheekiness and daring.

He was driving a load of whisky into Warrnambool one weekend, when the police bailed him up at Allansford Bridge. One policeman went to grab the horse's head, and the other began to climb in the back of the cart. Delaney whipped up the horse and both fell to the ground. One of them fired a shot which hit the steel stay of the back seat. Delaney sped away, dumped the whisky in a quarry and loaded the cart with cheese from a friendly farmer. Then he drove into Warrnambool police station to complain that two armed men had held him up at Allansford. On the following Monday, Fidler McKenzie, a quarry worker, turned up for work and found the whisky which Delaney had dumped. He and his mates had a spree for a week.

There is a Western District legend about Christie too. On his visits there, he sometimes stayed with Frank Allen, a member of the first Australian Cricket Eleven (1878), who was then a public servant. On the side, Frank Allen tanned skins and made furred rugs. On one visit, Christie handed him a piece of raw hide, and asked Mr Allen to tan it for him. Later, Mr Allen said: "Well, John, here is your hide, and a beautiful piece of leather it is; but I am curious to know what animal it was taken from." Christie replied: "Oh, you know So-and-so who was hanged at Pentridge; that is the skin off his back."

The Nirranda seizures earned Christie a £20 reward from the customs department; it was a high amount and a rare event. Christie became well-known for clearing out the moonshiners. Not that he needed fame; he had made his fame years earlier in the police department. This second career, in customs, was fame's bonus.

CHAPTER 2

Take that, you bully

Christie joined the detective force in 1867 by walking in off the street with a character reference. This was a normal way to do things. You did not need to be in the police force first. In fact, detectives and general police were different entities, despite answering to the same chief commissioner. Even their premises were different; the detectives were in Little Collins Street, and the general police were a couple of blocks away, and they were happy to keep each other at a distance. As years went by, they grew even further apart; they became enemies. But things were not too bad when Christie arrived. He walked in off Little Collins Street, presented his reference, demonstrated that he could read and write, passed a medical test, and that was that. Most of his colleagues became detectives the same way.

They received no training. They learned their job by going out to arrest people, and by listening to the older detectives gossiping in the muster room. One of these older men when Christie arrived was William Henry Manwaring, a grumpy-sounding man who had led a life of high adventure. He had served with the London Police, been decorated in the Crimean War at the Battle of Alma, taken part in capturing Mad Dog Morgan at Peechelba, and served as a mounted constable at Castlemaine under a different kind of madman, named Robert O'Hara Burke.

Manwaring had been among the Melbourne police called in to quell the convicts who assassinated their penal superintendent John Price at Williamstown in 1857, and he had once locked up a suspected horse thief named Thomas Castro. At that stage, the name meant nothing to Manwaring. Years later it hit him like a thunderbolt that Castro was the fraudulent Sir Roger Tichborne. Despite this crowded life, Manwaring was still only 42 when Christie met him. Christie was 21.

One of Manwaring's stories would almost certainly have reached Christie, for Manwaring was tremendously proud of it. It was the custom then to arrest wife deserters, and Manwaring had been assigned—or, in the detectives' language, 'told off'—Manwaring had been told off to bring in a man named Frost whose only known address was Geelong. The problem was that Geelong was too big a town in which to tramp the streets in the hope of tracing someone.

Manwaring was smart; he managed to get the name of Frost's former employer in Melbourne and, disguising the fact that he was a detective, he wrote to Frost care of the Geelong post office. The former employer, he said, had recommended Mr Frost as a reliable man to take a job looking after some dairy cattle at Essendon; was Mr Frost interested? Three weeks later Frost called at Manwaring's lodgings. Manwaring took him away and locked him up.

The story is important because of the way Manwaring remembered it many years later: "The success and the novelty of this capture gained me some reputation and it was described as one of pure detection, for frequently cases were got by impure detection, that is by one thief being secretly put away by another." Manwaring's tactic seems primitive now, but it was noteworthy then. The praise it earned is crucial to understanding the detective office in which Christie had just hung his bowler hat and sat down in the muster room.

Manwaring was speaking of the previous decade, but nothing had changed much. Primarily, the detectives were thief-catchers, and their method, almost without exception, was to use Judas criminals (whom they called fizgigs) to betray other criminals for reward. Without telephones, without fingerprints, without forensic science, without extensive criminal files, the detectives scarcely knew another way. It was a system that led to corruption, and it caused the detective force eventually to destroy itself.

But it was not a totally bad system in Melbourne of the 1860s, when the criminal class (which is what the detectives called crooks) was said to number 4000 in a population just above 140,000, and the city was still 20 years away from being labelled 'Marvellous Melbourne'. True, Melbourne was incredibly rich from gold, and it was among the jewels that the British Empire was proud to acknowledge as a product of its own magnificence; but it was a child among cities.

Melbourne was extraordinary really; it was still only 32 years old, carved from a wilderness. And now it sat in the beginnings of splendour; it had a university, handsome buildings, a parliament, lavish mansions, paved roads, reticulated water, gas mains, a railway system, a boisterous theatre life, a public service, a museum, an art gallery, an impressive public library, a growing sense of order and a powerful sense of destiny; but some of its habits were those of a village. Every morning, each detective would go to the watchhouse, look at the overnight prisoners, and try to memorise their faces. This was terribly important. Life was as simple as that.

Bourke Street at night, from the post office to Spring Street, was crowded with pleasure-seekers walking up and down. It was the favourite promenade of unwashed people, according to Manwaring who stoutly believed, as others did, that crime was a sickness, passed in a virus from one generation to another. Some of the ex-convicts from Van Diemen's Land displayed this virus in deformed bodies, and their hideousness, said Manwaring, was appalling— "hunchbacks, dwarfs, cripples etc. . . . a striking expression of their low type of character".

The lanes at the eastern end of Bourke Street contained "abodes of infamy", and when night fell, they spewed out their criminals who stalked forth unabashed and filled the bars and the vestibule of the Theatre Royal, in a noisy, drinking mob until midnight. Part of the Theatre Royal was a rendezvous of low-priced prostitutes, and was called the saddling paddock in Christie's day. The more elegant prostitutes walked Collins Street, dressing well and behaving with decorum, to lessen the chance that the businessmen who engaged them would attract notice. Prostitutes were everywhere. By 1870, the detective office had graded them into three classes, from the kept woman to the hopelessly low.

Both ends of Little Bourke Street were infamous, for the Vandemonians had spread their virus indiscriminately, and their progeny (according to the popular genetic theory) had inherited it unchanged. The Chinese drifters from the goldfields had not yet settled here in droves. At night the street was unsafe, and peaceful strangers were robbed quickly if they went there. "At night too the thief stole forth prowling all over the town and suburbs practising his guilty craft." Men were garrotted in Little Bourke Street.

Into such habitats walked a new detective named John Mitchell Christie, who was 21, well-born, well-educated and assertive. He had brown hair, blue eyes, a lordly manner and the voice and the bearing of a British gentleman. His clothes had style. A fawning member of the Melbourne Club once mistook him for a distinguished aide to the visiting Duke of Edinburgh—a peer perhaps. Christie had fun in keeping him guessing.

Christie often used his lofty appearance to fool suspects. At nearly 5ft 11ins (or about 180 centimetres) he was relatively tall, Ned Kelly's height. He was also a bit of a conman. In the back streets and alleys, in the rowdy, dangerous pubs, in the mean little houses and crowded pavements of criminal Melbourne, he could ease his way into anything. Disguised as a criminal, he lived like a criminal, drank and ate like a criminal and slept, it was said, with a criminal's wife.

On his first assignment with the detective force, Christie was told off to walk around the city and detect stray offenders. At the Eastern Market, where the Southern Cross Hotel was later built, he stood gazing at the first Chinaman (the universal word for a Chinese) he had seen. Something in the Chinaman's manner made him suspicious, and he followed him around the town.

The Chinaman came back to the market and stole two pairs of boots. Christie subdued him in a scuffle and set out to take him to the detective office, which was around the corner. New to Melbourne, Christie lost his way, wandered with the protesting Chinese for half-a-mile, and had the embarrassment of running into a police sergeant for whom he could not produce a detective's authority card. Sceptically, the sergeant took the two of them to the detective office, and sorted things out.

Christie was born into a military family at Clackmannan, Scotland, on 30 December 1845. His father, Captain James Christie, had served in India. His brother, also a captain named James, was later at the Relief of Lucknow with the Black Watch. Destined for the army, John Mitchell Christie was 17 when his father sent him to Taylor's

College, Woolwich. Because he was the only Scot in his group, other students taunted him and in retaliating, he found himself confronting the school bully in an organised fight refereed by a sergeant-major. Christie was beaten.

This is the beginning of a ripping yarn. Coming home on holiday, Christie learned that his father had heard about the fight and was sympathetic. His father took him to a London pugilist, Nat Langham, who taught Christie how to box with science, develop a straight left hand, and cope with the rough and tumble of Prize Ring rules, which pre-dated the use of gloves and rounds of a fixed time. Generally, a round ended when one of the contestants was knocked down.

In particular, Nat Langham showed Christie how to deal with brawlers who rushed their opponents. Returning to school, Christie fought the bully again, and this time his classmates carried him aloft after Christie won. Hooray, hooray; it was like a story from *Boys' Own Annual*. It was also the beginning of a notable boxing career which Christie indulged during his days as a detective, obviously in defiance of the law, for the open-air prize ring was illegal. Time and again in his memoirs, Christie talks about subduing offenders, and it is apparent that he is referring to his fists.

On one occasion, when larrikin pushes (gangs) were terrorising parts of Melbourne, Christie arranged with two visiting boxers, one of whom was the English champion Jem Mace, to go with him to Russell Street, a centre of trouble. Pretending to be drunk, the three men seemed an easy prey to the larrikins, who began to jostle them. The three stood in a triangle, shoulder to shoulder, and suddenly stopped acting drunk. As immovable as the Russell Street hill, they battered the larrikins to the ground, and routed them.

The worst push in Melbourne was said to be O'Leary's, which struck terror in Little Bourke Street and Stephen Street (later renamed Exhibition Street). Christie realised one night that O'Leary's gang had taken control of a low hotel called the Morning Star in Little Bourke Street, and its members were serving drinks and smashing the place up. Sending word to the detective office, he stayed watching. The larrikins learned the detectives were coming, and began to disperse.

Christie saw O'Leary coming up Little Bourke Street. As soon as O'Leary saw Christie, he lunged at him. Christie delivered one straight blow which smashed O'Leary's nose and knocked him through a pawnshop window. It was said that the detectives of these years, the late 1860s, inspired a fearful respect among criminals, who stood to attention as they passed.

Christie came to Australia because his mother's wealthy brother, Hugh Reoch, a Gippsland squatter and gold miner, wanted to make him his heir. The family held a conference and decided that Christie's future lay in Australia, not in the army. He arrived in Melbourne in 1863, and learned to ride rough horses and sleep on rough ground at Kilmany Park Station, in which Uncle Hugh was a partner. On the Gippsland Lakes, Christie became adroit in handling rowing boats, an experience that may have helped him later to become champion sculler of Victoria. He also became the friend of Tom Curran, a former boxing champion, who ran a boxing room next to a pub at Stringers Creek (Walhalla). Christie won local fame here by defeating a district champion called 'The Bruiser'.

Many kind and influential Gippsland men took an interest in Christie, and were on hand to support him in 1864 when he received news that his Uncle Hugh had been drowned in the Tara River. This part of Christie's life ceases to be a ripping yarn, and becomes a melodrama. The story is that Hugh's will, naming Christie as heir, was not dated (or not witnessed), and was therefore invalid. Christie stayed for about two years on various stations, but declined offers to settle in Gippsland among his uncle's friends.

Carrying good references, he went to Melbourne and took a job in which his employer, the stock agent Richard Gibson, wanted some private detective work done. Christie's task was to get information from a man belonging to a railway survey party, so he joined it as an axeman. This was his first experience of disguise. Not only did he get the information, he defeated the boxing champion of a rival camp.

Returning to Melbourne, he knocked out a well-known boxer called 'The Fighting Artilleryman' in a bare-knuckle fight at the Butchers Arms Hotel, and his admirers subscribed to a testimonial for him. Christie decided he wanted to become a detective. Richard

Gibson, who was happy about Christie's success in his one experience as a private detective, gave him a note to the chief of detectives, Superintendent Charles Nicolson: "The bearer cleared up the case I spoke to you about some time ago. He is good with head and hands."

This is all there was to it. Christie was taken into the force on 17 August 1867 and confirmed in January 1868 as a third-class detective on 9s. a day. When he became second-class, he would get 10s 6d, and when he became first-class, if he ever did, he would get 12s.6d. There was no such thing as overtime. Like all detectives, he worked a basic twelve hours a day, seven days a week. He could not marry without his superiors' permission, and he did not have the right to vote in the colony's elections.

The pay was not considered good, but detectives could legitimately supplement it in two ways. One way was through the Police Reward Fund, from which the chief commissioner, the sexually-liberated Captain Frederick Standish, doled out sums ranging from £1 to £5 to men whose good work was recommended to him by the head of detectives. Another way, far more lucrative, was the private reward. Private citizens or firms would offer £20, £50, even £100, in their anxiety to have cases solved.

This money was not directed at detectives specifically, but to people who might have information; however detectives got a good share of it. It was said at one stage that to be transferred from the country to Melbourne was worth £10 extra a week to a detective. But the private-reward system, like the fizgig system, led to corruption; detectives with knowledge that could solve a case withheld it until someone offered a reward; or they combined with criminals to organise a burglary, knowing that a reward was likely for the return of stolen goods.

Christie's colleagues over the next few years were an extraordinary group. Alcohol was one problem. Detective John Hudson, who was told off to go to Geelong to see a witness in a murder case, came back to Melbourne a day late, drunk, and freely admitted that he had been on a spree and had slept in some stables. When the question of punishing him was discussed, Nicolson made a plea to Standish: "I

17

would be sorry to lose so good a man and one so capable of doing his duty." Nicolson was telling the gospel truth, and Standish gave Hudson another chance. Then there was Thomas Walker who, finding his wife drunk in the kitchen, hit her twice on the head with a child's boot, and killed her. There was the unforgettable Fook Shing, the force's Chinese detective, who spent some of his time in gambling dens arresting his countrymen, and some of his time smoking opium and falling asleep on a form at the office. This was something which repelled the other detectives. Drink was one thing; but opium was not right.

A detective named Potts was sitting in the office in Little Collins Street one day when two mariners, Captain James and Captain Irving, who were talking in the street, annoyed him so much that he came outside and said if they did not go away quickly he would put them in the watchhouse. Captain James went inside to find out who this insulting person might be, and Potts came around the counter and pushed him out again. Once more it was Nicolson who interceded with Standish. Potts was guilty, but only to a certain degree, he told Standish; Potts had been interrupted in important clerical work; there had been fault on both sides. Standish thought differently. He ruled that Potts had interfered unduly with Captain James, and he suspended him from pay and reprimanded him severely.

Reading of such incidents—and there were scores—you can get the impression that of the 12 or 16 people who occupied the Melbourne detective office, only Superintendent Nicolson was thoroughly stable. This is wrong. Nicolson was stable all right, and he was an attractive human being of fairness and probity, but he did not run a crazy office. He had taken charge of the detective force in 1858 and reshaped it, and its reputation was high. People spoke of it as the Scotland Yard of the southern hemisphere. But in a drifting, murky population, it could not pick and choose the men it wanted.

Manwaring's early colleagues had included three or four ex-convicts from Van Diemen's Land (useful in catching thieves) and others who had failed as clerks and shopkeepers. "Some were quite unfit for anything," Manwaring said. Some legacy of this situation remained for Christie, and you can see why Nicolson fought to retain

Detective Hudson who had gone on a spree and slept in the stables: Hudson was a drunk, but he was competent. Christie, in turn, must have seemed a godsend: a sharp, intelligent, educated, physically-capable, articulate and personable young man, who was never in trouble over liquor and who knew what fork to use with dessert.

The colony's biggest event in 1867 was the arrival at Sandridge (Port Melbourne) of His Royal Highness, Prince Alfred, the Duke of Edinburgh, Queen Victoria's second son, who at 22 was a few months older than Christie. This was the first time that English royalty had visited Australia; and the Duke, who was a Royal Navy captain in command of *HMS Galatea*, was a figure of glamour, reverence and power to the largest crowds Australia had ever known.

The adulation was astonishing. On the day he stepped ashore in November, the crowd stretched from Port Melbourne to the Treasury, a distance of nearly four miles. From that moment, the Duke went through an exhausting round of balls, speeches, shooting expeditions, civic welcomes, inspection tours, theatre visits, race meetings, a levee, a torchlight parade and a country tour. Wisely, he avoided a free banquet that was organised to feed about 100,000 people, who became impatient waiting for him. They stormed the food tables, tapped a 500-gallon keg of wine and created an orgy.

Wherever the Duke went, the newspapers recorded his every move. Melbourne was besotted. Almost every building, even the smallest of the houses, carried a decoration that was illuminated at night. One of these illuminations was at the lunatic asylum at Yarra Bend. It said: "Welcome to our royal guest." The decorations at the detective office were Chinese lanterns.

The Duke had an irreverent streak. He called the Victorian Governor "a snuffy old bloke", and he shocked the Bishop of Melbourne after dinner one night, when the ladies had withdrawn, by referring to someone getting a kick in the backside. Bishop Perry looked grave. Perhaps the Duke knew he was being shocking, or perhaps he didn't, but he went on to say that the fellow who had done the kicking was induced to apologise—"but it's poor satisfaction, I should say, to get an apology after having one's backside kicked."

The Duke was coarse in other ways. Someone counted eleven

19

rings on his hands one night, massive gold affairs, such as those that earthy miners might wear. The rings were so thick that the Duke could not close his fingers. As the notable judge, Sir Redmond Barry, remarked, they made his hands look like the fins of a turtle.

By day, under the hot sun, as the Duke listened to speech after speech, and received endless gifts and scrolls of welcome, he seemed bored. But things were different at night. The Duke, a sexual hedonist, had found a companion in Captain Standish, the bachelor police chief, who lived at the Melbourne Club, the pinnacle of social acceptance for colonial men. Standish received an annual salary of £1200, and it was nothing for him to lose £400 at the racecourse. He gambled heavily, he slept little, he idled away his leisure playing billiards or cards, he dined in style every night, and once, at a particularly notable dinner, he sat naked women on black velvet chairs to highlight the whiteness of their skin. As an upper-class Englishman and a former officer in the Royal Artillery, Captain Standish was exactly the man to look after the Duke.

On the day that the Duke landed (the day of the vast crowd) Standish dined with the Duke's close friends from the royal party, Lord Newry and Eliot Yorke (the Duke's equerry) at the Melbourne Club, then took them to the most polished brothel in town, Sarah Fraser's, in Stephen Street, where no client did anything so crass as pay a fixed fee. At Sarah Fraser's, one availed oneself of the abundant liquor, and made various arrangements for an agreed consideration. It was in mid-December that Standish introduced the Duke to Sarah Fraser's.

They went to other places too. Standish's fellow member of the Melbourne Club, Curtis Candler, the coroner, wrote in his diary for 1 December 1867 that the Duke's party played billiards at the club, then: "He (the Duke) remained while a few strokes were played and then left with Yorke. Standish shortly followed and from what I hear this morning, I fancy they were cruising around town in suspicious quarters for some hours afterwards."

Candler wrote later: "I asked (Standish) what was done on Saturday night—or Sunday morning rather—after I went to bed; but he was disposed to draw a veil over the proceedings. He was very mysterious—from which I suspect that the trio—the Duke, Yorke and himself—had rather a fast night of it. It was whispered that the Duke went on board the *Galatea* with the milk. At the Casino, before I went home, I saw something going on that had a suspicious resemblance to pimping."

Standish and the Duke of Edinburgh did not break the law by going to brothels, which were not illegal in Melbourne; nor was prostitution. A prostitute could be prosecuted under the Vagrancy Act if she were creating a nuisance, but otherwise she was free to sell her body in the street, in her home, in a hotel or in a brothel. A belated attempt to regulate this situation was the Contagious Diseases Act (1878), which was proclaimed but never brought into force. Standish in fact used brothels as a device to gather intelligence. On his desk every morning, according to information given to the prominent lawyer, Butler Aspinall, a report of the night's patrons awaited him. In this way, Standish kept track of the high and the low. He also used brothels as a way to entertain visiting dignitaries.

One of Sarah Fraser's prostitutes followed the Duke to Sydney, and took a house in the city while he was there. A clue to her identity comes from Curtis Candler, who wrote in his diary on 15 December 1867: "That same evening I went to the 'Varieties', where I found Yorke, Standish (etc). The 'Psyche' was there in great force, and confided to me that she had been honoured by the Royal commands, with great exultation . . . . She leaves Melbourne for Sydney when the Duke goes there; so that I presume her fortune is made."

The 'Psyche' was almost certainly not Sarah Fraser, who was also known as Mother Fraser, a term that denotes somebody who is no longer young. Sarah Fraser, in an age when certain merchants proclaimed that they were under royal patronage because they sold goods to royalty, wanted to display the royal coat of arms outside her brothel, but she was dissuaded. There is no evidence to say Christie had a place in all this. Eventually, he and the Duke became surprisingly close, but at this stage they probably had not met.

The crew of the *Galatea* also enjoyed Melbourne. By December, 50 of them had deserted. At the Duke's request, the police searched high and low, but could not find them. The Duke stayed in Victoria for five weeks, then sailed the *Galatea* to Hobart and Sydney, where he continued to visit brothels. He was shot in the back during a picnic at Clontarf on 12 March. "Oh—my back is broken," he cried as he fell, seriously wounded by the bullets of a pathetic dipsomaniac, Henry James O'Farrell, who claimed he belonged to the Irish national movement, the Fenians, and had support from others. The poor man was mentally unstable, but the NSW government hanged him despite the Duke's protests.

Because O'Farrell had lived in Melbourne and Ballarat, Standish launched a huge hunt for Fenians in Victoria, and it was amazing how eager people were to point their fingers at innocent neighbors. At Stawell, someone reported, the Catholics were planning a meeting ostensibly to discuss their school debt, but really, the informer said, they were concerned with Fenian matters. Standish had already experienced an Orange-Green riot during the Duke's stay in Melbourne, and he was prepared to investigate anything. He sent a telegram to the Stawell informer: "You must concoct some plan for ascertaining what is done at the meeting."

Detectives dashed to dozens of spots where Fenian sympathisers were spuriously reported. Between Hanging Rock and Woodend, 25 men were reported to be drilling by night. It was pub talk. In country Victoria not one person out of the scores who were investigated could be linked to any revolutionary cause. The biggest scare was in Melbourne, where some of the Irish held a funeral procession to honour the recently-hanged Manchester Martyrs, and Standish authorised the cemetery gates to be shut. It did not make much difference that just before going to the gallows, O'Farrell confessed he had no connection with the Fenians and had acted without the collaboration of others.

The job of investigating all this fell to a few, notably Detective Tom O'Callaghan, one of the biggest larrikins in the force. Meanwhile, the other work of the detective office went on. It was surprisingly varied, but a lot of it was boring. Detective Kennedy, assigned to watch the ships coming in, reported there were no suspicious characters that he could see. Detective Martin Doherty took a steamer to Portland to investigate William Thompson's complaint that someone was setting fire to his fences at Lake Wallace; Doherty signed on as a boundary rider and slept in a hut with the other men.

Three men stole the poorbox from St Francis's Church, and Christie and Hannan caught them. Detective Peter Jennings, investigating lunacy, as was the detectives' custom, reported that G.F.Chapman, an inmate of the Immigrants' Home, was "much given to writing and labouring under the delusion that he has discovered a medicine which will cure all diseases," but this did not mean he was mad, Jennings said.

On any day of the year, the detectives were looking for what they called missing friends. From many parts of the world, people wrote to Melbourne to ask the police to find a relative or friend who had set off for Australia and not been heard of again. Sometimes a photograph of the missing person accompanied these pleas, and one cannot look at them now without feeling profoundly touched. These were of people so ordinary they were like the person down the street.

The photographs, now fading, were made with such hope and pride that one can imagine a whole excited family gathered around the photographer in his studio as the young son, or the father, took a deep breath to stifle his emotions and did his best to look indifferent. He was sailing away from England or Ireland to be separated from those he loved most in the world. How many mothers woke up sad every morning? How many sweethearts waited a lifetime? Standish was prompt in passing all of these pleas to the detective office.

In that constantly fluid society, people also became lost moving from colony to colony, or simply from town to town, or sometimes within Melbourne itself:

"Please look for boy named Matheson 14 or 15, light hair, weighs five stone, small features, sallow complexion, absconded from master's employ."

Robbery under arms was not uncommon. It came as close as the Treasury Gardens. There was also much talk about a series of crimes that became known as the Silk Robberies. Someone was raiding the great warehouses of Melbourne, stealing hoards of silk and other goods, and vanishing. This was unusually perplexing. At any other time, detectives could rely on gossip from the underworld to lead them to something, or to nothing, but now the underworld itself seemed baffled. Six months had passed since the last robbery, and not even rewards that reached the staggering sum of £250 could provide one clue.

It was surprising how many clues to various crimes came from the country, when men went on the run. All of the detectives did a stint in country districts, where they worked from smaller offices, travelled long distances in carts or on horseback, and handled cases that might not come their way in the city. In the Melbourne office, the chief of detectives issued bulletins which often reported their activities:

> "Detective Duncan arrived last night fromMaryborough with the stomach of a Chinaman (name unknown) for analysis where he was found dead in his bed at the Golden Age Hotel Maryborough."

At the end of 1868, there was a stir about Harry Power, a horse thief who was getting on in years and who had broken out of Pentridge prison where he was serving a long term. The stir became a sensation when old Harry took to the roads in north-eastern Victoria and began bailing people up. Eventually, the story spread that Power had an apprentice bushranger with him, a boy aged about 14, who held the horses. People liked this tale; it had a dash of romance and daring about it. When the boy was identified a few years later, he turned out to be someone called Edward Kelly, but nobody in Melbourne had heard this name.

CHAPTER 3

Fighting among themselves

It seems a pity that Christie joined the detective force when a man named Otto Berliner had already left it. The clash of their personalities might have been spectacular, for Berliner was eccentric on a grand scale; which is to say that he was a nuisance to everyone. He played a considerable part in the Christie story, yet some of the circumstances, as you will see eventually, remain mysterious.

But this is a good time to meet Otto Berliner. He was a Prussian who joined the detectives in 1859, aged 23. Manwaring relieved him once at Beechworth, and could not stand him. Manwaring called him a meddling, quarrelsome fellow speaking broken English with a squalling voice, ignorant and arrogant. But Manwaring did acknowledge that Berliner was an especially active detective. At Beechworth, Berliner "made himself a bore by obtruding into polite company, for he was unfit to associate with cultured people".

Captain Standish and Superintendent Nicolson could not stand him either. Berliner was one of the investigators into the notorious Margaret Graham murder at Daylesford in 1864. Mrs Graham's husband, a shift worker at a gold mine, came home late at night and found her on a bed with her throat cut from ear to ear. Police established that an intruder had come down the chimney. It was a hard case to solve, and the police, suspecting an itinerant worker named David Young, held him in gaol for the outrageous time of seven months before bringing him to trial. The delay indicates how uncertain they were of their case; and indeed, even after Young was found guilty and hanged, many in the community believed he may have been innocent.

But he got a fair trial, and Standish had been glad to see the end of it. The Press raised questions after the hanging, but the fuss was quick to die away. Out of the blue, the Chief Secretary wrote to

Standish one day to demand why Berliner was spreading the story that he possessed information that David Young did not commit the murder. Standish was flabbergasted. On his own admission, Standish was a man naturally inclined to indolence, but now he moved at great speed, hurrying to the detective office to see Berliner, and sending a list of questions by telegram to Daylesford. Berliner offered no new evidence, but he was obsessed with the idea that paid informers had lied about David Young.

"I cannot sufficiently reprehend Detective Berliner's conduct in this matter," Standish told the Chief Secretary. "I attribute Detective Berliner's extraordinary conduct to the morbid jealousy which he entertains for every one of his comrades and probably to feelings of disappointment at not having been successful in tracing the culprit," he said. "This man, Detective Berliner, in spite of many good qualities, is becoming (so) crotchety and unpredictable to deal with that his presence in the detective force is a source of constant trouble and annoyance, and he is becoming worse that useless." Nicolson was equally insulting to Berliner in comments on his record sheet.

Berliner left the force within a couple of months, but Standish was not rid of him. Soon Berliner wrote to Standish applying for a "proper discharge", an expression which apparently referred to the unsatisfactory nature of a testimonial which Standish had written to the government. Berliner talked of "the everlasting stain which was unnecessarily embodied" in it. He was applying before Parliament for compensation for a back injury, and he wanted, he said, "a decent testimonial". He also accused Standish of debarring him from any future government service because he had written "a harsh but short sentence". The outcome of this is not clear. Berliner quickly opened a private detective office, claiming later that it was Australia's first.

Sometimes, his path crossed that of the detectives. In any dealings with him, Standish was correct and visibly polite, as if Berliner still made him wary. Probably Christie became aware of Berliner soon after joining the force, for Berliner liked to poke his nose into things. But the time was still far off when Berliner and Christie would become antagonists, and one would play a part in bringing the other down.

Third-class Detective Christie was confirmed as a permanent member of the force in January 1868. He had a companion in this: Mounted Constable Joseph Brown, of Sandhurst, who had been a detective-rookie with him the previous year. It would be good to say that the two young men became friends. Perhaps briefly they did. But within a couple of years, they split apart in ugly circumstances. Such enmity was not unusual in the detective office, but part of a fatal sickness of jealousy, antagonism and corrosion which lay incubating in this year and then spread its poison all around.

Much of the trouble began when J.D.Scott, the force's resident clerk, died in April 1868. The resident clerk, whose duties included handing out the assignments, was right-hand man to Nicolson, and thus wielded considerable power. J.D.Scott was half drunk on brandy much of the time, and he was said to want money from detectives in exchange for giving them the jobs they were keen on. But they coped with this. They could not cope with his replacement, Frederick Secretan, a first-class detective on transfer from Dunolly. Amazingly, Secretan was Nicolson's protege, an inexperienced detective, who was bad at handling men, hopeless at running an office, and inept at solving crime. It was bad enough that Secretan became resident clerk. It was a catastrophe that he rose swiftly, under Nicolson's patronage, to become officer in charge, occupying the post which Nicolson relinquished in 1868 to take promotion.

For the time being, however, the office continued to function well. Christie was among detectives assigned to solve a series of Carlton housebreakings which happened on Sunday mornings when families were at church. Wealthy people lived in Carlton. Having failed to identify any likely robber, the detectives divided Carlton into sections where each of them kept a different watch. Christie chose Barry Street, where the well-to-do looked out on public gardens. By a stroke of luck, his first Melbourne employer, Richard Gibson, the cattle dealer, had a high-roofed house here, and he said Christie could use it as a lookout.

Christie disguised himself as a parson, called at the house the following Sunday morning and asked to see Mr Gibson. "I was ushered into his presence in his smoking room, where he was having a quiet smoke with Messrs Robinson and Buncle, two well-known residents," Christie wrote. "I was well-known to the three, but my make-up was so complete neither of them recognised me till I made myself known to them."

They invited Christie to have a drink; and he was never one to refuse it. Then he climbed on to the roof where he sat with a pair of field glasses, scrutinising everyone who passed. On the second Sunday at this, he recognised two burglars coming along the street with a third man, whom he did not know. The burglars were Thomas Hall *alias* Belzie, and Thomas Evans *alias* Tommy the Dancer. As they were walking quickly and it was almost time for church to finish, Christie deduced that they were returning to their houses with some loot, so he climbed down to the street and, carrying a Bible, followed them. He stayed about ten yards behind, on the opposite footpath so that he could see which door they turned into.

He tracked them to a blind right-of-way containing about six houses off Madeline Street, but they turned in so quickly he did not know which house they entered. "So with my Bible and some tracts in my hand, I boldly entered the lane and called at the first cottage," he wrote. "There was a decent old lady in the front room and she asked me in. I told her I had come to visit one of my congregation who was sick, but I did not know the house the person lived in." When the woman explained who lived where, Christie learned that Hall and Tommy the Dancer occupied the last house on the opposite side. He was about to leave when the third man came out.

Christie tracked him to a house in Hotham (North Melbourne), went to his hotel and changed, and got the help of Detectives Hannan and Hartigan. They all went back to the right-of-way, and the woman said the two neighbours had just gone out. The detectives told her who they were, and she invited them to watch from her house. As Hall and Tommy the Dancer came back, the detectives were so close behind them that they went in the door with them, subdued them in a struggle and found an immense amount of stolen property. Christie and Hannan dashed to the third man's house at Hotham, burst in the door when he refused to open it, and found more loot. Hall and Tommy the Dancer each got five years. The third man, Arthur Johnson *alias* Charles Robinson, got three years.

Christie and Hannan were both rewarded, and they teamed again the following month in solving a case in which a sleeping North Melbourne householder awoke to find that a man holding a lighted candle was ransacking drawers. The intruder escaped, but left his hat, which the detectives thought they recognised. This man was George Smithers *alias* Liberty Collins. Even before the attempted robbery, the detectives had been keeping him under surveillance, by persuading one of his neighbours and her ten-year-old son to watch and follow him. On the night of the offence, the neighbours had seen Smithers in a hat go in the direction of the victim's house, and had seen him come back bare-headed. There was other evidence about Smithers' appearance and voice, enough to convince a judge to give him three years. Smithers was a mate of Hall and Tommy the Dancer.

Nicolson was so impressed by the detectives' tactics and the way they assembled evidence in this case that he recommended three pounds reward for Hannan and a promotion in class for Christie. Standish promoted Christie as soon as he found a vacancy, the following August. Christie had thus taken about twelve months, including his time on probation, to become a second-class detective.

As if he had suddenly unlocked the secrets of how to solve crime, Christie built on these successes in a brilliant year. One of his best cases began one evening when he was walking down Elizabeth Street from his lodgings at Seaforth House in Franklin Street. He noticed an elderly man, whom he recognised as an old burglar named Briely, carrying a ladder about 10 feet long. It was just getting dark, and Christie knew that Briely was up to no good. He followed him down Elizabeth Street and jumped in a cab, the driver of which he knew. He got the driver to lend him his heavy overcoat, a red woollen muffler and his wide-awake hat. He swapped the hat for his own bowler. Christie climbed into the driver's seat, telling the driver to follow him at a distance on foot.

In this way, Christie tracked Briely into Flinders Lane West, and into a blind right-of-way, where he saw him lay the ladder on the ground against Heymanson's warehouse, which was only one storey high. In an Irish accent, Christie asked: "Where is the Port Phillip livery stables?" and Briely said he was a stranger and did not know. Briely then went back up Elizabeth Street. "I knew if he was on a job that night, I had only to watch the ladder," Christie wrote, "so I called the cabbie and told him to go to the detective office and get Detective Hannan and bring him down at once." When Hannan arrived, Christie told him to watch the ladder from a distance, then he got into the cab and went home.

Here he changed into the rig-out of a ship's steward, with bright colored buttons on the jacket and cap. He tied a handkerchief around his head over one eye, and put spots of red liquid on it and on his nose and mouth to resemble blood. Putting his ordinary clothes in a bag in the cab, he returned to Elizabeth Street and got out, pretending to be very drunk. He staggered down Flinders Lane, spoke to Hannan and lay down in a doorway near the entrance to the right-of-way in which the ladder was lying. A constable on his beat told him to get out of it, and Christie rolled down the street in front of him until the constable went to meet his shift relief. (This means that the time was about 9 p.m., for it was then, and again at 5 a.m., that beat constables changed shifts).

Christie returned to Flinders Lane and dropped down in the same doorway. Almost at once, Briely came back. He grabbed hold of Christie and shook him, saying: "Hello mate, what's up?" In a drunken voice, Christie asked if this was the lodging house, and dropped his head on his knees and rolled over. Briely said as he left: "Bug hunting ain't my game" (meaning robbing drunken men). Briely put the ladder against the wall and climbed on to the roof. Then he put a rope through the top of the ladder, pushed the ladder away and lowered it to the ground. He freed the rope and pulled it up after him.

Christie met the new beat constable, explained what was happening, then changed his clothes in the cab and summoned Hannan with a peculiar whistle they both knew. Listening at the front door of the warehouse, they heard noises inside. Christie put the constable at the front door and Hannan at the back, and put the ladder against the wall and climbed on the roof. Inspecting it with the constable's dark lantern, he found where corrugated iron had been prised up, leaving a hole through which he crawled onto the ceiling. He found a square hole cut in the lining, and beside it, a rope tied to a rafter and knotted about every foot. He turned the lamp's bullseye all over the store and saw it was filled with merchandise silks. Briely was obviously the inside man who went in overnight and packed the loot ready for removal at 5 a.m., when the beat shift changed again.

Dousing the bullseye and using the rope, Christie let himself down into the store and lay flat. "Just as I did so, I heard something whizz past and strike the wall," he wrote. "We afterwards found an alderman jemmy with the sharp end stuck in the boards which lined the partition. Alderman is the slang name for a peculiar and powerful jemmy." Christie turned the light on again and caught sight of Briely, who rushed him. "We had a desperate fight for some minutes which the police outside could distinctly hear but could not assist (in). At last I got his head in chancery and throwing him over my hip, fell on him, knocking all the wind out of him."

Briely gave in and was handcuffed. Because the doors were locked and padlocked, the only way Christie could get Briely out was through the roof. Christie put a large packing case on a counter, stood Briely on it and called to the constable to lift him by the handcuffs while Christie pushed from below. When that was done, Christie went back to search the store, and found four skeleton keys which Briely would have somehow passed to his accomplices to unlock the doors when they arrived. Briely was sentenced to five years. His attempted robbery of Heymanson's was not part of the Silk Robberies, which were still a mystery.

A new gold rush occurred at Spring Creek, from where Detective Alexander, of Heathcote, reported that he could identify 40 criminals in a sudden population of 9500. Christie was assigned to go to Spring Creek, but at the last minute word came from Superintendent Hussey Malone Chomley, of Sandhurst (Bendigo), that crime was quiet in his district. He could spare Detective O'Leary for Spring Creek, he said. So Christie stayed in Melbourne.

A few months later, in February 1869, Standish was confronted with a problem new to the detective office: some of his detectives seemed to be trying to destroy one of their own. The rot had begun. A woman named Esther Green was taken to the detective office after pawning some stolen silk for a few pounds, and she carried a tall bottle of lavender water. Neither the bottle nor the money was found on her when a woman later searched her. Detectives Moore, White, Black, Crooke and Marshall were associated with this simple case. The question raised at a police investigation was: which one of them, if any, was a thief?

There seemed to be an attempt to unload the blame unjustly onto Detective Hudson (the one who had got drunk and slept in the stables). Two detectives, Barnfield and Moore, gave evidence that they heard Esther Green say she gave the money to Hudson. The inference was that he accepted a bribe to get the woman out of trouble.

Hudson stated bluntly that he was being victimised by men who were under suspicion. He offered to show his superiors a convoluted letter which he had received from an unnamed colleague. It purported to prove that a different colleague (also unnamed) knew of a plan by Esther Green to incriminate Hudson, but was saying nothing. Should the plan go ahead, the first colleague would "fix it on the right person": that is, clear Hudson's name by identifying the real culprit. The case had come a long way from an inquiry into a missing bottle of scent.

Whether the relevant names reached Standish is not known, but he had no hesitation in clearing Hudson of any wrong-doing. Standish said the evidence pointed irreversibly to the conclusion that Esther Green gave the bottle to Detective Black who, after foolishly accepting such a present, did not have the moral courage to admit the truth. But the evidence was not conclusive, he said. As for the money, there was no proof it ever came to the hands of any detective. Standish considered Esther Green's statement about Hudson was a base attempt to injure him.

Less than a month passed before some of the detectives began outright war against their new resident clerk, Frederick Secretan. This time, a man had come to the office wanting a detective to go with him about a forged cheque. Secretan sent Henry Daly, and the choice angered Detective Peter Jennings and some others who believed this was favouritism. Secretan asked Jennings: "You mean to imply that Daly is shown favouritism from this office?", and Jennings replied: "Yes, everyone knows that."

Secretan promptly put himself on a charge of being accused of greater familiarity with Daly than was consistent with discipline, and of so marked a character as to have attracted general attention. Further, Secretan charged himself with having put into Daly's hands certain cases, the proper charge of which, according to right and precedent, belonged to other detectives.

An inquiry was unavoidable, and it was conducted by Sub-Inspector Ted Ryall, standing in for Nicolson, who was ill. In his evidence, Jennings quoted no specific case of favouritism, but said he had noticed that Secretan always treated Daly in a more friendly manner than he did any other detective. He had seen the two of them in close conversation. The voice and manner of Secretan, when he addressed Daly, was more that of an equal than a superior. Secretan used to call Daly to the door of the inner office about 5.30 of an evening and speak to him in so familiar a manner that it was bad for discipline.

Manwaring testified that he believed the charges against Secretan were true. Several times in his evidence, Manwaring linked Christie's name to Daly's in talking about the jobs they were given. A watchhouse sergeant said that after Daly arrived in Melbourne (from Ballarat) the conversation of nearly all the detectives had been of favours shown towards Daly and sometimes towards Christie. Daly told the inquiry he had been in Melbourne only five months, and during that time, he had received no rewards or gifts from the Police Reward Fund or from private persons.

Somebody called for a list of arrests, and when it came it was a revelation. Between June 1868 and March 1869, Christie, who had been in the force for only 15 months, topped the list with 56 arrests. The nearest to him were Kilfedder with 38 and Daly with 29. For a man who had been in Melbourne only five months, Daly's figure was remarkable. The list after that read: O'Callaghan 28, Lomax 15, Fook Shing 14, Jennings 13, Black and Manwaring 12, Hudson 11, (indecipherable) 10, Crooke 9, Brown 8, Williams and Christen 7,

Barnfield 6, Moore 4, Quinton, Southall, Hartney, Kennedy and Eason 1.

Standish cleared Secretan, saying there were not the slightest grounds to impute his impartiality. Jennings had made a frivolous and vexatious charge against his superior officer, he said, but he refused to demote him from second class to third class as Secretan had urged. He would not single out Jennings for punishment, he said, when it was evident that several other detectives thought as he did. He praised Jennings for having had the manliness to speak out.

Standish was outstanding at sifting a mass of evidence then forcefully and lucidly isolating the important points and imposing his own view, which sometimes was surprising in its fairness. He may have been a libertine and a hypocrite, and sometimes he was foolish, and in later life he may have been lazy, but he also possessed certain strengths, which included a sensitivity to trouble and the ability to command men.

Here he let it be known that he was sensitive to something in his detective force that was new and alarming. "I must caution all those concerned," he said, "against a repetition of similar conduct, as I would sooner dispense with the services of the most useful members of the Detective Force than allow conduct which threatens to destroy subordination and to introduce jealous bickerings and ill-feeling which have hitherto been comparatively unknown." He directed, in the interests of harmony, that no entry be made on anybody's record sheet.

All of a sudden—hallelujah!—the Silk Robberies were solved. They turned out to be an extraordinary story of one man's criminal cunning and, at the very end, bungles by two detectives which nearly let him go scot-free. The Great Silk Robber—not a gang, but merely one man who hugged his secrets to himself—was Thomas Griffiths, living at 56 Stanley Street, West Melbourne.

He had been transported to Van Diemen's Land in 1843 and assigned to an emancipist tanner whose daughter he subsequently married. She was much younger than he. When he had served out his sentence, Griffiths moved to a Victorian country town with his wife and small family, and then moved to Melbourne. His robberies were expertly planned, and they were carried out so well that he left not a trace of his identity or the loot; and this was one of the aspects that had stumped the detectives: the loot simply vanished.

The biggest of the robberies was at Clarke and Adams, next to the south-west corner of Elizabeth and Collins Streets. On the corner itself was an insurance office. At neither building did anyone sleep at night. Clarke's building was not attractive to a burglar because the front door was plainly visible, but the insurance office next door was surrounded by a verandah, which at night concealed any loiterer. Before the robbery, Griffiths entered both buildings with skeleton keys, examined the interiors and left without trace.

When he was ready to act, he and one of his sons entered the insurance office, and began driving through a brick wall to get at the warehouse. A second son stayed hidden outside to warn them to be quiet whenever a constable passed on his beat. Griffiths had spent so many nights observing the locality that he knew the exact length of this beat.

Having got through the brick wall, he picked out the goods he wanted from Clarke's, let his son out the front door, and stayed behind locked in while the two boys went to fetch the family's horse and spring cart, which they drove to the door just after 5 a.m. when the constables changed shifts and the coast was temporarily clear. The cart carried three milk cans, as if it were a milk cart. Griffiths loaded it, locked the door and drove home to 56 Stanley Street.

For several years the family had lived here as civic paragons, in a large, double-storey stone building near Spencer Street. They made no friends, and had no acquaintances. They regularly attended the Wesleyan church, and the children went to Sunday school. Not even old lags from Van Diemen's Land, of whom Melbourne had plenty, knew that Griffiths existed. The family lived well, but the neighbours did not wonder why, for the information had been dropped that Griffiths owned valuable mining shares.

No receiver of stolen goods had ever heard of him. It was Mrs Griffiths who disposed of the plunder. Well-spoken and quietly mannered, she drove out in a hooded, two-wheel buggy with one of her boys beside her, and knocked on the doors of women in Toorak,

Caulfield, Brighton, Hawthorn, Balaclava and Elsternwick. Mrs Griffiths told them the goods were presents from her father who was in the trade at Home; that is, England.

Pleased at getting a bargain, the women did not question this, nor did they question why she kept coming back. From all accounts, they did not care where the goods came from, even when Mrs Griffiths brought them brand-new sewing machines which her husband had stolen.

Some of the monied people of Williamstown were Mrs Griffiths's customers. About once a month she would leave the buggy at Sandridge and take the steamboat across the bay to see them. But one day, she sold a fichu to a woman who showed it to members of the Eckroyd family, owners of a warehouse that had been robbed in October 1868. Eckroyd identified it at once, and told the detectives. They watched for Mrs Griffiths on her next visit. Unobserved, Detective Richard Quinton stuck with her all day, and shadowed her home in a cab to 56 Stanley Street.

Then came the blunders. Nicolson told Manwaring on Friday, 22 January 1869, to get a search warrant and execute it. Manwaring did not obtain it until the following Monday, and then he held it for two days. On the first day, he allowed the Griffiths family to drive away, and he came back to the office. On the second day, he knocked at the door and was told that Griffiths had gone out. Manwaring, Quinton and Detective Barnfield returned to the office. Almost incredulous, Nicolson ordered them back, and told Christie to go with them.

As the four detectives watched the house, Christie saw an old man (Griffiths) come out in a belltopper hat. Christie went to Manwaring, who was his superior, and said: "The old man just came out of the house. Will he be taken back?" Manwaring said no, and sent Barnfield to follow the old man.

Then a woman came to the door. Christie said he thought it was the woman they wanted. "Oh no," said Manwaring, "that's the daughter." Christie said: "I thought you told me the daughter was only 16 years of age. That woman is much more likely 30 or 35." (When Christie subsequently met Mrs Griffiths, he had no doubt she was the same woman).

Christie asked Manwaring: "What is to be done?" Manwaring: "Oh, we must shepherd (watch) the place until the cart comes home." Christie: "You will never see that old man again. From the way he looked I know he is an old hand (crook or convict). He seemed to know Barnfield from the peculiar way he looked at him." Christie asked Quinton if this were Griffiths, and he said: "Yes, that is him."

A little later, Christie saw a head above the fences at the corner of King and Stanley Streets, and the old man came round the corner. Christie said: "There's the old man," and Quinton replied: "Yes, that is him." The old man went down King Street. That was the end of him. He was not seen again for more than two months.

Just then, Detective Barnfield, who had been sent to watch Griffiths, returned from Spencer Street, telling a lie. "I saw him down at the corner," he said. "He suddenly got in a cab and drove off. I ran after the cab to try to get the number. It was 230 or 240." Why Barnfield told this outrageous lie was never explained. He was young; and perhaps he was nervous.

Christie said: "You had no right to leave him." Barnfield said he could not follow Griffiths, because there was no other cab. Christie: "A few minutes ago, we saw him at the corner UP THERE" (Christie's emphasis), pointing to King and Stanley Streets. Barnfield: "Oh, I met him at the corner. He went away in a cab." When the case was over, this lie cost Barnfield his job.

Manwaring's indecision put him in serious trouble. He claimed later that he behaved as he did because Nicolson had ordered him explicitly to be cautious; Nicolson, he said, had feared a terrible blunder because he could not believe that such a quiet family was criminal. For the same reason, said Manwaring, Eckroyd was so nervous that he had to be talked into laying an information for a search warrant. Even then he did not want to see it executed. When Manwaring and Eckroyd finally plucked up the courage to knock on Griffiths's door, a beautiful young girl of modest demeanour opened it, and all their doubts returned. But they carried out a search, and they found more of Eckroyd's goods. They took Mrs Griffiths away as a prisoner.

She told Manwaring she had long grown weary of being her husband's accomplice, and had dreaded the day that the police would call. Griffiths had kept the whole family in subjection, she said. Mrs Griffiths gladly accompanied the detectives around the suburbs in a cart, pointing out fashionable houses at which she had sold the loot. She was a modest, fresh-complexioned, attractive woman, and the detectives regarded her as a sort of pet. They let her visit her house in custody by day, and they returned her to gaol in the evening, for she was being held pending her husband's arrest. With her help, the detectives accounted for several robberies and they easily put together three cases against Griffiths.

Acting on a tip-off, Manwaring and other detectives caught him on the night of St Patrick's Day at the Old Cemetery (later the site of the Queen Victoria market). Griffiths was creeping through the darkness, carrying toys for his younger children, whom he had not seen since going on the run. His capture led the detectives to a another pile of stolen goods, this time in Brunswick. In April Griffiths went to gaol for eleven years, but was transferred later to the lunatic asylum, where he died. Mrs Griffiths became a nurse, and opened a hospital in a mansion in Madeline Street, Carlton, near Elgin Street. Financially, she did well.

Nicolson told Standish that Manwaring's lack of judgment and decision had caused one of the most disgraceful and lamentable failures on record. Standish rejected Nicolson's recommendation to reduce Manwaring from first to second class, but only because of his long and good service. Manwaring lost pay and received a severe reprimand. Dealing with Barnfield, Nicolson said he had given repeated proofs that he was unfit for the detective force, and he recommended that he be discharged at once. Standish agreed. There was a formula about the way such a discharge was done. Barnfield wrote to Nicolson:

"Detective Barnfield begs to submit his
resignation as a third-class detective at once."

Nothing more. This was accepted. Such a note, disclosing no reason for a resignation, almost invariably meant that the writer had been sacked. Conversely, Detective H.J.Christen, submitting his resignation soon afterwards, had felt impelled to say why:

> "Detective Christen is obliged to seek the protection of the Insolvent Court and begs to resign his appointment in consequence."

Standish let him go the same day.

Recommending how the private reward money should be distributed became a nightmare for Standish and Nicolson, because it was in several parts: some from the warehousemen of Melbourne, some from Eckroyds and some from Clarke and Adams. Some of it was conditional on the return of stolen goods. Some of it was for a capture only—which made the indecisive Manwaring pre-eminently eligible.

Nicolson was furious that a large part of this money—for the capture—could have been split only four ways, between Manwaring, Christie, Quinton and Barnfield, if only Barnfield had done his job and Manwaring had listened to the wisdom of Christie and Quinton. Because this had not happened, the money for the capture was to be split eight ways. Probably Christie did get some reward in the end—in addition to the laudatory entry on his record sheet—but he was not even present at the Old Cemetery on St Patrick's night 1869; he was looking after the Duke of Edinburgh, who had unexpectedly come back.

CHAPTER 4

Life with the Duke

The Duke of Edinburgh sailed *HMS Galatea* back to Australian waters in February 1869, on his way to an official New Zealand visit. From Adelaide the Duke telegraphed to Standish, who met him at Sandridge and escorted him to Government House, which was then at Toorak. Next day they played billiards all day, dined at the Melbourne Club, gambled at whist for most of the night then went to Sarah Fraser's brothel. Standish came back to the club and played cards until 6 a.m., losing £92. If the two men had been close on the Duke's previous visit, they were now almost inseparable.

They dined at the club next evening, and went to the Theatre Royal. Standish got home just after eleven, perhaps intending to sleep, but he received a message from the equerry, Eliot Yorke, and went out to Sarah Fraser's again. And so it went on. The Duke and Standish lunched together, dined together, played billiards or pool, shot rabbits or went whoring. At the mayor's ball, Standish stopped dancing to join the Duke in his private room to play blind poker. He lost £94.

Somewhere in all of this was Christie. The Duke is reported to have asked Standish from Adelaide if the Victorian detective force contained a Detective Christie, brother of Captain James Christie, of the 42nd Highland Regiment (the Black Watch). If the answer were yes, the Duke wished to see Detective Christie when the *Galatea* reached Melbourne.

In this way, Christie became the Duke's bodyguard. This unofficial royal visit to Melbourne, from 22 February to 8 March, enabled the Duke to avoid the strictures of Government House, which he was inclined to deride, and to go about the city incognito, presumably with Christie by his side. There is a photograph of Christie dressed

41

as a sailor (see page 58). This was sometimes his disguise when the Duke was on shore informally. If Christie were the Duke's shadow, dogging the Duke's every footstep, as newspapers later reported, he must have seen many unexpected activities. Not once in public, however, for the remainder of his life, did he betray any confidence.

Years later, a typical newspaper report quoted Christie as saying that he accompanied the Duke everywhere "very quietly, to races, balls, levees, pigeon matches, theatres, country trips, on board the *Galatea*, and the whole round of the royal visits." A reporter asked Christie: "You were practically one of the staff?" Christie replied: "It really amounted to that. Fortunately, I got on splendidly with the equerry (Eliot Yorke) which is half the battle in the position I filled. You see, we were always together, morning, noon and night, so much that I even slept under the same roof as the Duke, at Government House, on a warship, or elsewhere, as the royal residence might be for the time being."

When the brief Melbourne visit ended and the Duke was about to go to Sydney, he expressed the wish that Christie follow him as bodyguard in the steamer *City of Adelaide*, but because there was doubt about this, the Duke gave Christie a gold pin as a farewell gift. On the day the Duke sailed, he pressed Standish to let Christie go with him on the *Galatea*, and it was arranged on the spot, so quickly that Standish had to lend Christie 30 sovereigns to go on with, and Christie sailed with the clothes he stood in.

The Duke obviously thought much of Christie, for he requested his services again as he was about to leave Sydney on his New Zealand tour. This time Standish had a little more room to manoeuvre, but he was still hard-pressed, for Christie was in Sydney, without money. Standish needed to make some complicated financial arrangements with the Sydney police to enable Christie to be solvent, and on top of this, Christie sent a telegram asking for £15 more. These arrangements took a while to sort out when Christie returned.

Christie kept in touch. From the *Galatea* on 2 May he wrote to Standish that the Duke had received a magnificent reception at Dunedin. From Auckland he dropped a hint that the Duke was fornicating again:

"He visits the Prince of Wales Theatre publicly or privately almost every night. Miss Cleveland is THE STAR."

Christie emphasised 'the star'. There was also more serious news: "HRH has received some threatening letters and as there are numerous bad reports in circulation, it makes him rather timid and me very careful of his movements. I accompany him everywhere as part of his suite." Christie went on:

> "HRH has declined to visit the Thames goldfields after
> the report I made on the place. I was accompanied to
> the Thames by Captain Taylor RM. At a public dinner there
> the diggers refused to drink the Queen's health, and made
> a target of one of HRH's likenesses."

Apart from such incidents as this, you get the impression that the royal tour was all very jolly, rather like a succession of sixth-form japes. In Melbourne the light-hearted, or light-headed, young officers of the *Galatea* stole a statue of Venus from the Fitzroy Gardens, and were on their way to put it in Standish's bed at the Melbourne Club when a constable flashed his lamp. They ran off, and the constable fell in a gully chasing them.

At a theatre one night something came whirling through the darkness and landed in the royal box. Christie, whispering: "Sit still! Sit still!", snatched it up and took it away. It was a bunch of flowers. This incident is said to have greatly amused the Duke.

There was the young New Zealand woman who bet her fiance six pairs of gloves that she could walk up to the Duke and pinch his arm. Christie got wind of it, and when he saw her stepping forward from a crowd, he blocked her way and asked if she would like to meet the Duke. Yes, she said. Christie arranged it, and the Duke passed on to her a box of gloves.

To amuse the royal party, Christie boxed a New Zealand champion, and beat him over seven rounds in a 16 foot ring under Prize rules.

Whatever it was that the Duke was doing with the actress Miss Cleveland, Christie was an original party to it. When the Duke first wished to visit Miss Cleveland incognito, Christie found a way to the theatre's back door, but the streets were like a maze. He put chalk marks on each turn so that the Duke and he could find their way out after dark.

At the end of the tour, Christie declined the Duke's invitation to sail with him to England and join the royal household as a detective. He came back to Melbourne alone on 12 June.

A Melbourne reporter once asked Christie: "And what about all those interesting little stories told about the Duke?" Christie's face went rigid, and he pointed out that the duty of a royal shadow was "of a strictly special and confidential nature, only to be spoken of in generalities". He kept the Duke's secrets all his life. But everyone knew that secrets existed.

One journal wrote many years later that if ever the Christie memoirs about the royal visit were published, "say a hundred years hence, when the peccadilloes of Princes, like the backslidings of Saints, will have passed into perfections, the royal chapter in them will not be the least interesting to posterity."

It went on: "To us young men of the virile generation, the Australian tour of Prince Alfred is enshrouded in a piquant mystery, which the survivor of the old school will only hint at tantalisingly with a wink of the eye and a tactful changing of the subject whenever excited curiosity attempts a cross-examination. Christie's eye must have got very tired of winking by this time, and his agility in changing the subject must have become quite acrobatic. At any rate, the racy secrets of the Prince's Progress, if racy secrets there were, are safe and sacred in this loyal keeping."

Inspector Ryall was in charge of the detective office when Christie returned, for Nicolson had moved to a new post as officer in charge at Kyneton. The dreadful Secretan had been confirmed as resident clerk. Not much else was new, except that Standish had just issued some guidelines for detectives attending prize fights. The guidelines indicated that illegal boxing was the business of general police. Standish said that without special instructions from their office, detectives should not try to stop the fights. They should take notes, watch who was there, and note any disreputable or criminal classes.

Standish also sent a note to Ryall after a couple of weeks: "I wish to see Detective Christie at the Club before 6½" (6.30 p.m.). One has to assume that this was a social gesture, an extremely generous one, for there is no record that Standish issued such a command to any other detective. Nor did Standish record the visit in his diary. Nor is there a record of what Standish and Christie discussed, presumably the Duke. It would not have been proper for the two of them to gossip about him in a police office. Whatever the reason, Christie's presence at the club was a small acknowledgment of how far his career had taken him. The Duke's regard for him must have helped of course, but at the age of 23, Detective Christie (second-class, with only one step to climb) was also doing brilliantly at his work.

At this time, two crime reports from Christie landed on Standish's desk. On each of them Ted Ryall had recommended an award from the Police Reward Fund. The first report told how Christie and Mackay had solved a burglary at Davidson's clothing store in Elizabeth Street by tracing two women, Anne Moore and Elizabeth Weekes, who had sold some of the loot. Through these women the detectives traced a man, James Turner, and recovered the rest of the property. All three were sent to gaol. Standish approved the reward for this as a matter of course.

But the other case puzzled him. Christie, acting alone, had set out to find an offender who had bashed and robbed Samuel Dobbin, of Kensington. The only information Christie had to go on was Dobbin's description of the attacker. Almost at once Christie found him, a man named John Williams, and Dobbin identified him next day in a line-up. Christie's routine reports to his superiors were always succinct; he could say in one page what other detectives said in three pages; but the information in this particular report was so scant that Standish was prompted to write back to Ryall: "How did the detective find the offender? The report simply states that he received a description of him, went in search and succeeded in finding him."

Furthermore, the offender had only recently arrived from New Zealand, so it was not as if Christie knew his form. Christie was equally brief in the supplementary report he was now obliged to write. On receiving the offender's description, he said, he had gone to the taps and haunts where he knew criminals took refuge. You can almost imagine Christie becoming exasperated at having to write this; of course he went to the taps and haunts; where else would he go? Dobbin's description tallied exactly with Williams's appearance, he said. He had regarded Williams with suspicion since he had arrived in Victoria. End of message.

Standish approved the reward, which was one of several Christie received from the reward fund in 1869. The amount of money he received in private rewards is impossible to know. Two pounds here. Five pounds there. Fifty sometimes. These private rewards did not always pass through the detective office, although most did. Standish tried to ensure that any reward was apportioned justly if more than one detective had worked on a case.

Standish was a stickler for accuracy. A reward for capture and conviction was exactly what it said. It was not a reward for recovering stolen goods, or for working long hours, or for being in at the kill. Similarly, a reward for recovering stolen goods was not a reward for capture. In such a case, a detective who found the prey but not the goods went begging. But sometimes the smaller private rewards were not even posted; they were a matter between a detective and a victim.

One of Christie's police rewards this year concerned a man whom he saw in the watchhouse. They had never met, but Christie recognised him as someone who was wanted for a different crime under a different name. This was an outstanding feat, which showed how well he must have absorbed the information which came to all members of the force each week in the *Police Gazette*. Surprisingly, many did not bother to read it.

In August, Christie and Hudson arrested Thomas James on a charge of having raped a woman near Whittlesea, and this too might have led to a reward, but James did not face trial; he stabbed himself to death. Christie and Hudson teamed again in October, trying to catch coiners who had circulated a large number of fake half-crowns and florins. The only substantial clue from victims was that one of the suspects always had a little fair-haired girl with him.

Among men recently released from Pentridge, three were coiners: Robert Smith, Joseph Brooks and John Wilson; and the detectives eliminated Smith who seemed to be going straight. But while they were talking to him, he mentioned he had run into Brooks and his little daughter at the market. Christie said he did not know Brooks had a daughter. Smith said yes, a little fair girl, about five. Smith also said Brooks had told him he was working in a timber yard in Rokeby Street, Collingwood.

Dressed in old clothes as a labourer, Christie went to Rokeby Street, but there was no timber yard. He dropped into the Glass-house Hotel where he knew the landlord, a co-operative man who listened to Christie's story and said he thought he recognised the person Christie was after. The landlord put Christie in a room upstairs, and gave him the tip-off when Brooks came in for a drink that evening. Christie came unobtrusively down the stairs and saw Brooks drinking with John Wilson.

The landlord also told Christie where Brooks lived, in a courtyard down Rokeby Street. Christie went there in the darkness and saw three tiny cottages, on one of which was a sign, 'Mangling done here.' The door was open, and he asked the woman sitting by a fire inside if she knew where Black Johnson lived. "There's no niggers living in this street," she said, but she also revealed that two men and a little girl occupied the middle cottage, and that something queer was happening there: strange sleeping hours and a smell of chemi-cals. She paid six shillings a week rent for her cottage, she said, and there wasn't even a backyard, just a front door. This information pleased Christie; if there were no back door, there was no escape route.

Next morning, Christie and Hudson crept past Brooks's window on their hands and knees, and burst in the door. Brooks lunged at Christie with a ladle of hot metal, but Christie floored him with a left and handcuffed him. Wilson had thrown Hudson and escaped by crashing through the glass of the window. Christie chased and caught him, and held him until their driver, Detective Thomas Kidney, ran up. At their trial, Brooks and Wilson were sentenced to four years each. The little girl was charged with being a neglected child, and was sent to prison to be with her mother.

Old Harry Power had been at large for a year now. In December, Manwaring went with a police party in search of him in the Ovens district, but he might as well have stayed home for all the success they had. Manwaring came back to Melbourne and wrote a gloomy report saying he had been on tired horses for 15 days through Belvoir, Little River, Beechworth, Bright, Myrtleford and Yackandandah, and he had seldom remained two nights in the one spot, and they were in outlying districts and had to stop in hotels or shanties and were generally charged for two meals and a bed, 6s. He was a gloomy fellow.

Manwaring omitted to keep a memorandum of his expenses which amounted, he said, to £6/13/0. This was rather like today's Australian businessman coming back from London and saying he had kept no receipts. Ryall asked Standish to authorise payment, but the claim was filed wrongly, and was lost for more than a month. When Ryall was forced to ask again, Standish apologised, but delayed it even more by going through his usual procedure of pruning the pence and shillings. By the time he had pruned the claim to £5/10/0, Manwaring had waited three months, and the year was 1870.

Christie reads an arrest warrant in 1894 to Tom Delaney who surrendered himself at the Warrnambool watchhouse after eluding a big police hunt. (J.B. Castieau)

Christie (back row, centre) and other officers pose with police during the customs raids on illicit distillers in the Warrnambool district. (J.B. Castieau)

49

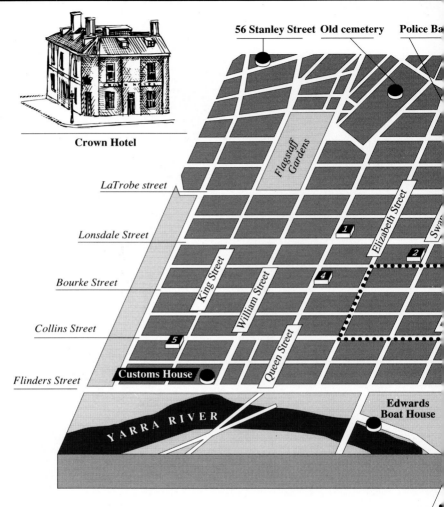

Crown Hotel

56 Stanley Street   Old cemetery   Police Ba

LaTrobe street

Lonsdale Street

Bourke Street

Collins Street

Flinders Street

Flagstaff Gardens

Elizabeth Street

Swan

1

2

4

King Street

William Street

5

Queen Street

Customs House

Edwards Boat House

YARRA RIVER

HOTELS

1 **Crown,** scene of a ludicrous police mix-up

2 **European,** where Christie was licensee

3 **Morning Star,** one of the lowest hotels in Little Bourke Street

4 **Sandhurst,** scene of Christie's brawl with Thomas Moore

5 **Admiral,** where Christie shouted drinks after his fight with John Sharp.

6 **Galatea,** one of Christie's lodgings.

Police Office and court

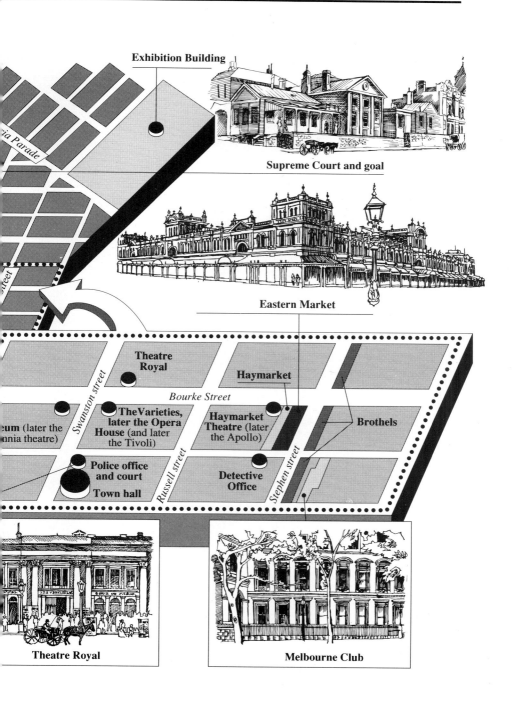

Exhibition Building

Supreme Court and goal

Eastern Market

Theatre Royal

Haymarket

Swanston street

Bourke Street

The Varieties, later the Opera House (and later the Tivoli)

Haymarket Theatre (later the Apollo)

Brothels

eum (later the nnia theatre)

Russell street

Police office and court

Detective Office

Town hall

Stephen street

ia Parade

Theatre Royal

Melbourne Club

An 1869 view of Melbourne photographed from the home of Dr. T. N. Fitzgerald in Lonsdale Street. The Crown Hotel is on the corner of Lonsdale and Queen Streets. (La Trobe Collection. State Library of Victoria)

Melbourne 1871, from Parliament House, Spring Street. (La Trobe Collection. State Library of Victoria)

The Duke of Edinburgh laying the foundation stone of the Melbourne Town Hall, Swanston Street, on 29 November, 1867. (Royal Historical Society of Victoria)

The Eastern Market as it was in Christie's day. The detective office was located in Little Collins Street, behind the market. (Royal Historical Society of Victoria)

Bourke Street looking east towards Swanston Street in the 1870s, taken from outside the building which today is David Jones. (Royal Historical Society of Victoria)

Bourke Street looking east in the 1860s. On the left is the Post Office with clock tower. (Royal Historical Society of Victoria)

Frederick Standish in his prime as gambler, libertine and chief commissioner of police.
(Victoria Police Historical Unit)

Superintendent Charles Nicolson, chief of detectives at the time Christie joined the force.(Victoria Police Historical Unit)

Superintendent Power Le Poer Bookey, who got rid of Christie after they clashed verbally at Geelong. (Royal Historical Society of Victoria)

Prince Alfred, Duke of Edinburgh, during the Australian tour on which Christie guarded him. (J.B. Castieau)

Christie disguised as a sailor from the royal yacht **H.M.S. Galatea.** (J.B. Castieau)

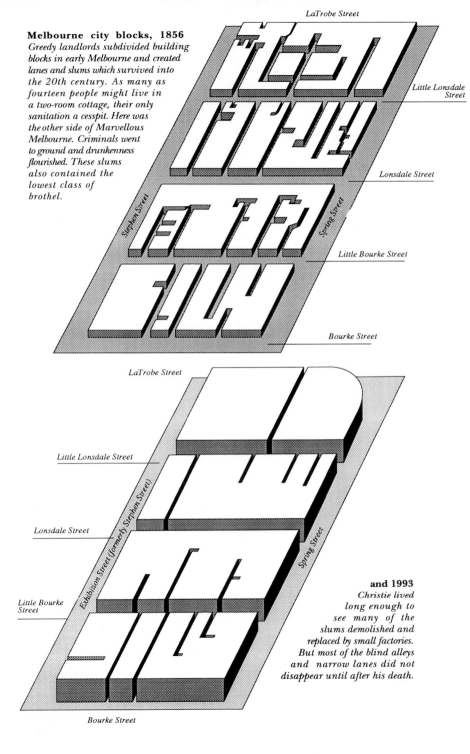

Melbourne city blocks, 1856
Greedy landlords subdivided building blocks in early Melbourne and created lanes and slums which survived into the 20th century. As many as fourteen people might live in a two-room cottage, their only sanitation a cesspit. Here was the other side of Marvellous Melbourne. Criminals went to ground and drunkenness flourished. These slums also contained the lowest class of brothel.

LaTrobe Street

Little Lonsdale Street

Lonsdale Street

Little Bourke Street

Bourke Street

Stephen Street

Spring Street

LaTrobe Street

Little Lonsdale Street

Lonsdale Street

Little Bourke Street

Exhibition Street (formerly Stephen Street)

Spring Street

and 1993
Christie lived long enough to see many of the slums demolished and replaced by small factories. But most of the blind alleys and narrow lanes did not disappear until after his death.

Bourke Street

*Inside the Theatre Royal,
Bourke Street, 1860. A
section was called the
saddling paddock.*
(Royal Historical Society
of Victoria)

*Olinda Dowling—a Mel-
bourne prostitute during
Christie's era. Photo-
graphs of prostitutes of
this period are scarce.*
(Victoria Police Historical
Unit)

CHAPTER 5

Driving the boss mad

Christie's first rural posting was to Geelong. Before he left Melbourne in January 1870, Inspector Ryall wrote on his record sheet: "A steady, active man with first-class abilities as a detective. Most trustworthy and reliable." Indeed, Christie's career seemed golden. But Geelong could not wait to get rid of him.

Christie stayed there for less than a month before Standish acceded to a plea to take him away. Christie's superior officer at Geelong, a superintendent with the unusual name of Power Le Poer Bookey, was driven to such fury and frustration by Christie's attitude that you can almost imagine him offering prayers of deliverance on the day that Christie left. On that day, in fact, Bookey was home in bed ill. Christie had not been at Geelong more than ten days before he complained to Superintendent Bookey that it was almost impossible to carry out his instructions and work satisfactorily if Sergeant Jeremiah Toohey, of the general police, wearing plain clothes, were allowed to undermine him.

The story here is that Christie went to the saleyards to search for a horse thief. When he arrived, he learned that a bystander had recognised the suspect and had said to a constable: "There is the man you want. Arrest him quick or he will go away." The constable replied he did not have the man's description. "I won't touch him," he said, "I was merely sent to make inquiries by Sergeant Toohey, who is on the way, but I will go and tell him." Toohey arrived just then and chased the suspect, who escaped. Fuming about Toohey's unwarranted intervention, Christie complained that the men in the yards had thought this was a great joke on the police.

Next day Christie went to the National Hotel where the suspect had been sighted, and he became angry again because he learned that Sergeant Toohey had just arrested the man and was taking him away. Christie had other complaints. One concerned a dud cheque which had been passed at the Albion Hotel. When the publican referred the matter to Sergeant Toohey, he failed to issue a warrant or notify a criminal offence. Another complaint was about the theft of a crumbcloth, a small thing, but important in the way it emphasised antagonism. Christie learned that a woman named Lorrie (known as Annie Lorrie) had pawned the crumbcloth for four shillings, and he rode out to Chilwell to arrest her at the Gold Diggers Arms. When he got there, he was told: "Oh, she has just been arrested by Sergeant Toohey and Constable Lynch."

Christie told Bookey that Toohey had made a threat to the detective clerks in Melbourne that he did not care who they sent to Geelong, he would give them just whatever work he liked. Christie pointed out that this was contrary to the instructions in the *Police Manual*, pages 39 and 40.

The sad thing was that Bookey did not know what Christie, this self-confident young man of 24, was talking about. He asked Christie what his actual complaint was. It seemed to him, he said, that Sergeant Toohey, knowing the area better, was making more arrests than Christie at that time, and it was Toohey's duty to apprehend any offender.

When Christie received this reply, he did something unthinkable: he answered back. On 20 January, in a letter so plain that Superintendent Bookey regarded it as insubordination, Christie repeated his complaint that it was not the duty of police to duplicate jobs to which detectives had been assigned. Furthermore, he said, when a plain clothes man was told off for a special job, it should be with a detective in charge so that they would act in concert and not waste time. All criminal cases should be placed in the detective's hands immediately a report was received, Christie insisted; a detective was held responsible for all crime in the district.

Finally, Christie asked Bookey to charge Toohey with neglect of duty over the dud cheque. If the sergeant were still allowed to do duty in plain clothes, he said, the whole correspondence would be placed in the hands of the Chief Commissioner.

One would like to know Sergeant Toohey's response to this. His letters are intact, but the handwriting is so bad it is impossible to read him with certainty, or for that matter, to read him at all. He was a grub. It is possible that even in the 19th century, his colleagues groaned or hid when they were asked to read Toohey's writing. You cannot blame time for distorting it; it was bad. Christie's writing, on the other hand, was so clear and well-shaped that it appears to have have been done only last week.

Unrelentingly, Christie now sent Superintendent Bookey another memo because he had discovered that a different dud cheque, uttered in the Thistle Hotel six months earlier, had not been notified until that day. Sergeant Toohey had been told of the crime when it happened, but his notice about it, posted in the police station, claimed it had not been referred to him until that day. Once again Toohey's response is illegible.

Christie was now too much of a problem for Superintendent Bookey, who sent an immediate letter to the Chief Commissioner, Standish, saying Christie's report of 20 January was "most improperly and disrespectfully worded. In fact," he went on, "he has taken upon himself to dictate to me, his superior officer, the manner in which I should manage the men placed under my command and actually threatened me with an appeal to the Chief Commissioner of Police should I still permit Sergeant Toohey to make inquiries in plain clothes."

Superintendent Bookey had a lot to get off his chest: "I had intended to have at once suspended him from duty on receipt of the report, as it is impossible for me to carry out the duties of the district in a satisfactory manner with such a man, but as he was engaged in a case before the court which has not yet concluded, I was unable to do so. I look upon a man like Detective Christie, who cannot agree to work with the general police and who moreover, as it appears from these reports, came down here with the intention of giving trouble and making himself disagreeable from the commencement (underlined), as more than useless in any district."

These were extremely strong words from a superintendent about a young detective who had reached only second-class rank. They exposed Christie to the department's wrath. But Bookey had not finished yet. When the matter was settled, he said, he wanted Christie withdrawn; he could get on better without a detective. Indeed, he had found detectives of little use in Geelong, and always inclined to show a petty jealousy towards the general police. He would sooner be without one; he would save his department more than £191 a year.

"The sergeant and men stationed here know the places and inhabitants so well, and being, generally speaking, sharp, intelligent men, offenders who are wanted are arrested by them while the detectives are considering the best way of proceeding to make inquiries, and this, it appears to me, is Detective Christie's great grievance."

This was an annoyance for Standish. He could not take sides against Bookey, whose rank was high and whose service was long, but at the same time he could not abandon Christie who was defending instructions in the *Police Manual.* In reply to Bookey, Standish wrote a letter that was a masterpiece of tact. He was superb at this. One extraordinary thing about Standish was that despite his debilitating late nights as a playboy, he retained his energy and mental agility. He could write lucid, beautifully structured prose, and he did so every day in reports, letters and notations.

Writing now to Bookey, he began by politely disagreeing that Christie had been disrespectful or had tried to dictate working methods. What Christie appeared to complain of, he said, was that Sergeant Toohey was to all intents and purposes a plain clothes policeman who did not work cordially with Christie, but placed himself in a position of antagonism to him. Christie had written a great deal of nonsense in which his account of how Toohey had frustrated him could not be pursued without considerable amusement.

Standish said he had long thought that Toohey should be in the detective force. He did not approve of general policemen appearing constantly in plain clothes, and he ordered Bookey to rectify this. In view of Bookey's remarks, Standish said he saw no necessity now to have a detective stationed at Geelong. Christie would be transferred back to Melbourne.

Having made these points with a subtle warmth towards the

general police, Standish felt free to deal with Christie. "In justice to the Detective," he wrote, "I must say that he has always shown the highest character, and has never at any time displayed that jealousy against the general police of which Mr Bookey now accuses him. Mr Bookey's remark that the Detective 'came down here with the intention of giving trouble or making himself disagreeable from the commencement (underlined)' is, I think, unsupported by any evidence and unjust."

This should have ended the fuss, but Bookey would not let go. He at once wrote back to Standish saying he had been in the police force since 1853, always in charge of a considerable muster of men, and never had he received such a communication as Christie's from any member stationed under him. Bookey refused to abandon the idea that Christie went to Geelong to make trouble, "and I daresay," he went on, "if the truth be known, he was put up by others." Standish sent all the correspondence to Secretan, saying he was to let Christie read it but not make a copy of any part.

Christie came back to Melbourne and found he had received £2 from the Police Reward Fund for his part in the arrest and conviction of Joseph Brooks, the coiner. One other case in which Christie distinguished himself was a robbery at Hawthorn. Christie reached the conclusion that two young robbers named Lindley and Bitson were the burglars who had in March robbed Michael O'Grady of a silver centre stand valued at 200 guineas .

Disguising himself in a dirty old suit and hat, and putting his arm in a sling and his head in a bandage, Christie loitered near their houses, and followed them to John Mannix's barber shop in Madeline Street, Carlton. Mannix had been the Pentridge barber on and off for the 19 years in which he had served time. Now he turned out to be a receiver.

When he eventually learned that Christie was after him, he tried to escape in a cab, and Christie and Detective Daly chased him in another. The cabs hit, and the detectives were thrown out, but they caught Mannix, found the silver centre stand in pieces at his shop, and finally arrested Lindley and Bitson.

Awaiting trial in gaol, Mannix wrote to Inspector Secretan: "The police tels (sic) me I am not the man they want. They know I have only been a tool in their hands. They (said they) will ask my discharge at the police court. Sir, I can and will give up the burglars and evidence enuf (sic) to convict them."

To the distress of most detectives, Inspector Ted Ryall had moved on and Inspector Secretan was now their officer in charge. When Secretan received the Mannix letter, he actually left his office that day and went out to Pentridge to take a statement from Mannix. There are so few records of Secretan going anywhere on a job that one wonders whether he was trying here to recruit a new fizgig by offering early release in exchange for future services. In any case, he came back and reported to Standish that Mannix had named Lindley and Bitson as the burglars. Secretan suggested that the government be asked to mitigate Mannix's sentence. (All three men subsequently got five years.)

Christie, Daly and Williams, when asked for their views, told Standish that Mannix's help had been valuable in corroborating the evidence against Lindley and Bitson. This was not enough to sway the law office. It said it was too early to suggest releasing Mannix, but a pardon might reasonably be sought when he had served much more of his sentence.

A different case soon caught Melbourne's attention. If the city needed a reminder that Little Bourke Street was still violent in 1870, Detectives Daly and Mackay provided it. They staked out an area in Little Bourke Street for three weeks, and finally caught two men in the act of garrotting an old man named Arthur Harvie. Garrotting did not necessarily mean throttling someone to death. Rather, it was a simple procedure in which one attacker, coming from behind, pressed an arm with great force across the victim's throat and held his hands. A second attacker went through his clothes. When the detectives interrupted John Moore and Thomas Bourke at this, the old man's eyes were already starting out of his head.

Moore and Bourke, described as notorious garrotters, received ten years each. The judge thought of flogging them, but said this destroyed self-respect, which often was the only good thing that remained in criminals' natures.

In a ramshackle way, the months ahead were eventful for the detectives. Detective Louis Murray, who walked out one day and did not come back, was marked down as an absconder. Secretan told Christie he thought Murray had absconded because he had a wife and children and was in considerable debt.

Joe Brown was in trouble because he went to Pentridge to ask a prisoner about the location of stolen goods, and gave him a chew of tobacco. The gaol's governor, Mr Castieau, wrote bluntly to Standish that he was disgusted. In his defence, Brown said the prisoner had told him he was dying for a chew, so he he gave him one, thinking something good might come out of it. Brown was suspended and severely reprimanded.

Detective James Crooke, who had the reputation of being irregular in his duty, came to work one-and-a-half hours late on a day when he was supposed to be relieving the early starter. He had been out dining, he said, and did not get to bed until 5 a.m. Crooke was allowed to resign.

None of this, however, matched the spat between Detective Alfred Lomax and Detective Tom O'Callaghan. Lomax read in a newspaper that a judge had heaped praise on O'Callaghan over the arrest of a thief. Lomax was furious, because this was his case as well. He thought O'Callaghan had double-crossed him. O'Callaghan and Lomax, seeking clues to a robbery, had detained a man who tried to avoid them in the Star and Garter Hotel, South Melbourne, and he turned out to be the one they wanted. But when the case came to court, Lomax was on another job and could not attend, and it was O'Callaghan alone whom the judge had singled out.

Trying to make peace, O'Callaghan wrote a report in praise of Lomax, and said he had already given him £1 from a private reward; but the report only made things worse because O'Callaghan went on to say that after all, Lomax's role had been subordinate. Worse still, Inspector Palmer of the Russell Street police, who had been in court and heard the judge's comments, wrote in to say he agreed O'Callaghan deserved praise.

Standish put a stop to the bickering by taking the trouble to write a long, amiable memo— another masterpiece of tact—in which he said nobody had been subordinate. Acting together, the men had been "in a position of perfect equality and should share equally in any praise or profit". He promised each would receive a glowing entry on his record sheet, and he directed that they share the one pound reward.

When people criticise Standish for the mistakes he made during 23 years as Chief Commissioner—a long time—they sometimes overlook the turbulent natures of the men he was forced to rule. An enormous amount of his time and energy was spent in settling such squabbles as Bookey's with Christie and Lomax's with O'Callaghan.

He was never free of the force's internal troubles. Detective John Carter, 31, who had been a groom before joining the detective force in 1868, ran into a horse cab in Russell Street on the evening of 21 March 1870. The shafts forced his breast bone and three ribs back into his lungs, and he died that day. There was no workers' compensation, no gratuity or pension for his widow and children. The only thing Standish could do was make up his pay to the day Carter died.

Standish was horrified next day to learn that Mrs Carter intended to hold a wake over her husband's body in the government quarters they had occupied. "I cannot permit this barbarous and indecent practice to be carried out in Government quarters," he told Inspector Secretan; if the woman wanted a wake, she must hold it elsewhere. "Let this be at once intimated to her," he said, "with every consideration for her feelings."

Standish obviously saw no unkindness in this attitude. But he was a snob. He was very touched, for example, when a Captain Wilson (half pay, Royal Artillery) landed in Melbourne with a drink problem. Wilson came to notice by being picked up for drunkenness, forfeiting his bail by not turning up at his court hearing, and then being found drunk again when people went to look for him. "This unfortunate gentleman" was what Standish called him. He ordered a "quiet surveillance" on Captain Wilson, but there is no record that he did such a thing for other drunks, of whom the town was full.

Christie was not long back in Melbourne when he was assigned to a murder case that gives us a glimpse of low-life Melbourne in 1870. Susan Egan, 17, *alias* Louey Brown, was a prostitute who lived with two other prostitutes, Fanny Bell and Elizabeth Sharp, in Flinders Lane. Their very names sound so old-fashioned that it is easy to picture them in long dresses, bonnets and boots, moving about their lively neighbourhood on a hot summer night just as the gas lamps were coming on and they were about to set off to sell themselves. In fact, a description of Susan's clothing survives. On 24 February 1870 she wore a black silk jacket and a white crinoline hat with a flower in it like a feather. Her dress was light calico with pink spots.

These were the clothes Susan wore when Elizabeth Sharp found her at home a bit drunk that day. Susan had slept the night out with a foreign gentleman, she told Elizabeth, and she was going out that night to meet him again. Fanny Bell, the third of the trio, said she saw Susan that night at The Varieties, sitting at a table alone, smoking a cigar. A waiter testified later that it was not uncommon at The Varieties to see an unaccompanied woman doing this.

By the light of the gas lamps, Fanny and Susan walked down Bourke Street to the Post Office, then turned around and walked up to the corner of Russell Street, because Susan wanted to go to The Varieties again to keep her date with the foreign gentleman. The time was ten to 11. Fanny said later that Susan told her several times she had been down to the Swamp (around West Melbourne) that day with gentlemen. Several people said later they saw Susan at The Varieties about 11 p.m. with Harry Edwards, a butcher, with whom she had kept company.

Susan was found dead next day, battered about the head, on a bank of the Yarra River. Christie and Williams interviewed Edwards two days later at a Flinders Street butcher shop. Christie asked Edwards if he knew whose body had been found, and Edwards said no. Asked again, he said: "Quite certain". Christie and Williams then took him to the morgue, showed him the body and asked him to identify it. Edwards hesitated and said: "I don't think I know her." Williams told him to look again and make sure.

Edwards then said: "I do know her, as Miss Brown, but her proper name is Susan Egan." Williams cautioned Edwards and asked: "Did you not promise to marry her?" and Edwards said no at first, then: "Yes, I did, if she would lead a better life." He denied he had seen her since the previous week. The detectives took Edwards's boots off, and compared them with marks on Susan's forehead. They fitted, a fact to which a doctor later testified. Christie and Williams took Edwards outside and charged him with murder.

An inquest freed Edwards from custody, but Christie and Williams immediately rearrested him on a warrant. At a police court hearing in March, he was committed for trial. Detective Walker went snooping and filed a sobering report. Elizabeth Sharp was said to have destroyed some of Susan's clothing, probably by burning it, on the morning the body was found. Elizabeth, Fanny Bell and Henry Edwards were on "most intimate" terms, Walker said; there was every reason to believe they had suppressed valuable evidence.

Another interesting fact came to light: Susan had gone to Edwards's workplace and made a fuss, and the proprietor had told Edwards he would have to get rid of her. Some of this evidence was hearsay, and all of it was circumstantial. The Crown dropped the case because nobody could bring forward the foreigner for whom Susan had allegedly been waiting. Standish heard later that Elizabeth and Fanny went to live in New Zealand, and that Edwards followed them. For a while, Standish kept up a correspondence with the New Zealand police, but nothing came of it.

A bigger case, and more successful, loomed for Christie. In the middle of July 1870, he was spending a few days leave in Geelong, and he received an urgent telegram from Standish to return to Melbourne. He caught the evening train, went to the detective office and ran into Secretan who seemed very pleased to see him. Secretan told him the city was in the charge of a desperate gang of burglars, who had committed some big cracks (robberies). Christie read the crime sheets, and the thought that crossed his mind was that the gang must have good fences (receivers) to handle such a swag of goods.

He called next morning on one of the victims, Halliburton & Co., cloth warehousemen, of Lonsdale Street West, which had been robbed a few days earlier of cloth valued at £1500. Christie theorised that the thieves had got in by using a well-known technique. They waited until the beat constable went to meet his relief at 9 p.m. They then had 15 to 20 minutes in which it was safe for them to work.

Two thieves stood talking near the front door while two others laid the padlock of the hasp on its back on a stone and hit it with a jemmy. This caused the back of the padlock to fall off, the works to fall out, and the lock to spring open. To deaden the slight noise of the blow, the men on watch coughed. The thieves undid the hasp and opened the door with a skeleton key. Two of them went inside while the others replaced the hasp and substituted a padlock similar to the one which had been forced. They locked this new one.

The two thieves outside the door went away, carrying their implements, the debris and the keys of the new padlock, which would pass any test by a constable who might walk by and feel it. Whenever the men inside heard the constable coming they leaned against the door to keep it firm, because the lock of this—the one opened with the skeleton key—was still undone. The two men inside the building used a dark lantern to select the goods they wanted to take, and piled them near the door. The men who had remained outside came back at 5 a.m., when the constables changed beats again. The police were so punctual at this that any thief could plan his night around it.

This time the thieves brought a spring cart, usually carrying milk cans. One man jumped down and unlocked the padlock, the goods were piled in the cart and it was driven away. The men who had been inside the building removed the padlock to use another day, then casually walked away in the direction opposite to that from which the constable would come. On discovering the robbery, the constable would send to the barracks for a second constable, who would remain on guard until the owner arrived. The owner would then report the matter to the detective office. It was a clumsy system, which gave any thieves a start of several hours.

Christie discovered an important clue at Halliburton's: at least one of the thieves was an excellent judge of cloth, for nothing but the best and most expensive tweeds had been stolen. Then he got another clue: the firm's cutter had cut an irregular shape of cloth from one of the stolen rolls the day before the robbery, and he still had it. He said he would know his own cutting if Christie could find the roll and match it.

Christie then went to a second burgled store, Davidson's, on the corner of Elizabeth and Flinders Streets, where someone had taken an immense quantity of ready-made clothing, blankets and other goods which, said the owner, would be hard to identify because so many people had them. Christie's examination satisfied him that the same gang had done the Halliburton job.

At Davidson's, too, he got an important clue: the owner said the thieves had taken a pair of shoe brushes of a particular pattern on which he had placed his private mark. There was also a private mark of the firm from which he got them the day before the robbery. Christie asked if the supplier, Fenwick & Co., sold the same class of brushes to other customers. Davidson replied: "They only received six pairs as samples, and they may have the other five pairs left."

"I went round to Fenwick's," Christie wrote, "and found they were just about to forward the five pairs of brushes to different customers as samples of goods to arrive from Home (England) shortly," so he detained them, believing they might be important in establishing the identity of the loot. Later that day, Christie told Secretan he believed one of the thieves was so expert in judging cloth he must be a tailor. "Well," said Secretan, "go to work and run them down . . . the other detectives are completely at sea over the case, and knowing these cases are a specialty with you, I determined to recall you from Geelong." In the muster room, Christie perused the names of men recently released from Pentridge, and took a list of those whose trade was tailoring.

"I strolled down to Harry Coyle's hotel in Queen Street (the Sandhurst), a notorious criminals' haunt," Christie wrote. "On going through the house I saw it was deserted. I said, 'Well, Harry, what has become of all the boys?'. He replied, 'The other D's (detectives) have been here so often during the last few days that they have scared them away to the country, and what few that is left have gone to graft (work).'

'Which of them have gone to graft?'

'Well, Harry Brooks is working at a tailor's somewhere in North Melbourne, Ben Long tells me. Ben has been doing some carpentering for me, and he is coming back this afternoon with a couple of new forms he has made for the bar parlour. Both these men are on the square (have turned honest) right now'."

Christie went home and examined his wardrobe of disguises. He selected an old rig-out, including blankets which he had once bought from a hard-up swagman. He dyed his hair and eyebrows a reddish colour, which he could quickly wash out with soap and water, then he got dressed and called in his landlord, asking how he looked. The landlord replied: "Well, if I had not seen you rigged out like it before, I would have collared you for a thief."

Christie sent for the cab he usually employed on these occasions. He pulled down the cab's curtains and went to the corner of Bourke and Queen Streets to watch Coyle's for the arrival of Ben Long with the forms. Long delivered them in a hand truck, left quickly, abandoned the truck (it had been stolen) in a right-of-way in Lonsdale Street and jumped in a North Melbourne cab (horse tram) that was passing. Christie followed, because he felt sure Long and Brooks were two of the men who robbed Halliburton's and Davidson's.

Long got out at Howard Street and went into the Volunteer Arms Hotel. "I watched the hotel carefully for about 20 minutes," Christie wrote, "thinking he had only gone in for a drink, but as there was no sign of him coming out I jumped down with my swag on my back." Then he walked into the bar parlour where he called for a nip of rum. He threw it in the fire when the landlady's back was turned. Speaking in broad Irish, he asked her to have a nip. "She did so. I asked her if she could give me a shake-down (a bed for the night). She replied, 'As you have your blankets you can coil up in the shed at the back, there is a couple more dossing down there'. Seeing she sold tobacco, I bought a couple of plugs, and the landlady, on me shouting again, got communicative, more especially as I told her I had just made a rise (come into money) and would like her to mind my sugar (money) for me.

"I said, 'I am looking for an old mate of mine, Ben the carpenter, do you know of any carpenter living around here of that name?' She replied, 'There is a Ben Long a carpenter living in the next right-of-way. His back door opens into a yard adjoining my yard, and he nearly always goes in and out through my place. Go out and leave your swag in the shed, and you can go in and see if he is your mate, but if you want me to take care of your money you had better give it to me now, or you will get robbed of it.' I said, 'Wait till I come back as I may want to shout for my mate and his old woman'. She replied, 'He has no missus but he has six or seven men living with him.' I said, 'Well, if he has no missus he ain't my mate.'

"I picked up my swag and went through to the back yard, and after putting it in the shed, I took a quick survey of the back premises. There was only two cottages whose back gates opened into the yard as described by the landlady. One had the window covered up with calico and the yard was in a very neglected condition. The other had the back door open. There was an old woman sitting on the doorstep and three or four children playing in the yard, and although the cottage was a miserably small one, everything looked neat and tidy. Lighting my pipe, I walked over and got into conversation with the woman and at once saw that she was respectable, more especially when she told me her husband drove a spring cart for Laurence Bros, grocers, Elizabeth Street, City.

"I ascertained from her that her husband would not be home till 7 o'clock. I said to her, 'Who lives next door? Their yard is in a filthy state'. She replied, 'I don't know but they are not much account, they sleep all day and only go out after dark and don't come home till all hours in the night, and when they do come home they bring big bags full of stuff, as we can hear them dropping them on the floor. The other morning, my husband on getting up found that someone had been using his horse and spring dray during the night. He had cleaned it overnight and next morning found it all dirty, besides there was wheel marks leading from their door to where the cart stands, so he is going to put the police on to them'.

"This was enough for me so I bid her good day, and passing out through the hotel, walked down the street into Victoria Street, at the corner of which my cab was standing. Giving the cabman the office to follow, I jumped up as soon as we were round the corner and drove direct to the Detective office where I picked up Detectives Brown and Harrington. We adjourned to my hotel where I peeled off my disguise, washed off the dye of my hair and resumed my ordinary walking clothes. With (Brown and Harrington) I returned to Howard Street. It was now dark. I was going to keep the landlady's attention attracted so that Brown would get through without being seen. I told him as soon as he saw me talking to the landlady in the bar he was to slip through the side passage into the shed in the back yard where I would join him after a drink and a few words with the landlady.

"I walked out into the yard. Brown and I slipped into Long's yard and crept up to the back door and found the keyhole stopped up. I pushed the piece out of the keyhole with my knife and there saw Long and two other men in the front room (the centre door being open) measuring and cutting up cloth, so leaving Brown to guard the back I slipped out through the hotel to the cab, whipped off my overcoat, threw it into the cab and told Harrington to follow me. We got down to Long's front door. I found the door locked. Keeping out of sight of the window, I gave a gentle knock, when a voice said, 'Who's there?' I replied in a low voice, 'It's me, Ben'. The door was opened when I and Harrington burst in. The latter locked the door when a desperate fight took place but we eventually overpowered the three men and handcuffed them.

"We then let Detective Brown in by the back door, through the keyhole of which he could see all that transpired. Making the three men—Benjamin Long, Henry Brookes and John Thomas *alias* Young *alias* Jack the Lagger—sit down on the floor of the back room, I placed Detectives Brown and Harrington in charge of them whilst I took a chair and sat down behind the front door to await the arrival of the other men. I may here state that a cursory examination showed me that the two rooms were full of stolen property, principally articles of clothing."

Christie did not have to wait long. He kept behind the door, and opened it to a knock. Two men walked in. There was no light except from a small fire. Christie locked the door, and the two men found they were trapped. "After a slight struggle, I got them into the back room with the others where there was a lighted candle," Christie wrote. The two arrivals were Charles Baker *alias* Young, and George Edwards *alias* Brown. The detectives handcuffed them together, and Brown and Harrington stood guard on the five. Christie shut the door between the two rooms, and again took his position behind the front door. "Who's there?" he asked when someone knocked. A voice replied: "It's all right Ben." Christie opened the door to a man and woman, and locked it. Harrington opened the connecting door and brought in the candle.

"I found I had secured two other notorious criminals, Henry McEwan *alias* Hugh Connor *alias* Denis Fogarty, and Elizabeth Waddle *alias* Wilson," Christie said. He had no more handcuffs, but made the prisoners sit on the floor and tied them together with a piece of clothes line. Christie now opened the front door and sent a boy for the cab, which was just around the corner. When the cab arrived, Christie sent the driver to Hotham police station for three constables and two furniture vans. When Christie reached the detective office and marched his seven prisoners inside, the other detectives were "very much astonished," he said, and their astonishment was greater when they saw the size of the loot.

Christie now had to get evidence that would show that the seven lived in the house where stolen goods were found. Next day he went back to the hotel in his ordinary clothes, and told the landlady that one of the men had left his swag, and she asked if he meant the red-headed one. "I knew that man was a thief," she said, "I would not let him sleep in the house. He had a lot of money and the scoundrel wanted me to take care of it for him, but as I thought it was crooked I would have nothing to do with it."

Getting his swag, Christie called on the old woman who lived next door to Long's, and took down a statement proving that the seven lived in, or frequented, the burglars' house. Others in Howard Street corroborated her evidence. When she realised that Christie was the red-headed man, she was thunderstruck.

Examining Long's house by daylight, Christie found Davidson's shoe brushes with the private marks intact; in the fireplace he found charred labels of Halliburton goods; and raising the hearthstone he found a jemmy, a set of skeleton keys, a dark lantern and a brass padlock. He also matched the irregular–shaped cloth that had been cut from one of the Halliburton rolls.

In August, the six men prisoners received gaol terms ranging from five to eight years hard labour. The woman, Elizabeth Waddle, was apparently not presented in this court case. Thomas and Brookes turned out to be tailors, and Brookes afterwards told Christie that they were the two who had been in Halliburtons all night selecting the goods.

Christie received a total of £75 in generous rewards from Halliburtons and Davidsons, and £5 from the Police Reward Fund. All this was equivalent to about three months' salary. A greater accolade, highly unusual, came from the court itself. The Crown Prosecutor, Joseph Dunne, wrote to Standish praising Christie's zeal, energy and intelligence, and recommended him for promotion. Judge Pohlman, chairman of the Melbourne General Sessions, wrote to endorse these views.

"I would further state," Judge Pohlman wrote, "that in all cases in which Detective Christie has been engaged in this Court, he has invariably shown great earnestness and intelligence." Standish received other glowing reports about Christie: from Inspector Palmer of Russell Street and from the prosecutor in the lower court case. Christie, still only 24, was a public hero.

CHAPTER 6

Did he sleep with Mrs Walker?

It is strange the way heroes fall so quickly. Within one month of Christie's stunning success with the storebreakers, his name was blackened and he came close to being sacked.

About nine o'clock on the night of 28 September, acting on a tip-off, Christie walked into the bar of Harry Coyle's Sandhurst Hotel—where he had begun his hunt in the Halliburton robberies—and looked around for a criminal named Tommy Scott, who was said to be carrying skeleton keys. Coyle diverted Christie by offering him whisky. As he did so, Tommy Scott hurried out the door and threw a bundle on the floor. During a scuffle, Christie was battered by Scott's mates. One mate, Thomas Moore, grabbed the bundle and ran off with it, but Christie chased and caught him and was bashed again. Bleeding from a 25-minute struggle to hold Scott, he managed to get the bundle, which contained the keys, and drag Moore to the detective office.

When Moore came before the City Court on 6 October, charged with having possessed the keys, Harry Coyle denied in testimony that any disturbance had taken place at his hotel, and he said indignantly that he was not in the habit of harbouring criminals. Thus Coyle branded Christie a perjurer. But this was minor compared with the sensational allegation which he made next. His barman, he said, had told him that Christie lived with the wife of a convicted felon named Levi Walker, well-known as the maker of burglars' tools, and now imprisoned at Pentridge. Christie kept Levi Walker's wife and dressed her like any lady, he said. Coyle was insinuating that Levi Walker made the skeleton keys, gave them to Tommy Scott, and then conspired with Christie to have Scott arrested.

Recalled to the witness box, Christie was asked whether he lived with Mrs Walker, and he gave a strange answer. He said: "I have not known that lady until a short time since." This was no answer at all, as *The Age* pointed out two days later in an editorial calling for an investigation into this claim and others; for the other claims were almost as damning. Christie admitted under cross-examination that he struck Thomas Moore in the detective office after arresting him, a fact that he might have shrugged off in the circumstances after a bloody fight. But then Christie's detective colleague Joe Brown got in the witness box and damned him. Brown, who had no reason to be part of the case and who had gone to court unbidden and without telling his office, said that Moore was handcuffed and seated when Christie hit him.

The magistrates dismissed the charge against Moore on the grounds that there was not enough proof that he knowingly had the skeleton keys in his possession; but they believed he assaulted Christie, and fined him ten pounds. *The Age* editorial called the case extraordinary, and it obviously had no time for Harry Coyle. *The Age* asked: "Is it true, as described by a virtuous and horror-stricken publican, that Detective Christie, part of whose duty is supposed to be to promote public morality, is himself leading a life of debauchery, in collusion with the criminal class, getting up criminal cases for his own advantage; or if not, why should the bench have allowed his character to be so traduced (by Coyle) and his barman in open court?" The editorial said that in justice to the entire detective force, all the claims ought to be rigidly investigated.

On Standish's orders, Superintendent Nicolson began an inquiry the following day, but curiously, it ignored the allegations about Mrs Walker and connivance at crime, and looked only at the allegation of assault. Christie pleaded not guilty. He had hit Moore in self-defence, he said, because Moore had raised his manacled hands to strike him in the passage leading to the muster room. He had not hit him after that. Joe Brown swore this was wrong; he said he had seen two assaults, not just one. This evidence was crucial. To strike a man in self-defence might be understandable. To assault him again, not in self-defence, was a shocking breach of regulations.

One detective who partly supported Christie's claim was James

Marshall, who said he saw Moore with his hands raised in the passage as if to strike Christie. Christie thrust Moore into the muster room, and at the same time struck him three blows. The first blow struck Moore's arm as he guarded his head. Christie was saying: "You brute, I'll teach you to assault me." The second blow, Marshall believed, struck the side of Moore's head. The third blow struck his nose and knocked him backwards against a form at the muster room table, where he remained seated. Moore was saying: "You dog, I can stand all this."

Detective Marshall's description of Christie was vivid. He said Christie took off his coat and said: "I never had such a tieing up in my life," adding that he had been knocked down at the hotel and kicked about the body. Christie's face was smeared all over with blood, he was bleeding from the forehead and apparently had been bleeding from the nose. His clothes were disordered and dusty and stained with blood from his chest to his knees. His knuckles were cut and one of them was bleeding. Christie said he got that while stopping a blow Moore made at him with the handcuffs. Detective Marshall was unshakeable in his evidence that he saw Christie assault Moore only once. He was also certain that Detective Brown was the only other person present.

Detective Marshall said he told Christie: "You are very foolish to assault that man before Brown," and Christie replied: "The brute deserved it." Marshall said: "It will be all over town tomorrow," and Christie said: "I thought of that the moment I struck him." (Brown, in fact, admitted in later cross-examination that he discussed the case with criminals.)

The next witness was Detective Patrick Mackay, who said he was present during only one assault, when Moore was seated at the table. (So this assault was different from that which Marshall had described; in the assault which Mackey described, Moore was seated; he was not being thrust through the door). Mackay said he heard Moore tell Christie: "You know damn well I know nothing about those keys", and: "You bugger, if I had the handcuffs off, you would not strike me like that."

Although Levi Walker was not part of this case, Superintendent

Nicolson saw fit to bring his name into it by asking Mackay if he knew him. Mackay said he did. "I have heard it asserted in the muster room that Levi was working for Christie," he said. "During the time Ben Long was arrested by Christie, I heard it mentioned. I have heard it said that Levi Walker put Christie on to those men, meaning gave him information to their being the persons who committed the robbery."

Christie himself then cross-examined Mackay, and tried to drag some more muck from him. Under questioning, Mackay said Harry Coyle was a reputed receiver of stolen goods, and the Sandhurst Hotel was a house of the lowest class and frequented by thieves. The men Mackay had arrested there in the past included Tommy Scott.

Christie pursued this questioning, and Mackay said: "You and I have not been on speaking terms for some time, particularly since the arrest of Billy Smart." He did not say who Billy Smart was. Mackay also said that a thief named P.Costello, whom he had seen staying at the Sandhurst, was now wanted for the assault on Christie. Mackay said he had seen Ben Long and the gang that Christie arrested sitting in the kitchen drinking. He admitted he went to the Sandhurst and spoke to the landlord after Moore was arrested, but he denied he mentioned Levi Walker's name or said anyone had put the case away.

Detective Joe Brown's testimony that he twice saw Christie assault Moore—within a period of 30 seconds—overlapped the evidence of his two colleagues. Detective Marshall had alleged assault No.1, Detective Mackay had alleged assault No. 2, and now Brown alleged both. As Brown was cross-examined, the muck kept coming. He admitted he did not tell Secretan anything of the circumstances, and did not tell him he was going to attend the court case. He had been on duty all the previous night, he said, but went to the court without being ordered to. He could not remember telling Secretan he went because he took a particular interest in the case; he went because he wanted to hear the cases generally and Christie's and another in particular.

Brown said he had mentioned the assaults to only two people outside the office, when he was inquiring into Tommy Scott. One was a criminal named Jones and the other was Mickey Lynch, now in gaol.

Coyle's hotel, frequented by thieves, was one of the lowest, and Brown said he did not know any respectable people who went there. Nor was he aware that Tommy Woods, the pickpocket, was barman. He knew Harry King, the present barman, but had never heard he was ever convicted.

Christie then seems to have tried to make Brown admit he was dissatisfied about the Halliburton reward. Brown said he remembered the case of Ben Long and the other five whom Christie had put away. "We have been on good terms since that case," Brown said. "I had not any dispute with you over that case. You told me that Mr Secretan knew the facts of the case and if I deserved any reward I would get it. There was £3 reward from the Police Reward Fund. I do not think I deserved any reward." Brown said he remembered asking Christie for two shillings which he had spent on the case. He had never said on seeing the *Police Gazette* (which routinely announced rewards): "It will be my turn next" or "I'll serve you out for this."

Christie's statement to the inquiry had a ring of truth. He said that at 7 p.m. on 28 September, near the Theatre Royal, he met a man called Thomas Greenwood, who told him he had just left Coyle's hotel and had seen the thief Tommy Scott with some skeleton keys. Christie replied he could not believe this statement, because Greenwood had several times misled him. When Greenwood said he would give the information to other detectives, Christie gave him one more chance, and went to the detective office to get some help, but waited there in vain until 8.45. On the way to the Sandhurst he met George Williams, a bank clerk, and asked him to accompany him in case Christie needed to send for help.

Going into the bar of the Sandhurst Hotel, he saw Scott showing something in his hand to Moore and another man sitting at a table, but Scott put it in his pocket as soon as he saw Christie. "The landlord then asked me over to have some whisky," Christie said. "Scott instantly got up and I went over to him and said, 'Come out, I want to speak to you.' On going out of the door, Scott threw back a small bundle into the bar. I then concluded it was the skeleton keys referred to by Thomas Greenwood, so I arrested him and dragged him over to where the bundle lay, and when in the act of picking it up, a man kicked it over out of my reach. The same man then laid hold of me, and with the assistance of others, rushed me into a corner. Scott escaped, and while running out, cried out, 'Collar them Charlie' (meaning the prisoner).

"I kept my attention as much as possible to the keys (bundle) on the floor. I saw Thomas Moore pick it up, and I instantly made an effort and succeeded in seizing Moore, but the same men caught hold of me, when a violent struggle ensued during which I was roughly handled and thrown on the floor. Moore escaped and I saw him run out by the back of the hotel. I endeavoured to follow him but was kept back by the men. I saw Thomas Moore come in by the back, run down the side of (the) bar and into the street. I made a desperate effort to free myself, I succeeded in knocking down the ringleader, and by that means I escaped from them and ran into the street.

"I passed Mr Williams at the hotel door. I ran down the street after Moore, came up with him 50 yards (about) from the hotel, I caught him by the collar, when he turned round and made a violent blow at my face, which took effect on my right ear. I struck him on the neck, we both fell and he attempted to throw away the bundle of skeleton keys. While on the ground I picked them up and placed them inside my shirt. As I was getting up, I received a violent kick in the belly, which took the wind from me. I received several kicks from one of the bystanders. I have no doubt but it was the same man who assaulted me in the hotel.

"When he kicked me he said, 'Let him go you bloody dog'. By this time I had the handcuffs on one of Moore's hands, and the man who kicked me called out to Moore, 'Smash him Charlie', when Moore struck me in the face with the handcuff which was loose. He also struck me several times with his feet. I was so weak from the useage I received and loss of blood that I could not overcome Moore till after we had been wrestling and rolling in the gutter for at least 25 minutes. I sent Mr Williams for the assistance of the police, and at his absence I several times called upon the people (telling them who I was) to assist me, but I could see no respectable person about. Just before the arrival of Mr Williams with the police, the prisoner sang out, 'I give in, I will go quietly now.'

"I then said to him, 'I arrest you for having these skeleton keys in your possession.' He replied, 'They do not belong to me, they are Tommy's'. I then conveyed him to the detective office after putting on the other handcuff. On going up the side passage of the detective office, Moore turned half round quickly and made a violent blow at my face. I threw up my arm to stop it, and received its full force on the back of my right hand, which was cut, swollen and stiff for several days. I instantly pushed Moore into the muster room, and instantly struck him three times, at the same time saying, 'I will teach you to assault me you treacherous brute'.

"He then fell on the form near the room door. I then shut the door, went into the clerks' office, took off my coat and hung it up, and said to Marshall, 'Will you mind my prisoner till I see a man outside'. I then went out by the passage. On opening the front passage door I met Detective Mackay coming in. I saw Mr Williams there and requested him to remain till I came out. I then returned to the muster room, went into the clerks' office for a towel and on going into the muster room I saw Mr Secretan come out of his passage. He went into the office, followed by me. After a small conversation I called Detective Marshall and asked him to mind prisoner while I had a wash. I left room and returned in about two minutes, when I removed my prisoner to the watch house.

"On my way up Russell Street with prisoner he threw up his hands and was in the act of striking me again, when I seized him and said if he tried that again I would warm him. I have suffered severely from the effects of the ill treatment I received in the Sandhurst Hotel and Queen Street. While I had Moore on the ground in the street, I never struck him, altho if inclined I might have injured him severely. I never struck a man in my life when disabled until this occasion, and from the treacherous manner in which he assaulted me in the dark passage on the spur of the moment. I though was justified in striking him. Had I not stopped the blow with my hand, I might have been seriously injured in the face.

"I stated openly to the magistrates at the Police Court that I had been assaulted and that in return I had struck prisoner several times. I held back nothing. I positively deny having committed a second

85

assault upon prisoner. I also state that Levi Walker had no connection whatever with the case, and that I received no information from him dealing with the case. Thomas Greenwood my informant can be produced at any time if necessary."

Nicolson handed Standish the evidence on 12 October, and remarked that the second assault had been proved by Brown and Mackay. Nicolson made his usual plea for leniency towards men junior to him. He asked Standish to bear in mind Christie's good conduct and efficiency, the meritorious entries on his record sheet, and the severe treatment he had received from Thomas Moore and his friends. Standish replied that the evidence showed Christie had committed two distinct assaults on Moore.

Standish wrote: "The first, which took place in the passage at the Detective Office admits of some justification—for though members of the Force are strictly enjoined to employ the utmost forbearance on all occasions and not to allow their feelings to get the better of their discretion—Detective Christie may be said to have been acting almost in self-defence on that occasion. But even then I look upon his impetuosity as most censurable, as no danger of the prisoner escaping or of his committing a serious assault on the Detective could be reasonably apprehended within the precincts of the Detective Office and with assistance at hand.

"The second assault on the prisoner while he was sitting down handcuffed in the office is proved by the testimony of Detectives Brown and Mackay. This assault was both cowardly in a man and unjustifiable in a member of the Police Force—whatever the previous provocation may have been. Brutality to prisoners is an offence which I never gloss over. It is an offence calculated to bring the whole Department into disrepute and to engender an angry and hostile feeling on the part of the public against all members of the Force.

"If I do not order Detective Christie's dismissal from the Force it is because his conduct has not only been exemplary since he joined the Force but he has been on all occasions conspicuous for his zeal and efficiency and has rendered valuable services to the Department. His record sheet, which contains numerous entries of meritorious service, shows that he has never been even punished for misconduct. Superintendent Nicolson's recommendation in the Detective's favour has, I need not say, received the consideration which it is entitled to.

"It is necessary however that the Detective be severely punished and I have therefore to direct that he be reduced to the rank and pay of a third class Detective with loss of pay during his suspension from duty. I think that the narrow escape he has had from the disgrace of expulsion from the Force will be a lesson to him and that his subsequent conduct will show that the leniency with which he had been dealt has had a beneficial effect."

Despite delivering this stern sentence on Christie, Standish could smell a rat; he was not a fool. And he went on: "The conduct of Detectives Brown and Mackay—more especially that of the former—must not escape censure. They are much to be blamed for not at once having reported to Mr Secretan what they subsequently describe as a savage assault by Detective Christie. Moreover, Detective Brown appears to have talked about it to members of the criminal class and I cannot but entertain the suspicion that he was in attendance at the Police Court when the case against Moore was heard solely for the purpose of giving evidence against Detective Christie.

"There appears to be a very unwholesome state of feeling between these several members of the Detective Force to which I must draw Superintendent Nicolson's special attention. I trust that he will take the necessary steps to suppress anything of this kind by prompt and vigorous measures as the existence of these jealousies and animosities must be most detrimental to the efficiency and well–being of that branch of the Department."

But what about the allegations that Christie conspired with a criminal and slept with the criminal's wife? *The Age* was not going to let this matter drop, and as soon as the assault verdict was made public, it called for an inquiry conducted by a board free of police influence. It said: "That Mr Christie has enemies in the force is plain enough from the suggestive alacrity with which some of his colleagues testified against him when charged with assaulting a prisoner; that he has firm friends is equally certain, because he appears to have many likeable qualities; it is extremely desirable to save him from the intervention of either." Christie, too, was pressing for an inquiry.

Actually, Standish had already acted. On 14 October he asked the Chief Secretary for an early board of inquiry into Coyle's three allegations that Christie (a) was cohabiting with and keeping the wife of a felon, (b) gave false and malicious evidence about Coyle's public house, and (c) concocted a plan with a felon to arrest Thomas Scott. The Chief Secretary immediately appointed a board that included the senior magistrates Joseph Panton and Evelyn Sturt; and one would like to think that when they dealt with allegation No.2—that Christie told malicious lies about the Sandhurst Hotel—they all fell over laughing.

One would also think that in order to demolish allegation No.3— concocting a plot with a felon—Christie merely had to produce his informant Thomas Greenwood, as he said he could do. The remaining allegation—of living with Mrs Walker—well, who knows? Surely the board would have summonsed Coyle and his barman to substantiate the claim. What a duo they would have made: a perjurer and a pickpocket. It is difficult to see fair men giving them much credence.

It is just possible that the allegation about Mrs Walker was accurate, and it is just possible that Christie may have been forced to admit it; but he still had a way out. Constable Ernest Flood, of Greta, faced something similar in 1872. He was accused of having a boisterous relationship with Ned Kelly's sister Annie Gunn, whose horse-stealing husband was in gaol; Flood was also accused of stealing a gold watch and of urinating in another man's fireplace—all on the one remarkable day —but he was never found guilty or penalised. His superiors took the view that Flood had a duty to get close to the Kelly clan.

On 3 November, the Chief Secretary's office sent Standish a note: "The Governor-in-Council has been pleased to place on record that Detective Christie is quite exonerated of the charges." It is easy to imagine that after this, the muster room took a long time to relax. As for Standish, he could never relax. Old Harry Power was becoming more of a pest, galloping around the hills bailing people up. Sergeant Montford, of Benalla, passed on information from a man named Billy Love, just out of Pentridge, that Power was sheltered by the Lloyds, who were Kelly relatives. Billy Love claimed he could put Power away easily. Montford made him an offer, which he did not disclose, and Love was thinking it over.

Montford had a second suggestion, not about Power. This was that a suitable prisoner be discharged from Pentridge at the same time as a prisoner named Billy Lowry who had boasted to Love that he would go on the roads again (become a bushranger) as soon as he got out. The prisoner would go on the roads with Lowry and put him away. Standish thought the idea was plausible, but difficult to carry out. "Besides," he told Ryall, "the Police Department must avoid entrapping such a dangerous man . . . into the commission of crime."

It was the Chief Secretary, Sir James McCullough, who finally goaded the police into doing more about Power. Using his most friendly and civilised language, Sir James wrote to Standish to say that if Power were not caught soon, the officers in charge at Beechworth and Benalla would be removed. This was not quite the way Sir James put it. His words were that it might be necessary to see "whether there were not the officers who will display greater ability".

Educated men of the 1870s often used such eloquence when making threats. Standish, too, could do it. Backed by the words of Sir James McCullough—and by implication, under threat himself—he could have hurled thunderbolts at Beechworth and Benalla. But no. He wrote a charming letter to the two officers, pointing out that he could not fairly blame them for Power's continued freedom; it was not their fault, he said. The fault lay with Power's bushcraft, the terrain and public sympathy for him. At the same time, however, the public saw the lack of success as reflecting on the force's efficiency and reputation. And so on, and so on. Then—almost as an afterthought—Standish said that he himself was taking special steps in this matter. He was sending two experienced officers to the area.

These two men were experienced indeed, probably the pick of the force: Superintendent Charles Nicolson and Superintendent Frank Hare. They confirmed where old Harry's lair was from an informer, Ned Kelly's uncle, John Lloyd, who received £500 for this.

Some sort of information came from young Ned himself, who had been arrested as Harry Power's accomplice.

Ned was aged about 15, and had been held for five weeks awaiting trial at Kyneton on charges which at first included highway robbery. It was a scandal to hold a boy for so long, or to hold anyone, but Nicolson had persisted and had weathered the newspaper fuss. Finally, the police presented no evidence against Ned, and he was freed. Within a few days, Power was caught. Many people thought this was a strange sequence of events. It was an equally strange letter that Ned wrote soon afterward to Sergeant Babington, of Kyneton:

> "I write you these lines hoping to find you and Mister Nickilson in good health as I am myself at present I have arrived safe and I would like you would see what you and Mister Nickilson could do for me I have done all circum stances would alow me which you now try what you can to answer this letter as soon as posabel direct your letter to Daniel Kelly gretta post office that is my name no more at present"
>
> Edward Kelly.

> "everyone looks on me like a black snake send me an answer me as soon as posable."

When the time came to pounce on Power, the glory went to Nicolson. It was he who took Power, at his hide-out on the Lloyds' property in the ranges at the head of the King River. The rain was so heavy on that night that the guard dogs did not bark and the guard peacock did not scream. Nicolson, Hare and Sergeant Montford crept past the Lloyd house and seized old Harry as he slept in a mia-mia. A blacktracker, Donald, who led the police in, was later awarded ten pounds. The following year, Standish was still writing to the law office to try to get it for him.

Power went quietly. As they brought the old galoot to Pentridge, he turned to Detective Henry Daly who was part of the escort, and said: "There Daly, take this," handing him his meerschaum pipe from his pocket. "I present it to you," said Power, "Smoke it for my sake until I come out again." Poor old Harry did come out, but he had one rum too many one day and drowned in the Murray River. Daly took the pipe to Secretan, not being sure what to do with it. Secretan told Standish he proposed to keep the pipe in his office until it could be sold at auction. Standish approved. "I am sure that Daly will see that his being allowed to retain the pipe might (expose?) the Department to misrepresentation," he wrote.

Little things like a pipe could bring odium to the police. So could little newspaper reports; they did not have to be big. On 29 December, as 1870 closed, Melbourne read about a fuss over John Hayward, the former rate collector of the borough of Fitzroy. He had defaulted, and a warrant was out for his arrest. And yet, there he was walking around the Royal Park as large as life and the detectives were doing nothing about it. A Fitzroy councillor named Delbridge was so disgusted he brought the matter up at the council meeting. He had even gone to the detective office within 15 minutes of a Hayward sighting, and still nothing had been done.

He could only account for this, he said, by supposing that (a) someone wanted Hayward to escape, or (b) the detectives would not try to arrest him until a reward was offered. Cr Delbridge was not the only person angry. His colleague, Cr McLean, said many people had seen Hayward.

Manwaring, Christie, Walker and Parker, who were on the case, all denied doing wrong. What a coincidence it was that Parker went out and arrested Hayward that very morning.

CHAPTER 7

Doing a dirty deal

The Age had many reasons to campaign against the police force. One of them was the detectives' habit of basing their prosecutions on the words: 'from information received'. For example, a detective would enter the witness box and say that from information he received, he went to a house in Richmond and found stolen goods.

There was no way to test this claim. *The Age* had long believed that in all court cases, police should be compelled to disclose their sources of information. Anything less than this, it said, threatened the liberty of innocent people, gave immunity to criminals who betrayed their mates for gain, enabled policemen to concoct crimes, and put them into a partnership that condoned one part of a crime in order to solve another part.

In February 1871, *The Age* reported a court case so explicit in its evidence about this corruption that it seemed incredible. The case was brought by Detective Daly and Detective Mackay, and it showed they were deeply involved in a scandalous practice. Daly had been subsidising an old thief called Henry Jackson who would tell him about a crime that was coming up and give him a 'programme of operation'.

"Daly never plucks the fruit before it is ripe," said *The Age*. "Jackson tells him of a burglary to be perpetrated in the St Kilda Road 'this very night'. 'Good,' says Daly, 'find out where it is and meet me again by the Burke and Wills monument.' But somehow it does not suit Jackson's game, or perhaps Daly's game as Jackson understands it, for the locality to be found. Daly has, according to the practice, been to the detective office and reported that a robbery is coming off, but he does not know where.

"Not a word is said to any of the other detectives except Daly's companion Mackay. One would think that when anything had been sprung, the word ought to go round; but no, each pair of detectives keeps its own secrets and nurses its own burglaries. Jackson does not keep his appointment at the monument. What then? It may naturally be suggested that the detectives take a walk down the St Kilda Road. Not they. The affair is in Jackson's hands and is safe.

"Their confidence is justified, for, although the news of the burglary is published next day, a letter comes to Daly from Jackson with the 'programmed operations'. Webb, one of the robbers, is to be caught in the evening crossing the Falls-bridge with a pair of chandeliers on his shoulders, and caught he is, according to the programme. Next day the papers duly record the clever capture made by Detectives Daly and Mackay. Jackson can afford to do without his share of the glory. And what does he get? Is it not immunity for himself?"

The practice was rife, but there is no evidence that all detectives were part of it. Whatever his own methods were, Christie continued to collect rewards and commendations in a string of successes as a thief-taker. And now, for a second time, the bench of a court wrote to Standish singing Christie's praises. The chief magistrate, Mr Evelyn Sturt, directed by the mayor and a bench of magistrates, drew Standish's attention to the "praiseworthy zeal" and good work done by Christie and Detective Bailey, who had secured the conviction of two shopbreakers (Nat Dwyer and William Turner) and a receiver (William Robinson).

This was a remarkably swift result. The men were arrested on 8 July and sentenced to gaol terms ten days later, a fact which delighted the bench. Mr Sturt almost tripped over his own eager words in saying so: "Immediate detection and punishment falling on criminal offenders following rapidly on their offences must lead greatly to the suppression of crime . . . ," the letter said. The mayor and magistrates referred their view to the force for favourable consideration. Christie, among other things, had kept the offenders under surveillance for nine days. This does not sound like either entrapment or criminal connivance. Standish awarded Christie £3. The detectives needed such successes because *The Age* had looked in a copy of the *Police Gazette,* counted 37 robberies in and around Melbourne within a week, and concluded that "something must be wrong somewhere". "It may be asked," it said, "how many of these robberies will be traced home, and those who know will quickly answer not one-tenth." When this was published, Nicolson managed to count only 30. Secretan told him such a number was not uncommon for the time of year; in most cases there had not been time for a result, but the detectives had made 19 arrests.

To read this issue of the *Gazette* is to gaze at a Melbourne whose simplicity is now unrecognisable. One notice says: "Stolen from a buggy in Lonsdale Street West about 8 p.m. 25 June an oppossum skin carriage rug 8 feet long by 3 feet lined with rough green cloth. Belonged to the Rev. John O'Sullivan."

Dear oh dear, nothing was sacred. The *Gazette* also mentioned that Henry Johnstone had served his time at Pentridge and was free again. He was a sailor, thick–lipped, with a cast in both eyes and a small scar on his temple; he was 19 and not much more than 5 feet tall. One wonders if he ever found a woman to love him. Poor Henry. He did 12 months for stealing matches. Ah, one thinks, this would be because he had prior convictions. None is listed, although the priors of others are.

•   •   •   •   •

Christie was enticed into a boxing ring in August to fight for the amateur heavyweight championship of Victoria. This was a bout organised by Abe Hicken, well-known in his day as the Australian heavyweight champion, although the title was in some dispute. Hicken ran an athletics hall, and he called for all-comers to compete there for a cup valued at ten guineas. The only contestants who were willing to stand up to each other when the night came were Christie and a rangy boxer named Jack Thompson, whose reputation was high.

Thompson, at 6 feet 3 inches, was four inches taller than Christie, and his reach was longer. At 13 stone 4lbs, Thompson was almost two stone heavier. It was a weight difference which fitted easily into the era's liberal interpretation of heavyweight. In a hall crowded with men who had paid the high entrance fee of ten shillings, Christie and Thompson wore the new-fangled boxing gloves (four ounces in this case) which were slowly replacing bare knuckles in Australia. Not everyone thought gloves were a good thing.

It would take another ten or 15 years before they became thoroughly accepted. So this was a period when the bare-knuckle open-air prize fight, which was brutal and illegal, and which had no set number of rounds, co-existed with attempts to make boxing more disciplined. In this sense, Christie and Thompson were among pioneers in Australia. But the rounds were not yet timed or limited. A round ended when one of the boxers fell, was knocked down, or was too dazed to continue.

On this night, Thompson ended the first round by landing a heavy blow behind Christie's left ear and sending him tottering to the ropes. The second round ended when Thompson, his nose bleeding freely, slipped and fell during some furious in-fighting. Christie was using his left hand in the way he had been taught during the days of the school bully. The betting in the hall suddenly made him favourite at two-to-one on. This shortened to three-to-one on after the third round, in which Christie's blows sent Thompson to the ropes.

Thompson made the mistake in the fourth round of rushing at Christie, whose lessons from schooldays had prepared him for this too. He parried Thompson's blows, and dazed him with a right-hand to the jaw. When Thompson came at him again, Christie floored him with his left. This was the end of the championship fight. It was amazingly short for the times. The crowd cheered Christie, who had shown that technique could stop a taller, heavier, longer-reaching opponent.

In his work, Christie had another popular success in October. He demonstrated once again that, in the absence of scientific detection—of which he and the force knew nothing—the next best thing was a knowledge of individual criminals and their distinctive methods. Christie had developed a remarkable knack of looking at the aftermath of a crime and being able to nominate the culprit. About this latest case, he wrote:

"The renowned burlesque actresses, the three sisters Zavistowski, whilst on a professional tour through Victoria, drew great attention through their dressy appearance and the magnificent jewellery they wore at race meetings and public gatherings. Whilst in Melbourne they resided in a two-storey house in Nicholson Street, opposite the model schools, on account of its close proximity to the City and the Theatre Royal, at which they were performing. On the evening of 14 October 1871, they left their residence about 7 p.m. en route for the theatre, leaving all their jewellery in their bedroom upstairs. On their return from the theatre about 11 p.m., they discovered the house had been entered by burglars, and jewellery worth about £300 stolen.

"After reading the report describing the watches, rings, chains, necklets, bracelets etc, I proceeded to the house, and on a careful examination, I found that the robbery had been effected by the burglars climbing up one of the verandah posts on to the verandah, and the rest was easy. The catch of the window was shot with the aid of a knife, and once inside the bedroom they had merely to select what jewellery would suit them, and remove it. This was exactly what the thieves did.

"After carefully thinking over the case I came to the conclusion that the burglars who committed this robbery were the same gang who did the verandah-post trick in the burglary at Spann's the jewellers. The modus operandi was exactly the same, and thieves generally have their own particular line of work. I came to the conclusion that William Williams and William Smith *alias* Smart were the burglars. A careful surveillance of Smart led me to the conclusion that David Scott, a renowned fence, a jeweller in Stephen Street, was likely to be the fence.

"I obtained a search warrant for his shop, and on executing same with Detectives Hartney and Manwaring, we found nearly the whole of the jewellery, watches taken to pieces, rings minus their stones etc. When I asked Scott to account for possession of the stolen property he replied he had purchased it in the ordinary course of business from a man who was a stranger to him. I said, 'You must have known it was stolen,' to which he replied, 'How could I tell? He looked a decent man.' 'What did you give him for it?' He replied, 'Four pounds.' On searching the shop I found the pawn list (stolen property list) which had been supplied to Scott, as it is to all pawn brokers, dealers, watchmakers of an indifferent character. I also found a written list of the purchase of the stolen goods. Both it and the pawn list had been carefully tallied off."

William Smart *alias* Smith was subsequently sentenced to two-and-a-half years gaol for burglary. Scott received a similar term for receiving. William Williams was acquitted. After the Spann robbery, which Christie likened in this manuscript to the Zavitowski robbery, the Adelaide police arrested a criminal named George Holden *alias* Eyre with the whole of the loot in his possession. He was brought back to Victoria, tried before Mr Justice Molesworth, and given two-and-a-half years for receiving. There was little doubt, said Christie, that Holden and Williams committed their burglary, and that Holden absconded with the loot, leaving Williams in the mud.

Christie wrote that before Holden was arrested, Mrs Spann haunted the detective office with all sorts of ideas about how it was done. "She invoked the aid of a spiritualistic medium at North Melbourne with the view to obtaining a clue to the robbers," Christie wrote. "The medium informed her that he knew the man who committed the robbery, and on payment of two guineas he would give her the necessary information. The money was planked down, and the medium told her to stand under the Post Office clock on a certain night at 12 o'clock, and as the clock began to strike the hour, the robber would pass her.

"She was delighted, called at the office and told me the result of the seance and wished me to accompany her to the Post Office on the night in question to capture the burglar. I refused, whereupon she said she believed the detectives were in the robbery as she could not get them to do as she wished. She went to the Post Office and as the clock struck she seized a man who was passing and called out 'Police.' The man assured her he was a policeman, in fact no other than the celebrated Sergeant Dalton in plain clothes. A constable was soon on the scene, and right or wrong she wanted him to lock Dalton up. As he refused, she said, 'It's just as I thought, you're all in it'."

Williams had climbed the Spann verandah post, shot the lock of a window with a table knife and, on getting inside, discovered that the room was occupied by a Miss Grant, who rented it from the Spanns and used it as a registry office. Williams descended a narrow staircase leading to the jewellery shop, and at the bottom he found a door which barred his way. He was carrying no suitable tool to force it, so he retraced his steps. Just at that moment, Holden, who had stayed on watch on the opposite side of the street, saw a constable come round the corner of the Colonial Bank into Elizabeth Street and walk directly towards them.

"Williams feigned drunkenness and Holden pretended he was trying to get his mate down to their ship," Christie wrote. "The ruse was successful as the constable, after advising Holden to get his mate home, proceeded on his beat. When (the constable was) out of sight, Williams hurried home to get a brace and bit and a keyhole saw, whilst Holden watched the constable to ascertain how he worked his beat and the times he visited Spann's shop."

Williams brought his tools back, and cut a hole in the door big enough to pass through. He did this by drilling four holes in each corner of a door panel, sawing between them, then lifting the whole panel out. Once inside the shop, he chose what jewellery he wanted, then joined Holden. They went to the university grounds to hide the loot until they could take it to a receiver. Next day, Holden did not turn up to a meeting to arrange the sale. Williams, becoming suspicious, went to the university grounds to see if the loot was safe, and found it all gone. This, said Christie, upset Williams's idea of there being honour among thieves.

Under Standish's instructions, detectives remained alert for prize fights, but they found few. About this time, Detective Jennings charged five men over a prize fight at Caulfield. Four of them were fined £2 and bound over to keep the peace. The fifth, William Cockbill, who was said to be the referee, was discharged because nobody could prove he was there.

The detectives constantly managed to divert Standish's energies to solving their own messes. Daly and Mackay once charged two men with stealing jewellery from Madame Diane de Beaumont's house in Russell Street, and she gratefully paid £50 reward. When she came to get her diamonds back, five were missing because the setting had broken. Standish had to authorise £20 to replace them, and he did not like this at all; for while he was reckless with his own salary of £1200 a year, he was a skinflint with the force's money.

But his worst experience that year concerned Detective Tom O'Callaghan, a larrikin if ever there was one. Indignantly, the police superintendent at Castlemaine wrote to Standish in December with an unheard-of complaint. During a court case, a prisoner named George Wilson had claimed that O'Callaghan plied him with liquor in order to get an admission from him. This allegation sounded so outrageous that Nicolson at first refused to believe it. Alas, he was soon writing to Standish:" . . . the detective by his conduct has brought scandal upon the Force." And yet, at this distance—if one believes O'Callaghan's story—it is hard not to crack a smile.

O'Callaghan was taking Wilson from Maryborough gaol to Castlemaine on a writ of habeus corpus. The coach stop at Maryborough was outside a pub, and while the two of them were waiting for the coach to arrive, a mate of O'Callaghan's came along and they went inside. The prisoner, Wilson, referred to the fact that he had made an admission, and said to O'Callaghan: "Well . . . won't it run a drink?" They bought him a nobbler of brandy. O'Callaghan and Wilson said goodbye to the mate and boarded the coach, and at Carisbrooke, Wilson said: "I am very thirsty, let me have a glass of ale here, I will make it up to you." O'Callaghan bought him one.

On reaching Castlemaine, Wilson said: "Well, I don't want to trespass too much on good nature, but if you can give me a drink before you lock me up, I shall feel obliged to you, for I know I won't get anything in the watchhouse until tomorrow morning." O'Callaghan took Wilson into the Supreme Court Hotel, bought him another, then locked him up.

Standish was incredulous. "The conduct of the Detective is calculated to bring great discredit upon the Department," he said. "I have had serious doubts whether he should be retained in the Force, but I am influenced by his former conduct and usefulness to the Department to give him another chance." Like Christie earlier, O'Callaghan was reduced to the rank and pay of third-class detective.

Detective O'Callaghan's record sheet contains reprimands and severe reprimands throughout his career. He got into so much trouble that he did not reach the rank of first-class until 1879. But the record sheet is also studded with his superiors' generous expressions of praise for the work he did well. Such a situation was nothing unusual; almost every detective of that time had something bad against him, and something good.

CHAPTER 8

Hanging by a pigtail

The year 1872 was marvellous for Christie. In February he was reinstated as a second-class detective, and in March he was transferred to the important town of Beechworth in north-eastern Victoria. This was a dazzling town, which had gorged itself on wealth from gold. Like a prince from a fairy-tale, a man had once ridden the Beechworth streets on a horse with golden shoes.

The town had laid fine pavements and built handsome Georgian buildings. Beechworth flaunted enormous charm and order—even splendour—but all around it, in the bush and hills, and in the small settlements, there was country not quite tamed. Highwaymen were on the roads, and the area was still a frontier. Day-to-day life was so unpredictable that during Christie's stay there, Judge Hackett got in a coach at Benalla to go to Melbourne and found it occupied by four prisoners, two of whom he had just sentenced. He got straight out.

Beechworth was the centre of a vast police district called the Ovens, in which even the place names sounded wild: Yackandandah, Wahgunya, Whroo, Snowy Creek, Corryong, Wodonga, Wangaratta. But there were also names that sounded more familiar to Europeans: Mansfield, Bright, Violet Town, Sebastopol, Eldorado, Chiltern—and two which would soon burst upon the colony like an explosion: Stringybark Creek and Glenrowan.

Christie went to Beechworth almost seven years before the Kelly outbreak, at a time when all the trouble was building up. It is strange now to open the 1872 police documents and meet people whom one already knows from a future time. They are moving in their ironclad patterns of the Kelly story, which was yet to come. All of them, police and outlaws alike, are still captives. Ghosts of the Kelly story stalk these pages, although Ned Kelly himself does not. It is his relatives, friends and enemies whose names appear so often: Quinn, Lloyd, Wright, Reynolds, Montford, Brooke Smith, and all the others.

One could almost talk to them. "Mounted Constable Scanlon," one could say, "Ned Kelly will shoot you in seven years from now. Joe Byrne, of Woolshed, they will hang your body from a hook and take your photo. Robert McBean, the squatter, your fence is on fire, but this is nothing to what the flames of Glenrowan will be like. Constable Michael Ward, you will become a detective and you will be disgraced. Constable Robert Graham, you will become the peace-maker at Greta; you were a brave and admirable man. Constable Ernest Flood, Ned Kelly will say that of four men in the world he wants to shoot, you are one. Annie Gunn, Ned's sister, poor Annie, toyed with by Flood and dead at 19, you were misused."

The Kelly name was so familiar in the Ovens district that even Christie, the new chum, was using it casually soon after he arrived. He was sent out to find a man named Crane, who had left his job as an assistant to Reynolds at the Glenrowan post office, and had failed to acknowledge three letters sent to him. Standish had written to Superintendent Hugh Ross Barclay, of Beechworth, asking him to use great discretion in this inquiry. You get the feeling of murder in the air.

Christie set out through the bush and reported to Superintendent Barclay on 15 April that he tracked Crane to a splitter named Sawyer "between Mrs Kelly's shanty and Greta" and then to Winton, where he found him. Christie did not say, 'Mrs Kelly's home' or 'a shanty run by a Mrs Kelly'. He said "Mrs Kelly's shanty" as if the place were a landmark, which it was.

Superintendent Barclay seems to have been fascinated by Christie. When Christie quickly solved a straightforward theft of clothing from the Tanswell Hotel, Barclay asked Standish to reward him. Lord knows, Christie had not performed a great feat. Someone had roused him from bed at 2 a.m. and reported the thefts, and Christie had asked the sensible question of whether anyone had been seen acting suspiciously. Why, yes; a stranger staying at a different hotel, the Star, had been loitering all evening at the Tanswell.

Christie went to the stranger's room at the Star and found the loot. The thief got three months. The Star's proprietor then came forward and said a pair of double blankets was missing. Christie traced them to a dealer and then to a person who had bought them. The thief got another three months. Christie could do this sort of thing half asleep. When Standish received Barclay's enthusiastic recommendation for a reward, he took the unusual step of refusing it, saying that nothing less than this success could be expected from a detective so experienced.

Such rebuffs were part of Barclay's life. Standish constantly rebuffed him, but in the gentlest way, for it must have been difficult not to like Barclay. He was always doing something wrong, but only slightly wrong. Standish would write, in the politest way, to say that Superintendent Barclay's monthly returns were late again, or his forage report was wrong because he had forgotten to include the hay, or his vaccination report had not been received. The superintendent had forgotten this, or not done that. Or such and such a suggestion, while worthy, was not, all things considered, quite practicable.

One other trouble was that Barclay wrote to Standish on the slightest pretext. Did he have permission, he once asked, to get the office clock cleaned? But Barclay was good-natured, generous and enthusiastic, and perhaps Standish saw Barclay's difficult job in that wild country as a miniature of his own. Besides, the Ovens district had a splendid record of successes. Standish was always quick to acknowledge that policemen who worked in the Ovens faced special problems. Once, one of Barclay's men, Constable Crilly, alone at his remote station at Yarrawonga, refused to row a stranger across the Murray River. The stranger began to fight Crilly, and actually pulled out some of his beard. Crilly not only subdued him but, unable to get any back-up, got him to justice by himself.

Christie did some important work at Beechworth, including the remarkable case of two Chinese storekeepers from Sebastopol, Te On and Hung Yung. They reported that a fellow-Chinese, Ah Suey, had twice tried to commit suicide, once by eating opium and once by trying to drown himself in a waterhole. Mounted Constable William Considine, arriving from Beechworth with a warrant to arrest Ah

Suey, found him in bed in the middle of the afternoon. The two set off for Beechworth, Considine riding and Ah Suey walking. Ah Suey seemed distressed. "He was talking but I could not understand him," Considine said later.

Then came one of the few tender episodes in the history of police in that rough country. About four miles along the road, Ah Suey made signs that he should get on the horse. Considine dismounted, put Ah Suey in the saddle, and walked beside him, holding him tight. It is a touching scene which stays in the mind. Soon Ah Suey began to have fits. They reached a dairy two miles further on, and Considine hoisted Ah Suey on to his back and carried him inside. He gave him a drink of tea, then left to find a vehicle. When he got back, Ah Suey was dead.

In Beechworth that night, Dr Fox, performing an autopsy, was puzzled by what seemed to be scratch marks on several parts of the body. Another puzzle was that he could not smell opium in the stomach of a man who was supposed to have swallowed it. Considine left for Melbourne with Ah Suey's stomach in a bag, to have it analysed. Inspector Brooke Smith, who was standing in for Barclay, told Christie to begin some inquiries. What emerged was an extraordinary tale of brutality.

Chinese at Sebastopol who talked to Christie said Ah Suey had fled to Bright because he owed more than £21 to Te On and Hung Yung, the storekeepers. Te On's cousin had followed Ah Suey and convinced him to come back. When he came back and told the storekeepers he had no money, they knocked him down and kicked and hit him in the head and stomach. They dragged him from his hut and hung him by his pigtail from a hook on the verandah, tied his hands behind him, chained his feet, tore off most of his clothes and kicked and hit him while he "sang for his life". Nobody interfered, said one witness, Ah Lin, because "whoever untied him would have to pay the money he owed". Eventually, a gambler, Ah Leong, untied him, and Ah Suey dropped exhausted.

The two storekeepers put Ah Suey through the same ordeal later and again the next day, hanging him by his pigtail with his feet just touching the ground, as they beat and kicked him. Crying and dishevelled, Ah Suey came that night to the kitchen door of the publican's wife, Emma Harvey, who gave him bread and sugar, but he was too weak to eat it. It stuck in her mind that poor Ah Suey kept wanting to give her a one shilling piece; she did not know why. Joe Byrne, later to become Ned Kelly's lieutenant, was among witnesses called at the inquest. He said he had seen Ah Leong the gambler untie the victim. When Te On and Hung Yung stood trial at Beechworth on 17 October, each was sentenced to four years hard labour for manslaughter.

Full of praise for Christie, Barclay recommended a reward of £5, which Standish approved. When Constable Ward read this in the *Police Gazette*, he complained to Barclay that it was he who had made the first moves in the case; on the night the body was brought in, he said, he had heard rumors that Ah Suey had met with foul play at the hands of his countrymen, and he had gone out straight away to begin inquiries. Ward said he had also introduced Christie to the witnesses, and had helped to arrest Te On and Hung Yung.

Once again, Barclay had got things a bit wrong. He apologised to Standish for not having known of Ward's part (a considerable one) in the investigation; he had been absent, he said. He now recommended that Ward too receive £5 reward. This sort of inefficiency could infuriate Standish. But now he did not write a critical note; he paid the reward without demur.

The Chinese, who had arrived as gold-seekers in the 1850s, were always called Chinamen in the frequent police reports about them. You get the impression that by Christie's time their large number contained many who were desperately poor. One of them, Ah Shim, gave poverty as the reason he tried to rob the sluice boxes of European miners, Morris Doig & Co. He was wounded in both legs by a spring gun which Doig had set the previous night as a booby trap. Ah Shim managed to crawl back to his hut, and he lay there for several days before he was forced to seek help at Woolshed. Barclay had him taken to hospital, and then brought him to court where he was sentenced to six months as a vagrant.

For having set the spring gun, Doig was committed for trial, a situation that made Constable Ward and Superintendent Barclay uncomfortable. "The men are hard-working respectable men and will be put to some expense by Doig having to stand his trial," Barclay told Standish. He suggested bringing the case to the Attorney General's notice. A reply from the law office came back to Barclay, through Standish. It said the case would go on; a spring gun was illegal and could kill. Besides, "it would not do in a mining community to let the Diggers think they could take the law into their own hands".

When a different Chinese, Chung Sim, died at Upper Buckley, Senior Constable Coyne wrote: "He was in desperate circumstances and had no relatives in the colony." In death, Chung Sim was treated in the same way as any destitute white man: the government buried him.

The Chinese were everywhere in the Ovens. It was a Chinese, Ah Fook, who had caused the first arrest of Ned Kelly, in 1869, by claiming that Ned, then aged about 14, had assaulted him. Ah Fook had gone to Mrs Kelly's shanty and asked Annie Gunn for a drink. She gave him water, but this was not what he wanted, and that is how the fight started. Ned was exonerated. It would be interesting to report that Christie met Ned in 1872, but there is no evidence for it. The two of them might have got on, for Ned became an excellent boxer.

Christie was in Beechworth when he received news that Manwaring, Hartney and he had been rewarded with two pounds each for once again catching the coiner, Joseph Brooks. This was one of Manwaring's last cases as a muster-room detective, for the post of resident clerk had become vacant, and the grand old warrior of the Crimea and Peechelba was persuaded to take it. He was aged about 47 then, getting near the age when it might have been good to spend more time sitting down.

Joseph Brooks, the coiner, must have been extremely stupid. As soon as he came out of gaol from the last time Christie had put him away, fake half-crowns began to circulate. Brooks was the immediate suspect, and Christie kept him under watch. Raiding Brooks's house, the detectives found Brooks and a woman, Marrianne Hennessy, firing a batch of fakes. This time Brooks got seven-and-a-half years,

Marrianne Hennessy got three, and William Jordan, an accomplice, got two-and-a-half.

Interestingly, Christie paid a cabbie 9s. for being on three hours waiting time, in this case. Nine shillings was a day's pay for a third-class detective. We learn too that the cabbie was Thomas Carrol, who could not sign his name so he made his cross on the receipt. Christie often spoke of using a particular cabbie on his jobs. Was it Carrol? This is one of the few cabbies' names we have.

The biggest feather in Barclay's cap that year—and Christie's—was what became known as the Wooragee Outrage. At 9 p.m. on 15 October, the Wooragee publican, John Watt, answered a doorknock and found masked men outside. One said: "Come out here, or I will blow your brains out." Watt ran back towards the kitchen and was shot in the side. In Beechworth, Christie was about to return to Melbourne, but Barclay detained him.

News of the shooting immediately alerted Constable Arthur Strahan, of Eldorado. He had previously received information that James Smith and others who had come to Victoria after serving gaol terms in New South Wales, intended to rob the Eldorado gold escort, of which Strahan was guard. This information had not bothered him at the time, but now he went to his immediate superior, Sergeant Chadwick, to tell him about it. The two galloped for the house of a man named Peter Brady, where the ex-prisoners sometimes stayed.

Brady was alone. He answered their questions so evasively that Chadwick sent Strahan to Chiltern to fetch another constable while he remained on watch. Peter Brady seemed anxious to get in touch with his son and two other men who, he said, were working in the bush and living in a bark mia-mia. When the two constables returned from Chiltern, they rode with Brady and Chadwick to the mia-mia and found the three men. Chadwick took them aside one by one and questioned them about where they had been on the night of the shooting. Their answers conflicted, and he arrested them. They were Smith, Thomas Brady and William Heppenstein.

In Beechworth next day, Barclay took the three men from the lock-up, and placed them with several bystanders. The principal witness to the shooting could only partly identify two. Barclay then took the men to Wooragee and made them confront Watt, who lay dying. Watt said he believed Smith fired the shot.

This was not much of a case. But from this moment on, Barclay's men worked long hours over great distances to gather clues and eliminate other suspects. Constable Strahan rode more than 60 miles one night in search of a gun. On a different night he rode more than 90 miles with Peter Brady, still in search of a gun and other information. At one stage, his horse knocked up and he had to hire a horse and cart to carry on.

For a night, a day and a second night, Joe Brown, who was up from Melbourne, rode 70 miles in search of information. Police followed false scents over great distances, but they did not give up; and slowly they found evidence. After the shooting, two men had been heard riding past a neighbouring house on unshod horses. This clue was invaluable, because in a separate incident a six-year-old boy had seen two men on unshod horses. The police took him to Brady's paddock, where he picked out one of the horses running in a mob of six.

Bit by bit, other clues accumulated. The gunman's words to John Watt were found to be similar to words two men had used earlier in holding up a farmer to steal a gun, and in holding up the Wooragee post office ("Come out, you bloody mongrel, or I'll blow your brains out"). The gun stolen from the farmer was a German make, and its broken stock had been mended in a distinctive way. The police managed to find it, and link it to Smith and Brady. On the line of route used from Wooragee to the Brady house, Joe Brown found clothing worn by the offenders. Sergeant Baber found tracks of unshod horses going in the same direction. Horses were traced as arriving at Brady's paddock about 6 a.m. on the morning after the shooting. The police also discovered that the horses had been stolen from New South Wales.

Property stolen from a Chinaman's hut was in the prisoners' possession. This does not sound much, but it was linked to other evidence. Christie prepared a map which later played a part in the court case. What else he did specifically is not clear, but Superintendent Barclay left several records that indicate his work was considerable. Police also took in a fourth man, Jack Lewis, *alias* Black Jack, a mate of Smith's in Parramatta gaol. Barclay questioned him and said he was satisfied Black Jack played no part in the murder. He applied for Black Jack's discharge and immediately rearrested him for horse theft in New South Wales. Black Jack gave the police valuable information.

Letting his head go in a memo to Standish, Barclay said: "Numerous minute links have from time to time been discovered, making together a satisfactory chain of circumstantial evidence which may in itself be sufficiently strong to secure a conviction." This was absolutely correct. Smith and Brady, found guilty of wilful murder and robbery under arms, were soon afterwards sentenced to death. The third man, William Heppenstein, was discharged.

This had been a magnificent police effort. Rarely had the police, including detectives, worked in such harmony and with such dedication and relentless intellectual discipline. Barclay wanted to reward everybody. He singled out Chadwick, Strahan, Christie, Brown, Baber, Dorking, Ward, Williams and the Chiltern and Yackandandah police. At one stage he wrote: "It would be invidious to particularise any one member (of the force) more than any other, but I cannot speak in the highest praise of Sergeant Baber and Detective Christie as being most indefatigable." (Barclay obviously meant that his praise could not be high enough.)

One can picture Standish sighing when he received this. He wrote back and reminded Barclay that a £100 government reward notified in the *Police Gazette* was for the offenders' capture. This was the important word: capture. Barclay replied then that he did not think anyone but Chadwick and Strahan were deserving. They got £25 each. Standish told Barclay to make suitable entries on the record sheets for others, and he would do the same for Christie when the file was returned to Melbourne. Standish must have forgotten this promise; nothing about the Wooragee Outrage appears on Christie's record sheet.

By the time the rewards were posted, Christie was back in Melbourne, moving around the low haunts in which he seemed to thrive. He arrived at the detective office one morning in September to find a sorrowful Swiss named Pietro Zala waiting to tell a familiar story.

111

Zala had come down from the gold diggings at Stringers Creek (now Walhalla) intending to have a final spree before catching a boat to Europe. In his money belt, next to his skin, was £320 in gold sovereigns. He met a woman who took him home. He lost the lot.

Zala had gone the previous evening to Charley Wright's Coliseum music hall in Bourke Street, the rendezvous of thieves and the lowest-priced prostitutes in town, and here he had picked up with a notorious thief, Isabella Hartigan. They had several drinks, and Isabella suggested they should go to her place, where she would introduce him to some pretty girls. She promised him "a high time". Isabella's residence was the lowest brothel in Melbourne. Here Zala met Meg Stacey *alias* McDonald and Emily Brusher *alias* Sayers.

Zala shouted more liquor, and soon a stranger knocked at the door and said:"I hope I don't intrude. I have just arrived by the last train from Ballarat, and I am going to see life. What will you all have to drink?" When the stranger said he was a miner, Zala said: "Then we will make a night of it, and I will stand the racket as I am flush of money." Zala had set out with £3 in his pocket and had spent it all by now, so he took the stranger into the next room and said confidentially: "Don't let the girls know, but I have £320 in this belt, so we will have a good time." He took out ten sovereigns and replaced the belt round his waist. They returned to the women, and while they were all having another drink the lights went out.

Zala was knocked down and his belt was stolen. Half-dazed, half-drunk, he staggered into a lane and sat on the doorstep. The door was shut behind him. He took out his knife and scratched 'Zala' on the door, so that he could point out the house to police. At daybreak he went to the detective office, where Christie and Williams listened to his woes and were detailed to help him. Their first task was to find the word' Zala' on a door, somewhere in the labyrinth of lanes and blind alleys that made up central Melbourne.

"From what he told us, we soon arrived at the house," Christie wrote. "At the end of the lane leading to the house we found a cab waiting, the driver of which was an old lag. I said to him, 'Hello, George! Got a job on?' He replied, 'I am waiting for Bella Hartigan, she's going down to Kenny's baths to have a hot sea bath.' We passed on, and the door of the house in which she lived had Zala scratched on it."

Inside, the detectives found the three women half-drunk. Hartigan had her hat on ready to go out. The other two were in bed. The detectives found nothing during a search, and when they asked the women about Zala, each was positive he had only £3 on him when he came in. Deciding to shadow Bella Hartigan, Christie slipped away down a lane, climbed a brick wall and landed in the yard of an hotel through which he passed to Stephen Street. He told a cab driver to wait for him at a certain spot, then rejoined Williams at Bella's house. Christie wanted to throw the women off their guard, so as the detectives left he said: "I knew that damned foreigner was lying when he said he had been robbed of £300." The women stared at each other astonished.

Christie and Williams found their cab, waited for Bella to come out of the right-of-way, and followed her to Spencer Street railway station, where she bought a ticket, which they discovered was to Williamstown. The detectives hopped in the guard's van. At Williamstown, Bella got out and walked unsteadily to the Prince of Wales Hotel, closely followed by Christie carrying a box and wearing a porter's cap which he had borrowed from the station master. "I walked right into the hotel," wrote Christie, "and said to the landlord who was in the passage, 'This box belongs to that lady who came in just now. There is one shilling to pay'. He replied, 'Well, you had better get it yourself, she is in that parlour with a man who came here from Melbourne about an hour ago'.

"Williams having come in, and the landlord recognising him, said, 'Hello, Jack! On the job today?' Williams put his finger to his mouth for silence, and dropping the box and railway cap, we went into the parlour and there found Bella and her paramour, no other than the notorious James O'Neil, a noted criminal only a few weeks discharged from Pentridge for assault and robbery. He knew the game was up so took matters quietly. As he answered the maudlin description furnished by Zala of the would-be Ballarat miner, we arrested him, but allowed Bella to return to Melbourne to await further developments."

113

Searching O'Neil, the detectives found a new gold watch, chain and ring, which he had bought that morning at Gaunt's the jeweller. They also found a bank book of the Bank of Australasia, showing that O'Neil had lodged £240 that day. When the detectives wanted him to draw the money out he demurred, so they agreed to treat the money as if it were his own property and place it alongside the jewellery on his police property sheet. They took O'Neil by police boat to Sandridge, where O'Neil presented his £240 withdrawal cheque at the bank. Christie took the teller aside and asked how O'Neil had deposited the money. When the teller told him it was all in sovereigns, Christie asked if he could have the same ones, and the teller managed to give him half and half.

Christie and Williams now had £310 in money and jewellery. They locked O'Neil up, and later in the day arrested Meg Stacey and Emily Brusher. At the trial, the women were acquitted, but Judge Molesworth sentenced O'Neil *alias* Jack the Bushranger to three years.

Christie's old antagonist from Geelong, Superindendent Power Le Poer Bookey, died on 14 December. Standish asked all officers to wear the usual badge of mourning—black crepe— on their left arms when in uniform, for a month.

The year closed in Melbourne with a court case so unusual that *The Herald* of 21 December did not quite know what to do with it. It began reporting the case early in the day on Page 3, which was where the news started in those days; but as more evidence unfolded throughout the day, it was forced to continue the report on Page 1, which was sacred to its advertisements. This is to say, readers had to begin the case on Page 3 then turn to Page 1, a procedure in reverse of today's practice. *The Herald* cleared a column of advertisements on Page 1 to finish publishing the County Court case in which Mary Hanlon, a servant girl, sued Samuel L. Amess, the mayor of Melbourne. This case concerned Christie not one bit, except in the sense that it was one more piece of mud that stuck to the force. Mayor Amess's gold chain was too big for his safe, so he kept it in his wardrobe at home between two silk dresses. One day it was gone. Mary Hanlon, an honest, sober and industrious girl, according to a reference written by Mrs Amess, had recently resigned from her employ to become a servant in Sandhurst with a bank manager and his wife, the Hyndmans.

Poor Mary. In the belief that she was the thief, Amess and the blustering private detective Otto Berliner broke into her quarters in Sandhurst, searched and ransacked her boxes and other belongings, read her private mail and asked Mrs Hyndman all sorts of questions about what company Mary kept and whether she owned gold lockets, watches and brooches. The Hyndmans sacked her. An employment agency would not now place her. Mary, 19, wept in court. Amess was a wealthy man, said Mary's lawyer; and Mary was a poor woman who was ruined unless the jury gave her an exemplary verdict for trespass. He asked for 100 pounds, and got 35.

The story about a rich mayor and a ruined servant girl was itself fascinating, but Mary provided a sensation altogether different during her evidence. The mayor's lawyer asked her: "May I ask who first took you to your attorney?" Mary replied: "Detective Williams". "Surprise in court". wrote *The Herald*.

How could this be? How could a detective be so partisan? Amess's lawyer had an answer: "This is the way that detectives aid in the discovery of stolen property!" (The exclamation mark is *The Herald's*). When Amess came into the witness box, he admitted that Detectives Alexander and Foster had been present when Berliner and he went to Mary's premises, and he believed it was Detective Williams who had obtained a search warrant (which was unused).

So now Williams was accused of arranging not only the attorney for the defence, but the search warrant for the complainant. The warrant had been issued on the grounds that money had disappeared from the back of the bank manager's wardrobe.

After the verdict, Amess brought the evidence to the Chief Secretary's notice, and the Chief Secretary suggested to the Solicitor General that there be an inquiry. This news was leaked to the Press just as Secretan was asking Detective Williams for a report on his actions. Because an inquiry was possible, Williams had grounds to decline making a report, a situation which Secretan accepted. All these bits of evidence about dodgy procedure from the detective office were rising like milk slowly boiling in a sealed saucepan.

CHAPTER 9

Playing the old banjo

Twice in January 1873, and twice in the succeeding months, Christie received police rewards for catching burglars or tracing loot. One man he put away for housebreaking was Detective Daly's fizgig of 1871, Henry Jackson. A fifth case stood out for the sheer eccentricity of Christie's investigation.

"In March 1873," wrote Christie, "a contractor named John Pigdon was stuck up and robbed of a valuable gold watch, with chain and seal attached, also several sovereigns, and amongst some silver there were two rupees, one of which had a small round hole in it. As there had been several similar robberies about this time, I determined to disguise myself and have a look through the various drinking dens, so I blacked up *à la* Christy Minstrel, black skull cap, and when I put on my plantation clothes and old battered white belltopper, I looked the character. I got this rigout in a present from George Arnott, an old nigger minstrel.

"I got my banjo which was one of Frank Weston's worn-out instruments. This completed my make-up. I got a cab and on getting to the corner of Stephen and Little Bourke Streets, I instructed my cabman to go down to the Golden Fleece and wait for me. I walked down Little Bourke Street and into the Morning Star Hotel. The bar was full of speelers, magsmen, thieves and prostitutes. They hailed me with 'Now then Bones, give us a tune', so I played and sang 'Ten Thousand Miles Away' to a rousing chorus of thieves. I was taking stock all the time.

"After the song I made a collection, which amounted to about 2s 6d. They insisted on another song, so I gave them 'The Old Log Cabin in the Lane', after which I left and strolled down to the Star of the East, kept by an ex-sergeant of police named Andrews who had got very low down in the world, and his house was the resort of notorious burglars and highway robbers. There was only a few prostitutes in the bar with a drunken bushman, so I went round into the back parlour which was pretty full of thieves.

"They were having a barney about changing a coin. The barney was between the landlord and a desperate character named John Wallace *alias* Chinaman Jack. On seeing me, Jack said 'I say, Darkie, can you change me a florin?' I replied yes. He handed me what I saw at once was a rupee, but pretended not to notice it. I gave him two shillings, and they all, including Jack, heartily laughed at me, thinking I had been gulled.

"I played them a tune and sang 'Ten Thousand Miles Away' and went round and collected somewhere about 1s 6d after which, as I had a clue to Pigdon's robbery through the rupee, I left the hotel and went quietly down to my cab, and told him to drive me to the Detective Office, where I picked up Detective Hartney and we called at my hotel, the Galatea close by, where in less than five minutes I was dressed in my ordinary clothes (and the black face turned into white). Rejoining Hartney, we proceeded to Little Bourke Street.

"On the way we examined the rupee and found it had a hole in it (stopped up with lead) and was no doubt the one Pigdon lost with the hole in it. We strolled down Little Bourke Street, and outside Mrs Moore's boarding house we saw Wallace talking to some prostitutes. I went up to him and told him to get into the cab which was following us. He cursed dreadful and fought like a demon but Hartney and I got him in and although he struggled violently all the way we landed him in the Detective Office where we stripped and searched him. In his socks we found Pigdon's seal and some of the sovereigns, and in his pocket we found the other rupee.

"I never let on to him that I had the other rupee, but he swore mortal vengeance against the nigger who he said had put him away because he had done him with changing a rupee. I pretended not to know what he meant, but he swore he would get even on the nigger some day when he met him. At the same time he did not have the slightest idea that I was identical with the darkey.

"I took him to the watchhouse and charged him with assault and robbery on John Pigdon and next morning I was in waiting at the watchhouse to see if any of his pals would bring him some breakfast. I was right in my conjectures as a notorious character named Kate Laurence called at the watchhouse with some breakfast for him. After she had departed I shadowed her home and in searching the house, I found a quantity of stolen property including Pigdon's watch and chain all of which was concealed in a hole under the hearthstone which I had to raise. Both were tried and convicted for the robbery. Wallace got seven years and Laurence two years, and I got £25 reward from Mr Pigdon."

The sensation of the year in the colony was a man named Hugh James Vincent O'Ferrall, a clerk in the Lands Department, who was fond of dogs, dressed carelessly and walked with a slovenly gait. So dazzling was his crime that it was not announced to the public by the police but by a special report tabled in the Legislative Assembly. O'Ferrall had diddled the Lands Department of a stupendous £9000, and disappeared. Defalcations and swindles were commonplace, but this one was over the odds. O'Ferrall had struck at the structure of administration; he had robbed the State.

This is an interesting story not only because it is a ripping yarn, but because it shows Standish and the Victorian detective office ineptly trying to grapple with a man hiding overseas. Standish was to claim later that everything went according to plan; and that the reason he called off a detective who was getting close to O'Ferrall was to make O'Ferrall believe he was safe; but the files on this case show only confusion. Nobody seemed to know what to do next.

At first Standish had no idea where O'Ferrall was, but he took the precautionary step of sending a description to Sydney and New Zealand on 5 November, the day of the parliamentary report. O'Ferrall should not have been difficult to spot, for as well as having a slovenly gait he had sloping shoulders, black hair, a Dublin accent and a dark complexion ("a slight mixture of Hindoo blood", said Standish). And as well as all this, O'Ferrall stood about six feet two inches (perhaps 188 centimetres), which was not a common height for the times.

The first real progress occurred when Detective Charles Forster had the good sense to report a scrap of information to Inspector Secretan: a man had told Forster that another man in Melbourne had received a letter from O'Ferrall, and it had come from some foreign country, perhaps New Caledonia. Amazingly, this information was accurate. Standish sent Detective Mackay to Noumea, from where he reported in March that O'Ferrall was living with an uncle, but had got wind of Mackay's arrival and had hidden in the bush.

About this time, a court case in Melbourne gave *The Age* an excuse to attack the police over O'Ferrall. A Victorian constable named William Bayley, who had been an acting clerk of petty sessions, left the force, handed his books to a successor, stayed around for a few weeks then went to live in New Zealand where he joined the mounted constables. When an error of £5 was found in his books, a constable was sent from Melbourne to arrest Bayley on a charge of embezzlement. At his trial in General Sessions, Bayley was acquitted after evidence showed the £5 deficiency was a clerical error; in fact the Police Department had owed Bayley more than £3 in back pay when he left Victoria.

The Age thundered its anger about "a trumped up and baseless case that has about it an aspect of malice and a reality of persecution." It went on: "Not long ago there was a culprit in the Lands Department, against whom not a false charge of embezzling £5, but a true charge of misappropriating £10,000 was laid. Rumours of his deficiencies were rife long before he found it expedient to take a sea voyage for the benefit of his health. But warrants were scarce, or the Chief Commissioner was deaf to silly tales about his spotless friend. O'Ferrall was a jolly good fellow, free with his cash and free in his cups; he was a swell upon the turf, and a dandy on the block; he hobnobbed with the dignitaries of the force. So the big transgressor was allowed to slip quietly and safely away. And the dexterous detectives who failed to land this voracious shark have made up for it by catching a harmless sprat."

In New Caledonia, meanwhile, Mackay was getting nowhere. He was told eventually that although the French authorities were anxious to help capture O'Ferrall, the police influence outside of Noumea was small. In the countryside, a native police force held authority, and its chief was related to O'Ferrall by marriage. Standish brought Mackay back, and asked him to write to the chief of police in New Caledonia. An answer from Noumea came back in French from the acting commissioner, Inspector G. Audit, saying there had been difficulties in the case because Mackay should have been confidentially accredited to him. When Standish read this letter, he wrote in the margin, "How could this be?"

O'Ferrall was hiding on a small island. The commissioner and two police agents had set out to find him in a long range of mountains "where even the aborigines of the country could not have tracked him". The hunting party was stranded by flooded rivers, and on the ninth day their food ran out. Green bananas were the only food. Inspector Audit returned to Noumea with fever, and went into hospital.

Standish took the view that the French did not want to help. He sent a New Zealander, Frank O'Brien, to Noumea posing as an investor in copper and lead mines. Standish gave him a gun and ammunition, and swore him in as a constable before he left. O'Brien had a plan to kidnap O'Ferrall. Eventually, O'Ferrall made a break from Noumea in a small boat, and reached the New Hebrides. Here the commander of *HMS Sandfly* spotted him. The commander wrote to Standish that O'Ferrall had then boarded the schooner *Lady Darling* on her way to the port of Mackay in Queensland.

It is not always easy to follow what happened next, but O'Ferrall reached Queensland and, unhindered, boarded a steamer for China via Singapore. Detective Tom O'Callaghan, who was sent up from Melbourne to nab O'Ferrall, arrived in Mackay after he had left. The situation was so serious now that the Governor of Victoria, Sir George Bowen, sent a "very urgent" telegram to the governor of the Straits Settlement, Singapore, asking him to arrest O'Ferrall. The arrest was made with ease, and O'Callaghan went to Singapore and brought him back. O'Ferrall had been at large for more than a year.

The public disquiet about the O'Ferrall case merged the following year with two other examples of police inefficiency. The first case concerned three detectives, Dowden, Lomax and Lennon, who alleged in court that a man named Fulton had tried to pick the pockets of women during the Queen's Birthday torchlight celebrations and again the next day during a firemen's display at the Eastern Hill. They could produce no victims and they called no witnesses except each other. Lomax even swore that he had seen Fulton in the crush at the Theatre Royal and hanging about the streets on Saturday nights.

Happily, Mr Fulton could prove he was a person of good character and comfortable means who was often entrusted with large sums of money by men of high repute. The bench threw the case out. But "had the defendant been a stranger he would in all probability have been sent to gaol as a rogue and a vagabond," said *The Age*, and it added: "The maxim that the end justifies the means appears to have become deeply impressed upon the minds of the professional thief-catcher."

In a separate circumstance, Standish was already embattled over the behaviour of Detective Lennon. This circumstance was almost unbelievable. At midnight on 31 March 1874, Lennon, who had been with the detective force for only three weeks, was keeping a man under surveillance in the parlour of Molloy's Crown Hotel in Queen Street. A bootmaker named Henry Doherty, who had a criminal record, was being paid to help him. Constable Boyd came into the parlour with a woman for whom he was trying to find a bed because she was on the run from a violent husband.

In Boyd's hearing, Lennon remarked to the landlord that he knew the woman as a common prostitute. Boyd came up and said Lennon was too damned smart. Lennon said he was a detective; and one angry word led to another. Boyd went to the detective office to check Lennon's story, but the only person he questioned there was the groom, who said he had never heard of a detective called Lennon. Boyd changed into plain clothes for some reason, went back to the hotel and announced he was going to arrest Lennon for impersonating a detective. He refused Lennon's request to be taken around the corner to the Paddington Hotel in Little Collins Street, where Detective Joe Brown lived, or to the detective office. At either place, Lennon could have been identified.

Constable Boyd took Lennon to the watchhouse, charged him in the presence of an inspector of police, and locked him up for seven-and-a-half hours. After an inquiry, Standish sacked Lennon, saying the blame for this fiasco was his because he should not have interfered in the business of a policeman doing his duty. Standish also said that Lennon had encouraged the police assistant Henry Doherty to lie at the inquiry. The public got to hear of this mess when Lennon sued Boyd (and won). The idea of a constable locking up a detective was hilarious. But the employment of a criminal assistant who told lies under oath was sobering.

The Lennon case, the Fulton case, the O'Ferrall case, the employment of criminals—the whole suspect operations of the detective office—forced Standish to make a special report to the Chief Secretary, who tabled it in parliament on 2 September, 1874, along with a supplementary report by Secretan. Standish said some unpopular things in his report, among them: "It seems to be assumed (he meant by the public) that the detectives should never employ any but honest men; but honest and honourable men cannot generally be procured, they shrink from the performance of such duties."

This may well have been true, but in saying it, and in developing his argument about it, Standish invited the angry and intelligent letters which the Melbourne newspapers published next day. The whole workings of the detective force were now open to debate. Standish also defended the way detectives had handled O'Ferrall's escape, the disappearance of a witness in a pending court case, and the temporary escape from Victoria of a Captain Edgar, charged over deaths at sea. The fact that Standish raised these matters showed he was aware of public misgivings.

Standish blamed poor pay for the failure to attract a better type of applicant to the detective force, and he recommended—not for the first time—that pay be increased. He also asked that certain allowances available to police should be extended to detectives. By these means, he said, the detective force might be restored to its former state of efficiency. He more or less dismissed allegations of jealousy between the general police and detectives. He felt that "it originates in a not ungenerous rivalry between the' two, and only becomes objectionable when either party, instead of running fairly in the race, endeavours to trip up the other".

One of Standish's severest critics over all this was the unstoppable Otto Berliner. Berliner wrote to the newspapers, adding other cases to Standish's list of O'Ferrall, Captain Edgar and the missing witness. Berliner added Mayor Amess's gold chain, and the disappearance of a 16-year-old girl from her boarding school in East Melbourne. For the fiasco of O'Ferrall, Berliner blamed mismanagement at headquarters. For the fiasco of Captain Edgar, who was not under surveillance, he blamed the detective force. Here, said Berliner, was a man who caught a train at Spencer Street, and at every station passed a police constable; and at Castlemaine and Sandhurst, he passed detective stations. Nowhere was he molested, until he was arrested by a New South Wales constable. Would the Chief Commissioner labour under the idea that Captain Edgar could do this because the detectives were getting 12s 6d a day instead of 14s?

Berliner also attacked the use of police agents ("dangerous and untrustworthy"); the promotion in 1869 of Detective Secretan, on Nicolson's advice, over men of better ability; the promotion of inexperienced men "known to be utterly useless" to the rank of first-class, and the idea that jealousy between police and detectives was not rife ("they never worked united").

None of this was enough to cause any reform to the police or detective functions. Only Ned Kelly, seven years later, when he was dead, managed to do that.

Christie had one more big case in 1874, the theft of jewellery belonging to the wife of William Lyster, the opera impresario. Christie and Hartney gathered information that the jewellery was in the possession of George Meredith, who had boarded a steamer and was on his way to England. At Standish's request, the English police watched Meredith land, but found nothing.

Christie had not rested in the meantime. Early in November he went to see a Bourke Street pawnbroker named Phillips and asked him to buy any of the Lyster loot which might come his way, and to let Christie know. Phillips would be reimbursed, he said, and would get half of any reward reward Lyster might pay.

Christie as a three year old in Scotland in 1848. (J.B. Castieau)

As champion sculler of Victoria, 1876. (J.B. Castieau)

Sir Harry Wollaston, head of Victoria's Customs Department during Christie's time. At federation, Wollaston became the first Comptroller General of Trade and Customs in the Commonwealth. (Royal Historical Society of Victoria)

Smugglers and their dodges. Figure No. 9 may be intended to be Christie.
(The Australasian, 7 June, 1890)

1. The waistcoat with 170 inside pockets for watch smuggling. 2. The dummy umbrella, used for 'ring sneaking' over the border. 3. Chinese false-bottomed box, showing smuggled opium in skins. 4. Opium belt put on round the chest. 5. The hollow-backed jewel smuggler (the lines show the box held in position by the braces). 6. The improver dodge. When in fashion wearers had to be watched carefully. 7. Customs officer: "John, you welly fat." John: "Don't touchee me, me got heart disease." (He was suffering from two opium belts round his chest.) 8. Disguises of a customs detective. 9. Detective (To returned colonist who has brought out a few things for his tall friend Brown): All those clothes yours? You must have shrunk a good deal on the voyage, Sir." 10. Customs officer (After plunging his bayonet through the false bottom of Ah Sin's clothes box, and finding the point covered with opium): "Whose box this?" Chorus of celestials: "No savee." 11. A ruse lately played. Six chinamen draw off the two custoims watchers, while the seventh sneaks a big swag of cigars ashore. 12. On the overland trip from Sydney.—Suspicious detective: "I beg your pardon, Sir. Hullo! What's that in your hat?" (It was a diamond tiara.)

127

Hussey Malone Chomley, who succeeded Standish as chief commissioner of police. He did not take Christie back into the force. (Victoria Police Historical Unit)

Tom O'Callaghan clung to office as chief commissioner even after censures.
(Victoria Police Historical Unit)

Superintendent Frank Hare, Standish's favourite, who displaced Nicolson in the Kelly hunt
(Victoria Police Historical Unit)

Shiny hats, shiny shoes, perfect grooming. Christie (right) with the New Zealand commissioner of police during the 1901 royal tour.
(J.B. Castieau)

130

The Customs House, Melbourne, in the 1870s. Here Christie had his office.
(La Trobe Collection. State Library of Victoria)

Customs men arrest a Chinese smuggler. (Illustrated Australasian News, 2 December, 1895)

*How a Melbourne newspaper reacted
to the Harry Weenan drawback case
(Chapter 15).* (Christie scrapbook,
La Trobe Manuscript Collection,
State Library of Victoria)

*This autographed photo–
graph and gold medal were
presented to Christie by the
Duke and Duchess of York
at the end of their Austral–
asian tour of 1901.*
(J.B. Castieau)

When he received a note two days later saying Phillips wanted to see him as soon as possible, Christie and Detective Hartney went to the pawnshop. Phillips showed them two diamonds which he said he had bought from Dick Jones the tailor. Lyster identified them later as part of the loot. Armed with a search warrant, Christie and Hartney called on Jones, found his responses unsatisfactory and searched his premises without success. After this, the detectives were walking up Victoria Street on a routine call to a different pawnbroker, R. Allen, in Little Collins Street West, when Dick Jones the tailor drove past in a cab.

Not managing to hail a cab themselves, Christie and Hartney hurried on foot by a short cut to Allen's, where they found Jones in the back parlour with more loot. Mr Justice Barry gave him six years. Lyster's reward was £20, which Secretan wanted to split by giving £8 to Phillips and £6 each to the detectives, but Standish, ever correct in these matters, reminded him that Christie had promised Phillips half of any reward. It turned out that Lyster had already paid something to Phillips, who was happy to take the £8.

CHAPTER 10

Otto Berliner strikes again

Christie was promoted to the rank of first-class detective in February 1875. This was the highest that any man could go in the detective office unless, as Manwaring had done, he chose to become resident clerk, or unless, as Secretan had done, he allowed a powerful ally to advance his interests; but he could not simply step outside of the detective framework and become, say, a sub-inspector of police at a rural station. Christie had reached the limit in eight years.

Perhaps he was bored; or tired. His papers for 1875 do not show him doing much work. One of his manuscripts says that in October, he and Detective Black arrested the old enemy Chinaman Jack (John B. Wallace) who was living with his paramour, Eliza Wallace, among a hoard of stolen goods in 'Ivy Cottage', Islington Street, Collingwood. This arrest sounds strange, because it was only two years since Christie had put Jack away for seven years. The manuscript places the crime in 1875, but Christie, writing this in his later years, may have been mistaken.

Chinaman Jack is among the few criminals about whom Christie took the trouble to write a little sketch. Chinaman Jack was transported to Tasmania in 1848, he said, and was in and out of prison so much that by the time he died in Pentridge in 1886, he had spent only half of his life in freedom. When Jack arrived in Victoria from Tasmania, he was arrested for robbery and was lodged in a cell with a wooden floor directly above a police storeroom. While a prisoner in an adjoining cell made a noise by singing 'Old Joe Brown', Jack cut a hole in the floor, dropped through, forced the lock on the storeroom door, climbed an iron fence and ran free.

There is something touching about a man who came from a convict ship, survived for nearly 40 years in the rough society in which he landed, and stayed defiant to the end. Perhaps Christie was not insensitive to this. He ran with criminals long enough to know them or become like them.

One thing which Christie certainly did in 1875 was spend time rowing. It annoyed Standish, who wrote a memo in May: "Mr Secretan will be good enough to intimate to Detective Christie that I cannot allow him to engage in any further boating matches. Though I have no reason to believe that the detective has in any way neglected his duty, yet I think that the prominent part he has played for two or three years in certain sports is not calculated to increase his usefulness to the Department while it is certain to lead sooner or later to unfavourable comment."

This memo probably referred specifically to Christie's successes as a sculler that autumn in the Melbourne Regatta. Christie was building up to something more spectacular. He wanted the title of champion. In December, he issued a challenge to row a sculling match in outriggers against any amateur in Australia over a two-mile course. Christie took it on himself to name the event as the championship, and to offer a gold cup valued at £100 to the winner. This use of the word championship angered the committee of the Melbourne Regatta, the authoritative rowing body at the time. Christie had snubbed the system.

The sculler who eventually met Christie's challenge was James Cazaly, whose club was Melbourne. Christie's club was I Zingari. The Melbourne club was based at James Edwards's excellent boatshed just east of Princes Bridge on the city side of the Yarra. Probably I Zingari was also based here. It certainly was based here in the following two years. Its records are scant, for the club did not last long.

This stretch of water, called the Upper Yarra, was not the course the rowers chose, for it was already falling out of favour; the banks were up to ten feet high on the city side, and full of lagoons and swamps on the Botanic Gardens side; and just upstream from Edwards's boatshed was a bend of about 90 degrees called Baths Corner because it was the site of public baths. Here the Yarra was about half as wide as it is now, before public works in the 1890s altered its course. Only two craft could compete side by side, and even then they risked disaster. The conditions were so insane that there had been an attempt to formalise bumping matches.

Christie's 'championship' was held instead on the Lower Yarra, downstream near dockland. It is pointless now to say where it began and ended, for the landmarks are different. Christie and Cazaly were described as "two of the best, if not the very best rowers in the colony", and their match excited public interest. Cazaly led for most of the way, although Christie stuck close to him, preparing for a final spurt. When the two of them got to a point called Humbug Reach, Cazaly steered too close to the Sandridge (Port Melbourne) bank, gave himself trouble in making a turn, and yielded the lead to Christie, who held it to the end, rowing desperately.

Then Christie got his left hand caught in reeds growing from the bank, and was yanked into the water. The race had been so furious that spectators thought he had fallen in from exhaustion, and one jumped in to save him. Christie's time of 10 minutes 12 seconds, over a course that was not quite two miles, established him as probably the fastest Melbourne sculler in his day.

By contrast, his detective work slumped in 1875. In the months leading up to the sculling match, he seemed to be suffering from a prolonged languor. If only we knew the background to what happened on 15 November, the day that changed his life. On that day, Otto Berliner wrote a strange letter to Standish from his private-detective office. This was the General Agency and Inquiry Office, 78 Elizabeth Street, opposite to where *The Age* once had its building. Berliner began:

"I beg leave to inform you that Detective Christie called several times at this office and also this day, wishing to be informed if I had any interviews with other detectives lately. I told Christie that some months ago Mr Superintendent Nicolson spoke to me in my office, and that I had forgiven him for anything which he Mr Nicolson had ever injured me in (years ago) whilst I served in the Department, that Mr Nicolson and myself parted as friends and that I had no connection with any member of the Detective Force for some time previous or since."

Berliner said that as he presumed Christie's calls during duty hours were by the authority of the chief of detectives, he was bringing this matter under Standish's notice, trusting for an explanation. He wished Christie to be told that his visits were uncalled for.

What an extraordinary collection of mysteries this is. The explanation becomes no clearer when we examine Christie's reply which he wrote to Standish through Secretan the next day:

"Detective Christie reports that he never was in Berliner's office in his life till yesterday afternoon, when he happened to drop in by accident while in the act of looking for Mr Ellis who prosecuted Von Sanden, he having some further inquiries to make into the case."

(Baron von Sanden was a swindler, and Ellis was a victim. Ellis had sought Standish's help to lay a charge against him, and Standish had advised him to apply for a warrant. Obviously Christie had been assigned to the case).

Christie went on:

"The accident occurred through Ellis having changed his office. The Detective (himself) did not even know it was Berliner's office till he saw him in his office. The only conversation which occurred was the Detective said, excuse me I have made a mistake, can you tell me which office Mr Ellis has removed into? Berliner said, it is in the next staircase.

"The Detective had no other conversation with him whatever, and being very glad to get out of his presence, knowing he had a great antipathy towards him."

Before passing this letter to Standish, Secretan noted on it that Christie was prepared to swear to his statement on oath. Secretan added: "I had no knowledge of Detective Christie having gone to Berliner's office and have never yet sent a man there to try to make inquiries of any kind."

Standish wrote to Berliner, enclosing a copy of Christie's letter. Berliner wrote back repeating his claim that Christie had visited him "on various occasions upon his own accord under pretence of friendship". During his visit on 15 November, he claimed, Christie had said "he did not care for anyone, he could come to me as he liked as he intended shortly to leave the Force and go to England."

Sometimes misusing the English language, Berliner continued that he had told Christie he had no wish to see him if his authorities objected, but—

"As Superintendent Nicolson had some time ago met me and addressed me, complimenting me at been saved from the wreck of *SS Schiller* also as to my success etc (after a period of nearly 11 years, during which time we did not recognise each other) and as Mr Nicolson and myself apparently parted friends, I presumed that all ill feeling had banished. Detective Christie's report contains willfull and deliberate untruth as he was at my office for some lengthened time and asked me if I was vexed with him as I had passed him (Christie) several times in the street and did not look at him friendly."

Berliner said he considered that Christie's lying deserved more punishment than the original offence of molesting him at his office. Christie's statement "proofs him to be unworthy of any public position where truth is essential", he said. He had no wish to see retaliation against Christie, but the visits must stop because they were offensive to his mind.

On the same day, Standish replied. His letter announced almost casually that he would not be taking any more action, because on the previous day (17 November) he had accepted Detective Christie's resignation. This sent Berliner into a mild frenzy in which he said Christie had called at his office so often he was certain he was doing so on the authority of the police department. He questioned how any responsible government officer (he meant Standish) would have allowed a member of his department to resign two days after a complaint was made, without first investigating it.

We will probably never know why Christie submitted his resignation, but it was true that he did and that Standish accepted it:

> "Detective Christie tenders his resignation as a member of the
> Detective Force and requests that it may be accepted at
> the end of the present month."

Secretan told Standish that Christie could "be at once discharged". To his credit, Standish wrote a note on the resignation letter: "I regret to learn that this Department is to lose Det. Christie's services." Christie was finished. But he did accept Standish's offer to take twelve days leave and receive his discharge at the end of it.

On Christie's record sheet Secretan wrote: "This man has served eight-years-and-a-half with tolerable credit. During the last ten months his exertions appear to have abated." Thus, that lively career was reduced in the end to two words: tolerable credit. What a mean man Secretan was. All of the glowing references on Christie's record sheet meant nothing. Standish scribbled across the record sheet: Conduct "very good on account of his own request". The three words, "his own request", were management code to indicate that Christie was probably not leaving voluntarily.

Otto Berliner's letters and Christie's resignation occurred so closely together, and so suddenly, and with so much mystery, that one would be foolish not to link them. If an explanation ever existed, it is no longer in the relevant police file, although it could still come to light. Christie served his time until the end of the month, and then, at the age of 29, he walked away from Little Collins Street and was free of the police force. In this new freedom, he staged his sculling championship against Cazaly.

But Standish and Secretan were not yet free of Christie. On Thursday 11 May 1876, the mayor of Melbourne presided at a small celebration to honour Christie at the end of his career, in the mayor's room at the town hall. Some of Christie's friends had contributed to a purse of sovereigns (said to total 300), which the mayor handed to him after a pleasant little speech in which he praised Christie's courage, energy and gentlemanly conduct, and talked of the onerous and delicate nature of Christie's detective duties. The mayor also referred to Christie's "recent rowing achievements".

The guests drank Christie's health in champagne, and Christie made what *The Telegraph* next day called a brief and pithy response. It was more like a series of insults to the detective office. Christie said that at least £3000 a year could be saved in the detective department; there were about 25 detectives on the force when he left, he said, but really, only nine or ten efficient ones were needed. If the government chose to hold an inquiry into the matter, some strange revelations would be made.

Christie said his primary reason for leaving the force was that it had become disorganised because of the admission of persons whose presence in any body of men would simply mean degradation. A few good and efficient members remained, but these would also leave unless the government improved their conditions.

This little speech occurred at a bad time for Standish because the police force was coming under fire for one of its biggest blunders ever. A woman had been raped at Burrumbeet, near Ballarat, and the investigation had turned into a catastrophe. Police got it into their heads that the culprit was James Halliday, but they arrested Thomas Davis instead, and then they let him go because, once he had been cleaned up and given new clothes in gaol—which should not have happened—he was unrecognisable by people who had come to identify him. (But remember he was the wrong man, anyway.)

There were suggestions that bungling was deliberate because police were waiting for a reward to be posted. The powerful voice of W.J.Clarke MLA demanded to know if there were a feeling of jealousy between detectives and general police. Then police discovered they had issued the wrong description of the culprit, and had to correct it. They arrested Halliday at Swan Hill after a hue and cry up and down the colony, but he had an ironclad alibi and was patently the wrong suspect. It is difficult to believe now that we are not reading a script of the Keystone Cops.

Standish and Superintendent Henry Hill of Ballarat exchanged confidential letters admitting police mistakes. At Hill's suggestion, Standish decided not to publish the description of a third suspect in the *Police Gazette* on the strange grounds that it might be republished by newspapers, and if the suspect read it he would know the police were after him.

And yet, throughout all this, there was a valuable witness who had given police the correct lead from the first day, but they had got it wrong. In the end, they arrested the correct man, James Ashe, at Romsey, and he was committed for trial. It did not escape public notice that the police had arrested three different men for the one crime within the space of seven weeks.

In the meantime, Standish had to reply to Christie's town hall

141

speech, and he did so in a report containing five main points which he submitted to the Chief Secretary on 20 May. It was bad luck for Standish that the newspapers published the report on 2 June, the day the third suspect in the Burrumbeet outrage was committed for trial; for Standish began his defence of the detective force by denying that it was disorganised.

He did admit, however, that the force had lost some of its prestige in recent years. If pay and conditions were improved, he said, a superior class of men would enrol. In his second point, Standish agreed with Christie's proposal to employ fewer men and pay them more, but then he said this was a wild idea unless all of these detectives possessed "matured police experience"; otherwise, a lot of detective duty would be left undone.

Standish also agreed that the force had enrolled many men who lacked education, judgment, discretion and general ability, but he denied that respectable men would suffer degradation by associating with them. In his fourth point, he said he knew of only two detectives contemplating retirement, and neither of them was doing this for the reasons Christie gave, as both had served for more than 20 years.

Standish's fifth point was that he had nothing to fear from the "strange revelations" that would come to light in a government inquiry, but he was against inquiries because they could cause mischief.

Finally, Standish referred to recent newspaper criticism that when police knew where criminals could be found, they kept the suspect under surveillance until a reward was offered for an arrest. He drew attention to a recent notice in the *Government Gazette* which he said made it unlikely that a constable would delay an important arrest on the uncertain chance of being rewarded.

All of Standish's statement was predictable. It was only Secretan's supplementary letter that caused any excitement. Secretan claimed that "at the time ex-Detective Christie left the service, there was a very serious charge of untruthfulness made against him by Mr Otto Berliner, and which, owing to his resigning, could never be inquired into." This charge simply lay there, waiting for something to happen — nothing did.

The Argus backed Standish, but the rest of the Press, in varying degrees, backed Christie. *The Age* said Standish had failed to answer Christie's charges, and it called for a public inquiry. *The Leader* published a remarkable editorial which denigrated not only the police force but the immorality which it protected. (see Appendix page 245).

Christie himself had been out of the colony during this argument. When he returned, he wrote to *The Argus* to defend himself against Secretan's "unfounded charges". Christie wrote: "Mr Otto Berliner will, I am sure, confirm at any moment to your satisfaction that he has no serious or any other charge against me, but always was, and is, a personal friend of mine. If the Chief Secretary will appoint a board, I am confident that both Mr. Berliner and myself, besides officers at present connected with the detective and police departments, will be able to submit evidence to prove how grossly the department has been mismanaged for years past."

But if Christie ever had a chance of seeing an inquiry launched, it was now too late. On the day his letter was published in *The Argus*, a report in *The Age* said the government had decided to take no action. The grounds for this were that the setting of Christie's farewell function (the town hall) and the presence of the mayor, had given Christie's remarks an illusion of importance which would not have become attached to them otherwise.

The remarks which Christie made about Otto Berliner in his letter were odd: "...he has no serious or any other charge against me, but always was, and is, a personal friend of mine." This was an amazing turnabout on what Christie had written the previous year after visiting Berliner. At that time, Christie was "glad to get out of his presence," knowing Berliner had a great antipathy towards him. In one of these statements, Christie had to be lying.

One other incident in 1876 raised questions about Christie's probity. A prisoner named A.H.J.Bishop, who was doing time in Castlemaine gaol for forgery, had been arrested by Christie and Dowden the previous year. Now Bishop wrote to the detective office to say some of his property had disappeared. The detectives had taken him and his two trunks off a steamer at Sandridge, and had made an inventory of his property as they were locking him up. Many articles that were missing when his solicitor went to retrieve the property included field glasses, fur slippers, a portrait album, five novels, a silk umbrella and a smoking cap.

Christie, now out of the police force, denied "all knowledge and recollection" when Secretan wrote to ask him about this. Christie said Bishop must be mistaken, for when he made the inventory with Dowden, no such articles were there. Bishop wrote a dignified reply, thanking Secretan for his trouble, and repeating his claim that the goods had vanished the way he described. "Bishop's letter has the appearance of truthfulness," Standish told Secretan. "The whole matter leaves on my mind a most unpleasant impression as to the honesty of Dowden and Christie."

Standish had at least one reason to feel satisfied in 1876. At long last, the government agreed to his pleas to pay detectives more money. The Chief Secretary announced that he was creating four classes of detectives to replace the former three. The daily rates now were 15s., 13s., 12s. and 9s., partly to induce experienced constables to change forces.

It was much too late. And it was not the answer to the three real problems, which were bad leadership, formalised corruption, and antiquated methods of catching criminals. To rely on fizgigs alone was not enough now. Melbourne had grown, spread, and developed refinement. It was almost one of the world's grand cities.

CHAPTER 11

The nursery of crime

The story grew that Christie left the detective force because he wanted to concentrate on sport, and this was a reasonable explanation to the public, because he continued to scull with great success, and he opened an athletics hall, or gymnasium, in Little Collins Street, where he taught boxing and kept in trim for his own bouts.

The old dare-devil Christie stayed the same. Training as a sculler one day on the lower Yarra, he was hit hard between the bare shoulder blades by a rock thrown at him from the bank, and he bled profusely. In a weakened state, he pulled in and asked some workmen to catch his attacker, who was running away. When they brought the man back, Christie recognised him as John Sharp, a burglar whom he had put away in 1868 for robbing the mayor's house. "Well, Sharp," said Christie, "if you had hit me on the head instead of the back, you would have finished me. But if you will stand up and face me for four rounds, I will cry quits."

God knows why Sharp agreed to this, but he did, and the workmen formed a ring. Sharp faced a known, skilful, athletic, angry, bare-knuckle veteran capable of inflicting terrible punishment and staying on his feet for 30 rounds or more. Four rounds were nothing to Christie. But perhaps a beating by anyone was preferable to another spell in Pentridge. In any case, Christie won, and he was to say later that he had never settled with anyone so cheerfully as he did with Sharp.

After such an incident, other men in Christie's place might have said to the workmen, "Thank you, lads, I owe you a favour." Christie's gestures were more dramatic. He invited the foreman and a dozen of the men to the nearby Admiral Hotel, on the corner of Collins and King Streets, to drink his health. Twenty-two turned up. One can imagine them trooping excitedly up the street after him, talking about this punch or that. Other men might have bought them one drink each, then said goodbye. Christie stayed to buy them all a second.

Christie trained hard at his sculling. Melbourne people, favoured with two rivers, the Yarra and the Saltwater, had been familiar with water sport since the first regatta in 1841. By Christie's day, rowing ranked with football and cricket as one of only three sports which attracted big crowds; and now it was entering a great era, for in 1876 various oarsmen founded the Victorian Rowing Association, which is said to be the oldest of its kind in the world. It took over the Melbourne Regatta and for the first time provided a body to regulate all other rowing competition. This period coincided with Christie's new freedom to train and perform.

In 1876 he won the Victorian amateur sculling championship— the real one—competing against John and James Cazaly and P.J.Carter. Christie started as favourite and led by 100 yards before half-way. John Cazaly, who came second, made a late surge, but could not catch him. In the following year, Christie retained the championship against James Cazaly and W.Stout. But he was 32 by then—old for a rower—and when he was beaten in 1878, he readily acknowledged that his opponent was better, and bowed out. He did little competition rowing after that.

But his boxing career flourished. In October, six months after he first won the sculling championship, Christie climbed into a boxing ring at the Princess Theatre in Melbourne to fight Abe Hicken, who was still calling himself Australian champion. This was not only a bout for the championship and a gold cup; it was a way to raise money for victims of the steamship *Dandenong*, which had sunk off Jervis Bay that September, and taken 40 people to the bottom.

Spectators packed the Princess. The two boxers were using 3 oz gloves, and meeting under Prize Ring rules in a 16ft ring; and at the back of the theatre, playing a role that was never really defined, were the police.

Christie's seconds were his old mate from Walhalla, Tom Curran, former champion of Victoria, and Jack Cody. Hicken's seconds were

Jack Thompson and Ned Bitten. When it was announced that the referee would be Thompson's brother, Joe, who was a notorious bookmaker, Christie's supporters were disgusted, for Joe had laid bets that Christie would not last an hour. Today the idea of a referee laying bets is outrageous. But there is no evidence that anyone tried to lynch Joe Thompson or take any other action against him.

Joe Thompson's time span of one hour may explain why Hicken fought the first three rounds more furiously than Christie, and why, from then on, he seemed anxious to get it finished. In the fourth round, acting on a suggestion by the police, the seconds entered the ring to "prevent accidents".

By the end of the ninth round, Christie had repulsed most of Hicken's moves, and he went to his corner smiling. Both men were knocked down in the eleventh; and their injuries were obvious in the twelfth: Christie had lost skin from his face, and Hicken's lips were swollen; Hicken also seemed to be losing his wind. The crowd, perhaps hearing whispers that the betting was suspect, began rowdily supporting Christie, and they cheered him loudly at the end of the 13th round after he had landed several hard, precise punches and warded off Hicken's attempts to retaliate. Christie knocked him under the ropes two rounds later.

It was by no means a brawl. Both men were too skilled for that, and some of their sparring was excellent. But Hicken kept dragging his gloves over Christie's raw face as if to chafe the skin. He also drew blood from Christie's nose, and once this had happened, he continued to hammer it. Christie repeatedly hit Hicken around the ears. He had backed himself to last beyond an hour, and when his seconds told him he had done it, he showed his pleasure by unleashing powerful blows to Hicken's shoulders, and lifting him off his feet.

In the 29th round, Hicken delivered three blows to Christie's nose (which was fairly big, and hard to miss) and Christie seemed to be failing in the legs, but this was an illusion, because he pummelled Hicken so hard in the 31st that Jack Thompson, Hicken's second, interfered. The spectators were furious. One of them became so demonstrative in the 34th round that police stepped in and spoke to the referee, who closed the fight. Joe Thompson, having backed

Hicken, then announced an amazing verdict: the fight had been a draw, but in Christie's favor. Neither of the boxers seemed upset by this. They shook hands and left in good spirits.

Christie did well financially out of the fight, for he had managed to back himself to go beyond an hour, and so had his friends. They later gave him a benefit night of boxing at the Princess, and presented him with £240 for his courage. Tickets to the Christie-Hicken fight had not been cheap: £1; 10s. and 5s. As a result, the *Dandenong* fund received £350. Taking part in such functions was not unusual for Christie; he is said to have raised more than £30,000 for charity during his life.

Undoubtedly his fight with Hicken was among those which hastened the end of bare-knuckle contests, but gloves were still such a novelty in Victoria that *The Age* apparently expected miracles from them. It grumbled that gloves had not stopped the type of betting that had changed the fight's character and provoked rowdiness. If gloves were to become associated with coarseness and brutality, it said, the inevitable result would be prejudice in respectable minds.

None of it worried Christie. In 1877, soon after he won the second of his two sculling titles, he joined up with the English boxer Jem Mace, an apostle of gloves and the Queensberry Rules, who was touring parts of Australia giving exhibitions. Christie had to box with Mace every night for four rounds, and was expected also to fight anyone who challenged him. The greatest boxer in this troupe was Larry Foley, of Sydney, already a legend as Australian champion. Abe Hicken, in claiming this title, was on shaky ground, and when the two men finally met in 1879 in a bare-knuckle fight at Echuca, Foley destroyed him in 16 rounds.

The entrepreneur for the Mace tour was John Wilson, a Melbourne circus proprietor, who apparently paid well. J.B.Castieau wrote much later that Mace received £150 a week and Christie £75 a week. Both figures were fortunes. It seems more likely that Foley and Christie earned £50 a month—still a lot of money—and Mace earned £500 a month. This was a disciplined group. Dressed superbly in white flannel knee-breeches, patent leather boots and armless singlets, the boxers drew huge audiences in Melbourne, Adelaide and Sydney.

When Christie left the tour, he was without one of his back teeth. He had accepted a bet that he could not knock out a negro professional, Harry Sallars, in ten rounds. Christie took a tremendous blow on the jaw in the second round and had to be carried to his corner. He spat out the tooth, and Jem Mace, who was refereeing, kept it as a souvenir. Christie fought so ferociously in the fourth round that Sallars gave in.

For some reason, Christie agreed after the tour to a bare-knuckle fight with Jack Thompson, whom he had beaten for the Victorian championship in Hicken's athletics hall in 1871. The stake was £400. The fight was illegal, and was so secret that nobody associated with it got word of the final arrangements until 5 a.m. on the day. Then a cavalcade of vehicles drove out of Melbourne to a patch of bare heath at Red Bluff, Sandringham. Jack Thompson, who was an American Civil War veteran, stayed in his cab, singing 'Just Before the Battle, Mother' while others stamped the ground level and marked the corners of an imaginary ring by sticking four walking-sticks in the dirt. About 70 spectators gathered round.

Thompson was still heavier than Christie, and he knocked him down in the first few seconds. In fact, he knocked him down in every round. Dazed and spattered with blood, Christie continued to come back until, in the ninth round, his seconds threw in the sponge. He had been totally thrashed. Even Thompson's larrikin brother, Joe, said it was cruelty and murder.

Police had shadowed the cavalcade from Melbourne, and during the fight two mounted constables rode up, forced their way to the ring and demanded: "You must stop this!" but some of the crowd pleaded that the boxers should be allowed to finish, and the constables left the ring and sat watching until it was over. They took names, and summonsed several men to the City Court on charges of having assembled to offend the Queen's peace.

The question remained: why had Christie been beaten so convincingly? An explanation came to light years later. He had become so ill just before the fight that he lost a stone in weight. Not wanting to go ahead with it, he handed some doctors' certificates to a friend and asked him to arrange a postponement. The friend met Jack Thompson, but did the opposite of what Christie had asked; he said the fight should go ahead, and if Christie failed to appear, he should forfeit his share of the stake. So on the day of the fight, Christie turned up at 2 a.m. in bitterly cold weather , and stood waiting in St Kilda Road for a rendezvous with the referee, who arrived two hours late. Then they drove through the cold to Black Rock.

By now Christie was licensee of the Empire Family Hotel in Swanston Street. On 5 December, 1877, at the Presbyterian manse, West Melbourne, he married Emilie Ada Taylor Baker, daughter of a bookseller. The marriage was by special licence and with the written consent of the magistrate, Evelyn Sturt. Emilie was aged 20, and Christie 32. The marriage certificate describes his rank or profession as gentleman. The following year they had a son, who was also named John Mitchell Christie. Christie did not speak of his family publicly.

Around this time Christie received an unusual invitation, from a surgeon who sometimes entertained his friends by holding boxing matches in his Toorak home after dinner. The surgeon had arranged a match just before the beginning of the 1878 Melbourne Cup season. One of the fighters was Jack Thompson; the other was Abe Hicken, who could not take part when the day arrived. Christie agreed to take Hicken's place and fight Thompson for a cheque of £25.

Christie was 15 lbs heavier than when he fought Thompson in the open air, but he still conceded about two stone to him. When the dining room had been cleared and the chairs placed along the walls, the two men began a contest of six rounds, which lasted for 20 minutes. The referee, the man who declared Christie the winner, was Standish, a regular guest at these functions.

On this night of good cheer, while the swells of Toorak and the Melbourne Club watched boxing and talked horses, four young men were on the run in the Wombat Ranges, close to Christie's old police district, the Ovens; the Kellys had shot three policemen at Stringybark Creek. No police force in the British Empire faced such a task as Standish and his men did then.

They went out to hunt the Kellys on the Kellys' own ground, and they might as well have ridden into a foreign land. The police methods broke down here. The police could neither manipulate the events nor get close to the people nor find comfort in the terrain. Many of them had never learned to ride. The Kellys outrode them, outfoxed them, spied on those who were spying on them, tracked the trackers, laid false scents and moved at will through the hills and towns. Astoundingly, they actually captured the town of Jerilderie across the New South Wales border. Here they snubbed their noses properly: the Kelly brothers donned police uniforms and strolled the main street.

Nicolson, in charge of the hunt for much of the time, tried to catch the Kellys through using his old urban system of paying informers, but it did not work here. Only once did it come close to working, near the end, after 20 months, when a spy came in to Benalla to say the Kellys were making armour and were planning something big. But by then Standish had begun to go strange. He removed Nicolson, and replaced him with his favourite, Frank Hare, for whom he had developed an intense and unexplained affection.

What a farce it was. Hare refused to believe the story about armour. Nicolson refused to shake hands with Standish. Behind his back, Standish called Nicolson a vainglorious lunatic. This was the state into which the force had sunk. Its men were paralysed, and their leaders were squabbling and snorting like old-man possums.

The siege of Glenrowan was a lucky accident for the police; not something which they had engineered, but something which went wrong for the Kellys. After Ned was captured and his comrades were dead—but even before he walked to the gallows—the newly-elected Berry Government sacked Standish and appointed Nicolson as Acting Chief Commissioner. This was a praiseworthy act. This was the peak of a loyal and efficient man's career.

But Nicolson fell quickly, along with Hare. The two of them were asked to resign together. These two highly experienced men were dumped because a royal commission had been appointed to examine the Kelly business and the whole workings of the police force; and it needed to begin with a clean slate on which to write its many condemnations. Nicolson and Hare saw out their days with dignity as police magistrates. The new chief commissioner, the most senior man remaining in the force, was somebody the public had scarcely heard of: Hussey Malone Chomley, who was in charge at Geelong. He had not been in the Kelly hunt, and his reputation for integreity was high.

The royal commission sat for more than two years, delivering various judgments. Among the general police, justice was swift: the corrupt and the cowardly were sacked, and the inefficient were censured or demoted. The commission uncovered damning evidence about brothels and illegal trading at hotels and about the way certain policemen protected them. It was alleged that "there is scarcely a suburb, or a street in the city, free from open and undisguised prostitution."

Many hotels near principal thoroughfares were said to be "notorious brothels, the licensees of which were . . . no better than professional panders, the barmaids employed professional harlots, and the attendants thieves and bullies".

Several detectives came forward to expose their own woes. Suddenly, all the professional grievances which detectives had suppressed for years came pouring out like a torrent of filthy water. "I consider in my humble opinion that the whole of the detective force should be abandoned at once," said Detective first–class Charles Forster, "and that the man in charge is totally unfit for his position..."

David Rourke, a former detective, said: "I know a man once in Carlton, who is now doing a sentence of two years; he was one of the 'Nelson' gold robbery. He used to act as the hairdresser. This man was working with Mr Secretan, and none of the other detectives in the division dared touch him, notwithstanding that he was committing robberies and getting robberies up day after day and night after night. He was arrested by one of them once, and Mr Secretan interfered and got him out of it, and in the end he got two years in Pentridge. He was giving information to Mr Secretan, but if he told Mr Secretan to punish one of the detectives in a division he would do it."

Rourke was asked: "This man, although he may have been useful to the force, was a dangerous man to society?" Rourke replied: "He was a dangerous man to society, and such a person ought not to be allowed amongst the detectives." Rourke was then asked: "Is it not necessary sometimes?"

He replied: "It is, sometimes, but in a fair way; not like that, to induce a companion—a robber—to commit a robbery, and then give information. That is very dangerous, and that sort of thing has been in existence for years since he (Secretan) came into that office. There was the case of Detective Christie, who had been in the service and has since left. He used to employ members of the criminal class, and pay them. He would go to his bed every night, and those men would go and get up robberies and commit them, and call him up at the dead of night and tell him where the property was. He would wait some days till a reward was offered, and then go and get the property.

"He was considered a very good detective, but as soon as he went into the Supreme Court, those things were thrown into his face. But it was only the statement of a criminal, and Mr Secretan would not believe it, because he got the cases to suit him. But when he was thrown back on his own exertions, through being thrown out by the criminal classes, he was incapable of doing his duty as a first-class detective, so a quarrel took place between him and Mr Secretan, and he was obliged to leave the service."

William Manwaring, who was retrenched from the force for economic reasons in 1880, also came forward at the commission, and reeled off his background of London Police and the Battle of Alma. He had been retired at the age of 55 on a yearly pension of nearly £149. Manwaring condemned Secretan's appointment as chief of the detectives over the heads of men who were his seniors in service and class; and he believed Secretan's arrival had begun the force's deterioration.

But he found it hard to believe there were put-up cases. "I do not know of any particularly," he said. "The detectives do not like them if anything is suspected of being put up or anything beyond a fair trap. A man gets chaffed, and so on, by the others in the muster room, and the feeling in the muster room goes a good deal to govern the conduct of the men."

Otto Berliner was there. He emerged from his testimony as a garrulous man, who said the detective force had been very effective up to the time Nicolson left it; now there was no detective force in existence. "There are few in the force who are fit to bear that name (detective)," he said. "It takes a well-educated, free-thinking head, and a man who desires to do good—who would not go into the witness box and slander anybody."

Berliner also let drop the surprising information that Standish had come to his residence privately and asked for some advice on the Kellys. In a different part of his evidence, Berliner said: "In the Kelly business, if there had not been a difficulty between Captain Standish and Mr Nicolson, those men (the Kellys) would have been taken at once."

The accusations piled up: Secretan was called the most useless man in the service, he was accused of destroying official documents that might embarrass him, he was powerless to control his department's business, and his main care was to prevent quarrelling among his men.

Secretan, it was said, had established a notorious criminal nicknamed 'The Friar' in a hairdressing business in Carlton and had subsidised him. The Friar's shop was designed as the focus and rendezvous of criminals, who were enticed to co-operate in robberies which he concocted. When The Friar was brought to court as a vagrant and sentenced to two years' gaol, Secretan's intervention had ensured his release after eight months, on the grounds that he had been useful to detectives. But Secretan could not tell the commission what The Friar had ever done for him.

The detectives themselves were severely criticised by some of their peers. They were accused of committing perjury, organising put-up cases and manipulating fizgigs. O'Callaghan, Nixon and Duncan came out worst, partly because of their own testimony, which the commission regarded as lies. Nixon and Duncan had used a criminal to implicate a young man in a bank hold-up. O'Callaghan had condoned a felony rather than see his fizgig prosecuted. O'Callaghan and Nixon were accused of destroying documents to conceal their guilt in another matter.

In January 1883, the commission delivered its report and recommendations about the detective force. It called the force a standing menace to the community, and echoed Detective Forster's view that it was a nursery of crime. It urged that Secretan be retired, the force be disbanded, and the detective office closed.

In its place, plain clothes men would operate from the chief commissioner's office, and under no circumstances could anyone but the chief commissioner pay criminals for their help in arresting offenders or recovering property. There were other recommendations, but these were the main ones, and they were enough to ensure that the old detective force was obliterated. Out of its wreckage grew a new body called the Criminal Investigation Branch.

Dealing with O'Callaghan, Duncan and Nixon, the commission said it could not refrain from labelling them on the evidence as untrustworthy; and it added: "Their retention in the force is not likely to be attended with credit or advantage to the public service."

A year earlier, O'Callaghan had been reprimanded and suspended from duty for "disrespectful demeanour" towards the royal commission. One would think that when this newest condemnation fell on him, he would have been dismissed. On the contrary, he rose to become the next Chief Commissioner of Police, succeeding Hussey Malone Chomley in 1902. O'Callaghan is said to have been the model for the corrupt Melbourne police chief, Thomas Callinan, in Frank Hardy's novel, *Power Without Glory*.

During Christie's time in the detective force, no other member had a similar-sounding name, such as Christy. The closest was Christen. When Detective Rourke testified that a Detective first–class Christie conspired with burglars and delayed recovering stolen goods until a reward was offered, he meant John Mitchell Christie.

Whether we believe Rourke depends on what we think of evidence by a different witness at the commission, Detective third–class Thomas Kidney. Here was one man, the commissioners said in their report, whose honesty was not impugned. Detective Kidney testified that the detectives were capable of unblushing perjury, and that if the commissioners sat till doomsday, they would never learn the truth, because what one man swore, half-a-dozen could be got to contradict.

Standish, showing increasing signs of ill-health and mental instability, died in his bedroom at the Melbourne Club two months later on 19 March 1883, aged 59. He had been born to an old and esteemed Catholic family in England, and had become a leading Freemason in Victoria. This had been his ultimate double standard. Whoring and boxing paled beside this. But he went one better in the end by dying in the presence of a priest and being buried as a Catholic. It was a double double-cross.

CHAPTER 12

Drawing his trusty Colt

The Kelly hunt was not the only great event which Christie missed as a former detective. Another was the 1880 International Exhibition in Melbourne, an event so enormous in its scope that there had been nothing like it in Australia. The police were deeply involved, mainly to detect pickpockets and other criminals. They actually ran a telephone line from the Exhibition Building to their headquarters in Russell Street, an innovation that was brilliant for the times; Alexander Graeme Bell had registered his patent only four years earlier.

To sanitise the approaches to the Exhibition Building, the police emptied the brothels and prostitutes out of Stephen Street and the neighbouring lanes, simply by telling the women to move. There was no fuss or coercion. In the old days, the old whore-mistress Sarah Fraser might have tried to pull some strings, but she was dead by now. Old Melbourne too was dead. The name Stephen Street was dead; it became Exhibition Street. If Melbourne needed a symbol to denote that the old was gone and the new had arrived, the International Exhibition, in a year of glory and excitement, enshrined it. Here was the symbolic beginning of Marvellous Melbourne.

Meanwhile, Christie got on with his new career as a publican. His wife Emilie, having given him a son, John, in 1878, gave him a daughter, Ada, in 1880. By then Christie had relinquished the licence of the European Family Hotel in Swanston Street. He soon became a partner in the Sir Henry Barkly Hotel in Punt Road, Richmond, where he remained until 1884. This was when he joined the customs department, but his reason for doing so is puzzling, for he joined at the lowest rank, which was called extra weigher, and he received the piffling salary of £132 a year. Under the customs department's rules, he later took out an insurance policy for £500 as a kind of bond to ensure his good behaviour.

If Christie were restless for excitement, he did not find it. Within a year he applied to rejoin the police force. Supporting this application, his superior wrote a personal letter to the police commissioner, Hussey Malone Chomley, whom he addressed as "Dear Chomley", a term which implied that here was one mate writing to another for a favour. Christie had apparently set his heart on becoming an inspector of licensed premises and liquor, but the Public Service Board could not appoint him to this job. There was no scope for Christie's ability, the superior said, and Christie deserved a better position than the one he now held.

Chomley was not averse to this, but as a matter of course he asked his officers for advice. Superintendent John Sadleir, a Kelly-hunter who had narrowly survived the wrath of the 1880s royal commission, ruined Christie's hopes. He wrote to Chomley that he could not speak much from personal knowledge of Christie, but:

> "I feel bound to say that, judging from the general
> feeling of those who were best acquainted with his
> manner of doing duty when formerly in the Service,
> and from the fact that since he left the Service he has
> followed the occupations of publican and professional
> pugalist, I think his re-appointment to the Service
> would be altogether inadvisable."

Besides, said Sadleir, twenty applicants to join the force were already waiting, and they had priority.

This was the third blow Christie suffered in 1885. The first was the death in March of his daughter, Ada, aged five, at Richmond. She suffered from debility and a spinal disease. The second blow was the death in July of his wife, Emilie, aged 28, at Prahran, from phthisis, a wasting disease associated with tuberculosis. Christie, not yet 40, was suddenly a widower, left alone with a seven-year-old son, and working at a job which he did not like. There was no way he could have known at this stage that Superintendent Sadleir had done him a tremendous favour, for in the years ahead, the customs department would give him power, money, adventure, and a public adulation on a scale he had not known. He had already taken the first step by moving up the customs ladder from the bottom rung of extra weigher to the next rung of weigher, but he waited two years to climb again, this time to revenue detective on 180 pounds a year. How the title 'detective' must have pleased him. By early 1888, he was also assistant inspector of fisheries. When one looks at the record sheets of Christie's many customs colleagues, it becomes apparent that his climb was unusually rapid; in four years he had doubled his salary to £264.

He had also become the friend and admirer of the emerging head of the Department of Trade and Customs, Harry Wollaston, whose subsequent career stamped him as one of colonial Australia's great public servants. Wollaston, who was roughly Christie's age, had joined the department as early as 1863 as a clerk, and had risen step by step through such ranks as tide-surveyor and landing waiter to become chief clerk, a post he secured in 1888. During this time, Wollaston graduated in law from the University of Melbourne, and in 1885 he was called to the Victorian bar. He became a Doctor of Laws in 1890, and permanent head of the department in 1891. It was a prodigious performance; and yet his best years were still to come.

Wollaston's promotion to chief clerk in 1888 coincided with Christie's appointment as a revenue detective. Christie's only detailed account of this period was the case of a Spaniard named Buenaventura Quiroga who, he said, had given the customs officers great anxiety because they believed he was regularly smuggling goods into Melbourne. Despite searching him and his luggage, they could not catch him at anything. The Collector of Customs, Mr Musgrove, asked Christie to handle the case. At this stage, Quiroga had just left Melbourne and gone on to Sydney on the *SS Lusitania*.

When the ship berthed at Melbourne on the return trip, Christie went on board and learned to his astonishment from the purser that Quiroga had disposed of an immense quantity of jewellery in Sydney. The purser said Quiroga came to Australia with eight packets of jewellery, one of which he sold in Melbourne and six in Sydney. Quiroga was not then on board, because he had decided to travel from Sydney to Melbourne by land, apparently still holding one of the eight packets, and rejoin the *Lusitania* when he arrived.

"Never having seen Quiroga," Christie wrote, "I determined to see the steamer off next day, to get a view of him if possible, so that I would know him for the future as I was determined to bowl him out if possible the next trip he made to the colony. Just as the steamer was about to leave, he arrived, and the purser pointed him out to me as he came on board. The purser said, 'Well, monsieur, have you done any more business?' He replied, 'Yes I have sold completely out. Come and have a bottle of wine'. I then went ashore."

Quiroga always travelled to Australia by the Orient line, and Christie did some calculations about when he would reach England and when he was likely to appear again in Melbourne. He watched the arrivals of various Orient steamers, and arranged with a clearing officer to telegraph him at once if Quiroga's name appeared on a passenger list. "So one morning, on the arrival of the SS *Oroya*, I received a telegram that he was a passenger," he wrote. Christie hurried to catch the Williamstown train to meet the steamer, but as the train came in to Spencer Street station, he learned that she had already berthed, and some of her passengers were on a train which had just pulled in.

"I cast my eye on them," he wrote, "and sure enough there was Quiroga. I turned around and, walking alongside of him up the station, got into conversation with him. I remarked what a nice trip we had round from Adelaide. He said, 'Did you come round from Adelaide by the *Oroya?*' I replied, 'Yes, I am going on to Sydney to my sister's wedding, and I want to buy her something nice here to present to her. Do you know any of the Melbourne jewellers?' He replied, 'Yes, but perhaps I can show you something nice and cheaper than you could buy it in Melbourne'. I appeared to be delighted. He said, 'We will go to a hotel where I can show you it'. I replied, 'All right', but suggested he might come with me to a friend's office first, as I wished to leave a letter.

"He readily assented. By this time, we had arrived at the Customs House. As we were walking in by the main entrance, Quiroga looked up at the building and said, 'This is a very fine building. What is it?'

I replied, 'The Customs House' (at the same time looking him straight in the face). He turned deadly pale and said, 'And who are you?' I replied, 'Detective Christie of the Customs Department.' He said, 'Then you did not come from Adelaide at all'. I replied, 'No, I was only joking.'

"We had now got to my office. I said, 'Show me the jewellery you have for sale.' He took three or four diamond rings off his fingers and handed them to me, saying, 'That is all I have. They are my private rings. I am hard up or I would not sell them, but before I sell them, would I be liable if I sold them?' I replied, 'We don't interfere with people's private jewellery, but have you no other jewellery on you?' He replied, 'No'. Pulling out his trouser pockets, he said, 'You can search me if you like. The customs house officer searched me as I left the steamer. They have an ill feeling towards me for some reason or another.' I accordingly searched him, but failed to find any other jewellery.

"Feeling sure he had some secreted about his person, I told him to take off his coat. He did so willingly. I examined the lining with no better result. He then got very excited and said, 'Would you like me to take off my boots?' I replied, 'Yes', so off they came. Still nothing. I said, 'Take off your waistcoat. He turned a pale greenish color and refused, so I took it off, when the swindle was exposed. Quiroga had a very hollow back, and he had had a chamois leather bag made to fit into it and fastened inside his waistcoat which, when on, defied detection. On opening the bag, I found a beautiful lot of diamond jewellery valued at £400."

Quiroga pleaded guilty in court, and was fined £100 and made to forfeit the jewellery. Quiroga paid the fine and boarded the same steamer to go on to Sydney. Christie saw him off and learned from the purser that Quiroga had given him a large quantity of jewellery to mind. The customs men could not touch it as it was under seal for Sydney, which was then a free port. If Quiroga had managed to sell the jewellery and another lot on his return, the amount of duty would have come to £220 for every thousand pounds worth.

Quiroga plotted revenge on Christie. When he next returned to Melbourne, he called on Mr Musgrove, the Collector of Customs, gave the false name of Gilliano, and said that he could give some valuable information about smuggling if Detective Christie would call next day at a certain time at his office on the ninth flat (floor?) of Broken Hill Chambers.

Christie had not come down in the last shower of rain. When he heard this news, he asked Musgrove to describe Gilliano, and the description tallied with Quiroga's. Christie reminded Musgrove that after the court case, Quiroga had said that someday he would rip that bastard Christie up. Musgrove remembered, and told Christie to be careful. Christie asked "a determined and trusty man" named Tom Brown to go with him and bring his revolver. "I had my Colt," wrote Christie. "On arriving at the top of the chambers, I left Brown handy and walked to Gilliano's door, having previously told Brown that if he heard any unusual noise to rush in. The door was opened by my old friend Quiroga.

"I said, 'I called to see Monsieur Gilliano.' He replied, 'I am the person. Be seated.' He locked the door and put the key in his pocket. There was nothing in the room except two chairs and a table. I watched him carefully. He sat down, and being assured that I had brought no-one with me, commenced a long rigmarole about smuggling and eventually about my kicking him out of the Customs House. I told him I did not come there to hear a lot of rot. Opening the table drawer, he took a large knife out and began flourishing it about.

"I drew my revolver, covering him. I said, 'Put that knife down or I will blow your brains out.' He put the knife down, whereupon I ordered him to open the door. He advanced again to the table, which I capsized, and knocked him down. Brown, who had been listening at the door, burst it in, and (Quiroga) then cooled down and said I had misunderstood him.

"I picked up the clasped knife, and as the blow I had given him I thought sufficient punishment, we left him and reported the matter to Mr Musgrove. There was no doubt had I gone alone and unarmed, he would have tried to murder me, as he would have thought had he accomplished his object all he had to do was leave me in his office, and as he had paid the rent for two weeks in advance, he would give himself time to escape by the outgoing steamer."

Christie became the smugglers' scourge. Almost everything that came into Melbourne by sea, or crossed Victoria's borders by land, was subject to duty: particularly such articles as clothing, lace, jewellery, cigars, and liquor. In this way, said the Victorian politicians, Victorian tradesmen were financially protected in their work. Sydney by contrast was a free-trade port. As a result of this difference, the price of, say, a piece of imported jewellery or a coat, was considerably higher in Melbourne than in Sydney; and the temptation for Victorians to shop in Sydney, then smuggle their purchases home, was considerable. Totally respectable people succumbed to it.

Respectable or not, they were all the same to Christie. On a train travelling towards New South Wales one day, he got talking to a fellow passenger who let drop the information that an acquaintance of his, about to be married, had bought his wedding presents for his bride and her bridesmaids in Sydney and smuggled them back to Melbourne. They were a fashionable couple, well-known in high society. Christie got off the train at Seymour, and took a train back to Melbourne. The marriage was taking place that day. He drove to the bride's house, and sent a message by the footman that he wanted to see the bridegroom.

Politely rebuffed, he then sent for the bride's father, a wealthy squatter, who greeted him affably, took him inside, opened champagne and asked what he could do for him. Christie said he had come for the customs duty on the wedding presents. But the bride and bridesmaids had already received them, the squatter said. In the end, Christie accepted an assurance that the bridegroom would bring the jewellery next day to the Customs House. The bridegroom did this, and was fined £200 and made to pay the full duty.

Such zeal may now seem more like persecution. Set in its times, however, it was considered praiseworthy within a colony devoutly determined to uphold a law that was seen to protect and encourage its emerging industries and crafts, and thus protect a living standard based on a working man's fair wage. Cheap imports could put Victorians out of jobs. For thousands of ordinary voters, protectionism was an ironclad article of political faith.

Christie may have held a serious faith in this view, or he may simply have been, as many policemen are, a dogged and impartial enforcer of the law, turning a blind eye to nothing. He seems to have put equal exertion into stopping small offences as big ones. Disguised as a Church of England parson, he would ride the overland express from Sydney to Melbourne, alert for any sign that a fellow passenger was trying to evade the customs check at the border town of Albury. If someone tried to stuff a package down a seat, Christie knew.

Most of Christie's big jobs concerned ships, particularly Chinese steamers, on which he sometimes made immense hauls of contraband goods. He worked with a team of nine men under him, three to search forward, three amidships and three aft. In each of these groups, two searched and the third kept watch and took charge of any goods uncovered. These third men also prevented offenders from shifting contraband goods from hiding places to cabins that had already been searched.

Once, while examining the cabin of a Chinese boatswain, Christie asked about a large picture of the Melbourne Cup race which had been taken from *The Australasian* and pasted on the wall near the porthole. When he tried to take it down, the boatswain objected, saying he liked horse races. Christie had the man removed. He took down the picture and examined the woodwork in vain for a false bulkhead. Then he got a wooden mallet and began beating. Soon he saw putty begin to crack around an area about 18 inches square.

Removing screws and pulling out a trapdoor, he found ropes fastened to wooden pins. He pulled up the ropes and uncovered 60 boxes, each of 100 cigars, made up like an endless chain and hanging between the inner skin and the steamer's iron side. In the lamp-trimmer's room he found three drums which the trimmer said contained oil, but they really held cigars and opium. Under the lower drawers in the steward's cabin, Christie found rolls of silk, silk handkerchiefs and cigars.

In the engine room, 2000 cigars were hidden among cotton waste. Christie ordered that about five tons of ashes be removed. He found what seemed to be five large chests of tea, but they contained cigars in boxes covered with Chinese matting and branded like tea chests. When a customs man examined a lifebelt, he found the cork had been removed and the space filled with tobacco. The airtight end compartment of a lifeboat contained cigars and silk. The raft on which four Chinese crew members were painting the side of the ship concealed six oil drums full of cigars and tobacco fastened underneath. The drums could be removed quickly and transferred to a boat after dark.

Such searches usually took from eight to ten hours. Offenders among the crew would be arrested and fined from £25 to £100, but they usually chose to go to gaol for six months, for this enabled them to evade the Chinese Restriction Act of 1890; when they got out of gaol, their ship would have gone, and they could not be removed from the colony. The authorities could take no action against the captain for leaving without the men. Normally, he could be fined £100 for every man he left behind, but if his men were in gaol, his defence that he could not take them was watertight.

The ship also could be fined from £5 to £100 and its clearance stopped until the company's agents paid the fine or guaranteed it. In turn, the agents unloaded the expense on to the captain. In turn, he unloaded it on to the crew, apportioning the cost among them according to their degree of guilt, and deducting money from their wages when they reached Hong Kong.

Christie uncovered a common immigration trick by Chinese. A Victorian resident wanting to return for good to China would swap identities with a man in Hong Kong wanting to settle in Victoria. The immigrant would sign on a ship for the round trip. Reaching Melbourne, he would remain at work until nearly sailing time. The resident would then go on board and the immigrant would walk ashore.

When the crew was mustered in Hobson's Bay to see if the ship had its complement, the resident would answer to the immigrant's name. Even if the officers spotted the swindle, said Christie, they would say nothing. Otherwise, the ship would be delayed until the other offender was found. At Hong Kong the crew would be paid off and discharged, and this was the end of it.

Customs authorities, who were the immigration authorities as well, knew that the Chinese trafficked in naturalisation papers, and they tried hard to stop them. Sometimes the papers were sent to China to buyers wanting to emigrate, and sometimes they were taken out of the colony by Chinese going home for a visit and wanting to come back. The law required that when a Chinese wanted to leave the colony and return, he must submit his naturalisation paper to the customs for inspection. He must also submit two photographs, one of which was attached to the paper. The customs men would keep the second photograph so as to identify the paper when the holder returned.

Christie was marginally concerned in the case of a Chinese who presented himself to the customs office and said he was Yee Jug, the name shown on the document, and he was aged 40. But the document was 13 years old, and Yee Jug's age was given as 42. Yee Jug should now have been 55. The holder turned out to be Ah Moke.

In working this swindle, many Chinese seem to have been prey to their own simplicity. Tue Sing, Wong Ah Gee and Chin Puk arrived on the *SS Guthrie* and brought their naturalisation papers to customs. The papers, elaborately sealed and signed with the names of the Victorian governor and premier, were not fakes. But the men, when questioned, knew nothing about Victoria. They were imposters trying to migrate on the papers of dead men. When they finally understood they would be returned to their ship and sent back to China, they broke down, "wailing like men demented." They said they had borrowed a fortune to pay their fares, and now they would have to work like slaves all their lives to repay the lender.

The Chinese were around Christie throughout his career, and it is noteworthy that he left no derogatory description of them as a race or as individuals. He seems to have enjoyed their company, even when he was arresting them. Many is the time he stood in court watching them take an oath by blowing out a lighted match. The assumption was that if a man lied, his soul would blow away as the match was blown out.

To Christie and to many other Australians, every Chinese man— every Chinaman—was called "John," a term which would today be

166

considered patronising but which in the 19th century was matter-of-fact. Christie's attempts to record Chinese dialogue might also be considered offensive now. But he could hardly have depicted them speaking perfect English.

"I caught a Chinaman coming off the steamer *Changsha* carrying two baskets of what appeared to be ginger," he wrote. "John with a bland smile said to one of the customs officers near me, 'You come and lookee my baskets, all ginger, me no smuggle'. The officer said, looking at the green ginger lying on top of the basket, 'John, you got any cigars at the bottom of the baskets under the ginger?' He replied, 'No fear, me too muchee honest to smuggle'.

"I told the officer to take out some of the ginger and see what was underneath. He did so. Then John got very fidgety and said. 'Me think me brought the wrong basket ashore', and when the layer of ginger laying on the top was removed, the baskets which were large ones, were found to contain 3000 cigars. John said, on seeing the cigars, 'That no my baskets. You keep him and me come back shortly and look for my right baskets.' I said to him, 'That's not good enough, John. Me lock you up for smuggling.' He replied, 'You too muchee clever. You think me bad man. No fear. Me no have cigars.'

"I took him to the police station where I searched him and found 200 more cigars concealed in papers round his body. I locked him up. Next day he was tried by the magistrates at the South Melbourne Court, when all that could be got out of him was, 'No savee. Me no speakee English.' The bench found him guilty and fined him £100 or six months. He suddenly forgot himself and called out, 'What for you give me six months? Too muchee gammon. Me no pay fine'.

"He was removed to the police cells. I went out and interviewed him, saying, 'John, you give me £100 and you can get out.' He replied, 'No fear. You take me dam'd fool. Government keep me six months for nothing.' "

Christie claimed that one of the cleverest and most daring smugglers he met was Christopher Johnson *alias* Joe Brown *alias* Tom Wilson *alias* Copper Johnson. Their association went back to 1875 while Christie was still in the police department. In August that year, he arrested Johnson for robberies from ships in Hobson's Bay.

Johnson usually landed the goods at a small pier known as Donaldson's Pier, between Town and Station Piers, Port Melbourne. Christie discovered a plant of stolen property, kept the place under surveillance with the local police, arrested Johnson and put him away for six months.

Next, Johnson and a man named Stream were caught with 4000 cigars, which they had smuggled from the *SS Tsinan*. Packed in empty oil drums, the cigars were lowered from the ship during the night, and made fast under the raft that was used in painting the ship's sides. When the raft was not in use, it was floated around the end of the wharf and moored in a quiet part of the dock, from where contraband could easily be shifted in darkness. Johnson's penalty was another six months.

Some time later, again at night, a customs officer detected him on board the *SS Menmuir*, with his clothes laden with cigars and tins of opium. Johnson knocked the officer down, jumped overboard into the Yarra, swam downstream and landed at the ferry steps, or rather, he was hauled out exhausted by the ferryman and the customs officer who had chased him on foot. Johnson was gaoled this time for smuggling and resisting an officer.

In January 1889, Christie caught him red-handed smuggling 50 lbs of cigars. Christie said: "Well, Copper, you are to rights again." Copper replied: "It looks like it, but you can never tell till the numbers are up." His numbers next day were a £50 fine or six months' gaol.

One morning, Christie received information that an old man had been locked up at South Melbourne for smuggling cigars. A customs officer had met him carrying a sackful of them, and had asked what ship the old man had brought them from. The old man looked astonished, and said he was carrying the bag from the wharf to the Golden Gate Hotel for a man who was to give him 1s.6d for the job. He gave a precise description of this man, and the officer and the police believed him. They immediately said: "This is some of Copper Johnson's work. He was afraid to carry the bag, so he got this old man to do it. It's a shame to get this poor old man fitted like that. A warrant should be obtained for Johnson's arrest."

Christie went to the South Melbourne police court, and "when the poor old decrepit man, with white hair and beard, hobbled into court limping, nearly doubled up, and told his tale, everyone including myself, sympathised with him," he wrote. The old man gave his name as Wilson. Christie was talking the matter over with Sergeant Monckton, when he noticed that the old man's hair at the back seemed a reddish color, in contrast to the rest, which was white.

Christie got the case adjourned for a few moments, and everyone thought he was going to ask for the charge to be withdrawn. He took the old man into the sergeant's room. As the man walked, he was scarcely 4 feet 10 inches high. Christie could see red hair clearly. Christie began questioning the man, who suddenly stood straight up to a height of 5 feet 10 inches, and said: "I was all right till you came. The moment you set your lamps on me, I knew the game was up, although you need not be too hard on me, as I was only playing off one of your own disguises on a customs officer."

Sergeant Monckton and Christie took Copper Johnson into the yard and washed his head with soap, soda and water. His hair turned red. When the case resumed, Johnson astonished the bench by saying: "I plead guilty." He was convicted, and as he was being taken to a cell, he said: "Well, Christie, you were not hard on me. It's the last time you will ever have me. I am on the square after I come out."

In August 1891, customs men gave the steamer *Guthrie*, moored at South Wharf, a good scan and took nothing, but Christie learned later that some of the Chinese crew had been walking the city selling a brand of American tobacco called 'Stolen Kisses'. On a Sunday morning Christie and a customs officer named Joyce searched the crew's quarters and found a lot of tobacco, cigars and earthenware. They cautioned the crew not to try to land any, and left *Guthrie* but kept her under surveillance.

They sent a man on board to see if the sailors would try to sell him any uncustomed goods, and they fell into the trap. The man paid three pounds for 800 cigars and 15 lbs of tobacco. The crew told him they still had 1000 cigars and 50 lbs of tobacco on board. Christie organised another raid, and the government confiscated the lot, after fining offenders in the crew £25 each.

It was typical of Christie not to stop at this. On the same day that he raided *Guthrie,* his party surprised a group of Chinese on board the steamer *Tsinan,* berthed in the Yarra. They had cigars and tobacco hidden in their clothes, and were selling silk handkerchiefs to visitors. There was hardly a week now in which Christie did not organise a successful customs raid, and his name appeared more and more before the public.

Interestingly, the customs office developed a special method in searching women suspected of smuggling. They employed two women searchers who were strangers to each other. Christie explained this by saying that women smugglers would square matters (provide a bribe) when only one woman searched them. This practice was not likely when two complete strangers did the searching. "If we have any doubts about any particular searchers, we put up a job and try them," Christie said.

By 'we' he meant himself. The innovations in his work were his own, and the harder he worked , the more money he received under a system of automatic reward. According to *The Herald* at the time, all fines, penalties and forfeitures under the Customs and Excise Act were split three ways. One–third of the proceeds went to the consolidated revenue of Victoria. One–third went to the person suing. The remaining one–third went to the informer.

As Christie was sometimes both suer and informer, and generally one or the other, his rewards must have been steady. Now and again they may have been considerable. Over the years, some kind of stigma has attached itself to him because of this. But Christie did not write the Act. Whatever reward he received under this system was an acceptable procedure of the day.

CHAPTER 13

Whisky on the rocks

A month after his raid on *Guthrie*, Christie was sent hurriedly to the Western District of Victoria where the barque *Fiji* was breaking up on rocks at Moonlight Head. It was one of the most dramatic wrecks in Victorian history, later to enter folklore because of wild and drunken scenes said to have been enacted by looters trying to pillage cases of liquor among the uncustomed cargo. Christie's party carried life-saving apparatus and rockets. Their main task, however, was to safeguard the revenue from goods washing onto a strip of beach.

The *Fiji* was 107 days out from Hamburg and was travelling to Melbourne with a cargo which included whisky, gin, schnapps and brandy and 250 cases of dynamite. She also carried tobacco, pianos, pig-iron and such toys as rocking horses and rubber balls, intended for the Christmas trade. At 2.30 a.m. on Sunday, 6 September 1891, apparently off course with the Cape Otway light, she struck rocks about 250 metres from shore.

On the sparsely settled coastline, nobody saw the rockets which the skipper, Captain William Vickers, sent up, or the blue distress signals which he burned. Waves crashed over the ship, and the crew of 25 huddled together on the forecastle deck. At dawn, they gazed at cliffs up to 400 feet high. Two young sailors volunteered to swim separately to a small strip of beach with a line. The first of these men was Julius Gebauhr, about 17, whose line became entangled. He cut it and returned to the ship.

Daniel Katlien then set out, but he was swept away and drowned. Gebauhr tried again. Once more his line was entangled, but when he cut it this time, he swam to shore, climbed the cliffs and began walking in a direction he believed might bring him to Melbourne. More than an hour later, a group of Warrnambool men who were in the area by sheer chance, inspecting land which was being thrown open for selection, found him dressed only in his socks, a singlet and a belt, lapping water from a pool like a dog. They thought he was insane, and made him throw down a knife stuck in his belt before they would come near him. Even then they could make no sense of him; he seemed to be speaking gibberish (which was actually broken English, for he was German). Eventually, Gebauhr made them understand that he came from a shipwreck.

The land-selectors galloped in different directions to raise the alarm and organise help. Some went to the wreck and wrote in large letters on a cliff: "Help coming in an hour." The survivors, who had been standing on the *Fiji's* forecastle deck, climbed on the bowsprit in a long line of 24 as the sea rose. Some sat cross-legged, some stood, some clung to ropes. Huge waves occasionally battered them. The men stayed there for more than five hours, in constant danger of being swept off.

As time went by, Captain Vickers realised that death was near for all of them, and said: "Someone must go ashore." The ship's carpenter, John Punken, volunteered. There was no line for him to take. He told his shipmates that if he reached shore, he would wave his hat to indicate there was no help. They were then to jump into the sea and do what they could to save themselves.

Punken swam about three-quarters of the way to shore, and was in some distress, when he encountered a young man swimming out to him. "It was like the face of an angel," Punken said later. "He told me not to be frightened, and to keep up, as we might be able to get ashore. Three times he swam away, and three times he came back to cheer me on." But at last the ordeal was too much for both of them. Punken swam back to the *Fiji* and was hauled on board. The young man headed for shore, but he obviously turned back, for soon afterwards, he too was hauled up, exhausted and dying. His name was Arthur Wilkinson. He lived at Port Campbell, and he had dived into the wild sea from the shore to save a seaman he did not know.

Rescuers on shore finally managed to get rocket apparatus from Port Campbell, and they fired a rocket line across the *Fiji*. The crew gave a cheer heard clearly on the beach. The crew expected a big rope to follow the rocket line, but the men on shore had none. They expected the sailors to put one on. The sailors had none either. At either end of the rocket line, men were pulling in a see-saw action, expecting that a thick rope would appear at the other end. The ship was sinking fast, and the sailors decided to try to reach the shore along the rocket line, which was less than the thickness of a clothes line. They had tied it to the mast.

One by one, hand over hand, they set out, clinging to the line with fingers numbed by cold. Waves knocked them back and forth. Some men dropped off almost at once. Punken said he left the *Fiji* after making sure nothing could be done for Wilkinson. "I got safely on shore after a terrible struggle," he said. He came out of the sea naked like every other survivor, and was taken to one of several fires blazing on the beach, and attended to. Later, it was here he heard the news that 11 of his shipmates had drowned. Punken and 13 others were alive.

At 7 o'clock on Sunday night, about 17 hours after the *Fiji* had hit the rocks, the last man was rescued. Those on shore saw him clinging to the line, shouting: "Save me! Save me!" and someone went to get him and bring him in. They asked: "Is the captain still on board?" and he replied: "I'm the captain." Half-an-hour later the *Fiji* broke up with a great roar. Captain Vickers was so exhausted that it was not until after midnight that he and a few others could be taken up the cliffs to get proper attention and rest.

The Age and *The Argus* in Melbourne both published reports that looters became drunk at the scene and ignored the suffering of the *Fiji's* survivors. Horses and buggies were alleged to have arrived from miles around, bringing sacks to carry away booty. Drunken men were said to have roamed the countryside offering bottles of liquor to strangers, and "brandy was cheaper than water at Princetown. Multitudes around soon discovered that drink was to be had, and down the narrow pathways of the high rocky headlands they crept back and forth like ants." Police horses were said to have been taken to remove stolen goods. Worst of all, men were said to be rolling about drunk among the bodies of the drowned.

When these reports came back to the coastal towns of the Western

District, they provoked fury. Reputable men who took part in the rescue denounced the reports so convincingly, and gave such detailed facts to disprove them, that the orgy stories at Moonlight Head come out badly under scrutiny. It is significant, for example, that the police made not one arrest for drunkenness, and that during the hours in which liquor was said to be strewn along the beach, the *Fiji* had not yet broken up.

One rescuer wrote that the only liquor on the beach when the sailors were being rescued was his own flask of brandy and a bottle of whisky brought by someone else. "My God," another rescuer had remarked to him, "what a pity we have not more spirits; we have only your flask of brandy and a bottle of whisky to relieve these poor fellows." They had to send a messenger to Princetown to try to buy more.

Over the next few days, the scene at the beach was poignant. Rocking horses sat there as if guarding the rest of the flotsam. Scores of toy boats rode the crests of the waves, "floating gallantly on the breakers as if in mockery of the larger craft which had come to grief." Wreckage was strewn everywhere, and it included cases of dynamite and cases of spirits. Only a few visitors were reported to have got drunk. Many others left the area carrying parcels, and were stopped by police. Very few parcels contained spirits. Most of them contained rubber balls and other toys. Somebody said: "Anyone who can scale the cliffs with a case of spirits on his back earns it." Even for a strong man, this would have been hard.

Christie's part in all this is ambiguous, for he left only a scrap of writing about it. It is possible that subsequent writers have confused him with Mr A. Christey, who was collector of customs at Warrnambool and who played a prominent role in the rescue of the seamen and the protection of goods. John Mitchell Christie could not have been on the beach the day the *Fiji* was wrecked, for he travelled by train from Melbourne to Camperdown, then rode with other customs men down the coast to Princetown. They stayed the night at Rivernook, where the Evans family was caring for survivors. Here Christie is said to have encountered "an Irish gang" whom he warned to clear out.

When Christie did reach the beach, he said he came across "a desperate band of smugglers known as the Kelly Gang", whose "only occupation was lawlessness". He named the leader as Tom Delaney, later to become famous when Christie captured the illicit still at Nirranda in 1894. "I was not long on the scene," Christie wrote, "when I found that the 'Kellys' were much in evidence, as they were boldly stealing the goods, and on one occasion, when the customs officer in charge, Mr Johnston, interfered, they assaulted him and he nearly lost his life through falling down the cliffs, which were nearly 400 feet high. He saved himself by clutching a bush, but not till he had fallen or rolled 50 feet. I took action and brought the offenders to justice . . . "

An incident like this certainly happened, but a contemporary version in *The Warrnambool Standard* had a different emphasis: Robert Johnson and Constable Michael Quinn, walking along the cliffs, halted a pack horse, behind which eight men were walking. Johnson held the horse, and Constable Quinn began examining the pack. Suddenly, one of the men struck Johnson, and a general attack was threatened. Tom and John Delaney stepped in to prevent any further trouble. Constable Quinn would have arrested the assailant, but he was unarmed and outnumbered. The officers managed to seize schnapps found in the pack.

In an incident which may have been unrelated, Johnson started to descend the cliff to get more constables, but he missed the beaten path, and rolled over and over. He tumbled over two or three precipices 15 to 20 feet deep and, still unable to stop himself, landed on the beach. He was not hurt.

When Christie wrote that he brought the offenders to justice, he meant that he prosecuted them for smuggling, not for pushing a man down a cliff. Christie was prosecutor at the Camperdown Court on 29 October when eight men were charged with having knowingly evaded customs duty on 11 September. Robert Johnston (sic) told his story about being struck, but said nothing about being pushed down a cliff. The Delaney brothers were among those fined £25, which was a hefty amount.

Tom Delaney was remanded to the police watchhouse, and he hailed Christie through the little square hole in the door. "Look here, Christie," he said, "I got that bit of breakfast you sent me in this morning, and I am thankful, as I was really hungry." Christie replied: "That's all right, Tom." Delaney said: "I will send you up a nice keg of poteen as a Christmas gift that will make your hair curl." Christie replied: "Thanks, and mind you do, as I never forget a man who breaks a promise."

In Melbourne, meanwhile, Dr Harry Wollaston, now the secretary and permanent head of trade and customs in Victoria, was beginning to spread his influence. He was already acknowledged as an authority on customs and marine legislation, and his reputation gained further lustre when the Western Australian government asked him review its own customs department. Wollaston recommended big changes, and drafted a Customs Consolidation Act for Western Australia, which parliament passed. He then consolidated Victoria's numerous customs Acts and ordinances. In 1892, he wrote his second book on customs law.

Christie maintained that Dr Wollaston's appointment as his department's permanent head was responsible for obliterating the practice of shanghai-ing seamen in Melbourne. Christie's word for shanghai-ing was crimping, and it usually meant forcing sailors to go to sea against their will, often by getting them drunk and kidnapping them. Melbourne had a terrible world reputation for crimping, which had been rife since the port first attracted sealers and former convicts from Van Diemen's Land. The gold rush had made the practice worse.

Not only sailors, but men who had never been to sea were drugged, bashed and kidnapped in the earliest days. Once on board a ship, they could be put in irons, and starved and beaten into subjection. One estimate said that three out of every four seamen who manned the windjammers and the early steamers out of Melbourne were sailing against their will. Publicans and low boarding-house keepers connived at the practice with criminals. The situation had improved in Christie's day, but it was still bad. Crimping had another side; it sometimes meant preventing a sailor from rejoining his ship after shore leave, if this was in the skipper's financial interest.

Two men were chiefly responsible for carrying out Wollaston's policy of suppressing the crimps. One was Christie, and the other was Captain Nichol, overseer of seamen, who had been an officer with the P & O line. They seem to have had a blank cheque. Between the three of them—Wollaston, Christie and Nichol—the crimps were gaoled and routed.

Seamen often came ashore in Melbourne with a lot of money due to them after a long voyage. The skipper could seize this if they left the ship without a proper discharge. This meant he had the benefit of their work over a long period for nothing, apart from food and the usual advance note of a month's pay when a man signed on. It was in a skipper's interests, therefore, to pay crimps to lure seaman ashore and keep them away from the ship until it sailed.

Keeping the sailor befuddled with drink, a crimp could then sell him to a different ship which needed a crew. The price for this could be as high as five pounds. Once more, the sailor would get a note authorising him to draw a month's pay as soon as the ship cleared port. Such a note enabled him to buy clothes or personal items. The crimp would get hold of this, sell the sailor cheap and inferior clothes and keep most of the advance for himself. Christie estimated that a crimp could make ten pounds a head on sailors unlucky enough to fall into his hands.

The masters of foreign vessels often protected their crews by anchoring in the bay and allowing few people to get on or off. This was not altruism, but hard economics, for the wages on colonial ships could be two or three times higher than those on European or American, and the crews were sometimes tempted to make a break, willingly forfeiting their accrued pay for the lure of something higher.

One night the master of the *Renown* called on Christie and said six of his crew had deserted, and he wanted them back before the ship sailed at daylight. Christie collected six constables and they drove to Port Melbourne to a pub kept by a crimp named 'Blueskin'. All crimps had such names: 'Flash Jack', 'Blue Nose', 'The Ghost', and a woman called 'Port Wine Mary Anne' because of a birthmark on her face. Christie said sailors knew her personally or by repute all over the world.

When Christie and the master of the *Renown* knocked on the pub door at Port Melbourne, all the lights went out. Soon, 'Blueskin' put his head out of an upstairs window, and Christie told him that if he did not open up, the door would be forced. At once, a ship's bell rang twice inside the building, obviously a signal to anyone on the run.

Sometimes in such places, whole walls were given a false façade with a door so cunningly fitted that it was difficult to find. Behind the façade, a ladder led to the roof. If a bell rang once, the runaways were to hide behind the façade. If it rang twice, they were to climb the ladder to the roof, drop down to a dark part of the street and flee. On this night, three men reached the roof. They scrambled over other rooftops, dropped into a backyard and eluded a constable who had seen them. The constable alerted Christie, who jumped into the wagonette which had brought the police party, and drove into a street where he thought the runaways would be.

"The police are after you, boys!" he called out when he saw them. "Jump in quick, and I'll get you away." They got in the wagonette, and Christie drove them to the police station before they knew where they were, and he locked them in the watchhouse. Back at the pub, he learned that three others had been found; they had been too drunk to climb the ladder. Under police escort, the six men were taken to the *Renown*, which sailed on time.

'Blueskin' also figured in Christie's story of the master of a clipper ship , an excellent boxer, who always made sure a good sparring partner was in his crew. When his current partner, a black, deserted, the master went to 'Blueskin' and asked him to shanghai a negro named 'Black Albert', a noted boxer in Melbourne.

'Blueskin' found the task too hard, so he invited a white boxer, Jimmy Shannon, to the pub on the pretext that they would arrange an evening of exhibition boxing. Jimmy turned up, succumbed to a drug in his drink, was robbed of his possessions and finally, unconscious, was carried on board the ship with his face, neck and hands blackened. In the darkness, he was dumped in the forecastle. The chief officer was at the gangway, and he told the master the black man had arrived. The master handed 'Blueskin' £5 and the man's advance note in exchange.

One by one, Christie and Captain Nichol picked off the crimps and put them away. The port became totally free of them. Runaways no longer tried to evade capture when police were chasing them, and decent seamen no longer feared to go on a spree.

Christie became inspector of liquor and excise and inspector of distilleries in 1893, and this heralded his remarkably active campaign against illicit distilling. It was now that he began tramping the Western District from Cape Otway to Warrnambool, disguised as a swagman or tinker. The capture of Tom Delaney and the Nirranda still was his most celebrated exploit around this time, but he had others in the city.

One of these was at No. 2 Bosisto Street, Richmond. Christie was puzzled as to why water ran almost ceaselessly in a gutter from the back of No. 2 to the street. The water looked clean, but Christie's nose detected refuse. To keep the house under watch, he disguised himself as a surveyor taking levels in Bosisto Street. Then he knocked on the door of No. 2 as a Salvation Army officer selling *The War Cry*. This gave him a chance to look quickly inside when the door was opened. Detecting nothing wrong, he went away and came back as a council labourer sweeping the gutters.

Finally, he appeared at the back door as a rouseabout looking for work. He noticed that the backyard tap was turned on, and attached to it was a piece of muslin, so that drips gently flushed the gutter without noise. He had now seen enough comings and goings at No. 2 to convince him that it hid a still. He raided the place and was proved correct. It was a simple case, but it made big headlines and aroused admiration in Melbourne. Perhaps Christie's exploits were ideal reading for the 1890s, when the colony was gripped by a deep economic depression; Christie gave the population something to marvel at. People said the same thing about Phar Lap in 1930; he was ideal for his time.

It was Christie's capacity to notice small details, and follow his instinct about them, that set him apart from many of his colleagues. He found it odd that a Melbourne grocer was selling whisky and gin at ridiculously low prices. The grocer told him that competition was tough, and that this was his way of attracting customers, who paid for

179

the loss on the spirits by the money they spent on groceries.

One thing led to another, and it turned out that the spirits were illegal. Christie took some constables to a small Richmond house and searched it after rousing the occupant from bed. In a back room they found a complete distillery. A pipe leading from this room to the chimney in the kitchen carried off the smoke from the distillery fire. It mingled with smoke from the cooking fire, and caused no suspicion.

Smugglers continued to compete with moonshiners for Christie's attention. At Williamstown one day, rushing to catch the *Gem* ferry, he rounded the Customs House corner and ran into a man carrying two portmanteaus. The man said: "Where the hell are you going to?" Christie said: "To catch the *Gem*." The man said: "Hurry up or you will miss her." They recognised each other. "Hello!" said Christie to Copper Johnson, "leaving the colony?" Johnson replied: "No, I am taking my duds to the washerwoman." Christie said: "What, two portmanteaus full? Open them."

The portmanteaus were packed with cigars and tobacco. Christie locked Copper Johnson up and, while searching him, found a letter hidden in one of his socks. It contained an address in Collingwood. Christie told the watchhouse keeper, Constable Bolger, to prevent anyone communicating with Johnson, even a solicitor, for three hours. Borrowing a cab and disguising himself as the driver, Christie went to the Collingwood address, where an Irish woman opened the door. Christie adopted an Irish brogue, and said that Mr Johnson had told him to call at six o'clock for a parcel; was Mr Johnson in? The woman said: "He has a parcel to go to Robinson the tobacconist in Spencer Street. He is not home yet, so you had better wait. He is sure to be in in a few minutes for tea."

Christie said he had another place to call at, and would be back later on. He drove to a neighbouring hotel, changed his clothes and, after having tea at the London Hotel, returned to the house without the cab. Now his accent was Scots. The woman did not recognise him. Christie said: "I am Detective Christie. Johnson has been arrested by me at Williamstown for smuggling. Have you any cigars or tobacco in this house?" She said yes. Christie searched the place and found what he called "a great quantity". Copper Johnson's penalty this time was £100 or six months.

In March 1893, Christie visited the *SS Tsinan*, lying at No. 3 shed South Wharf. His attention was attracted by a Salvation Army man having a close conversation with the boatswain and a shore-going Chinese. Christie looked into the cabin, and said to Copper Johnson: "Hello! Playing off one of my disguises again?" Johnson replied: "Oh, no! I am just trying to sell *The War Cry.*" Christie ordered him off the ship, and placed a watch on the shore Chinese. As a result, Ah Gow *alias* Sun Goon was arrested and convicted of smuggling 224 lbs (*2 hundredweight*) of cigars, valued at £100.

Despite Christie's string of successes and the acclaim which came his way, there was probably nothing that equalled the happiness and pride he must have felt when he learned of his next promotion in the department of trade and customs. This was the ultimate he could have hoped for. Dr Harry Wollaston, the customs chief, appointed him Revenue Detective Inspector and Senior Inspector of Excise.

Detective-Inspector Christie! Melbourne came to know him as this from the beginning of 1894. He was a Melbourne identity, whose celebrity status was confirmed constantly, even in such a small thing as a newspaper advertisement for a Children's Hospital bazaar: "Grand Assault at Arms (is) kindly arranged by Detective-Inspector Christie." There was no need to say who he was.

CHAPTER 14

Bamboozling the lawyers

Hundreds of court cases turned Christie into a skilled prosecutor, relying not only on his gift of the gab and his knowledge of customs law, but on his cunning. He could be looking at certain defeat, and turn it into a win. One case he enjoyed talking about was the prosecution of 14 offenders for selling sly grog in 1895 at Korumburra in Gippsland. Senior-Constable Johnston had carefully assembled the briefs on the evidence of two men whom he had employed as informers. Then he had let them go to Melbourne on the understanding they would return the next Friday on the evening train. The court case was for Saturday morning.

Senior-Constable Johnston was waiting at the railway station on Friday when Christie arrived at Korumburra to prosecute. The two informers were missing. Christie said: "Well, we will be in a pretty mess and will have a job to get the cases remanded, as they are all defended. No less than three lawyers for them. They will also get costs against us in each case." But he told Senior-Constable Johnston: "Don't let on until I see how the land lies."

In about half-an-hour, a lawyer interviewed Christie about four of the prisoners, against each of whom were two charges. All four had previous convictions. If they were found guilty now, they would go to gaol without the option of a fine. The solicitor had a proposition: if each of his clients pleaded guilty to one charge, would Christie withdraw the second charges and not prove the previous convictions?

Christie said the cases were glaring, but he would consider the proposal and let the solicitor know in the morning. In the meantime, the solicitor might see the other solicitors to find out if their own clients would agree to plead guilty to one charge; he could not make

183

fish of one and fowl of the other. "Oh," said the solicitor, "they must fall in and do it, as we know the two men who have joined as informers, and as they are never out of the shanty, we are in queer street this time." To Christie's surprise, the solicitor wrongly named the informers as Joe Connors and Pat Dooley.

Christie told Senior-Constable Johnston what had happened. and asked: "Who are Connors and Dooley?" Johnston replied: "Two larrikins who prowl about the hotels and shanties." Christie said: "If you can find them and bring them to me, I can use them as a bluff, and by that means get as many prisoners as possible to plead guilty. Those that don't, I will make some excuse to the bench to remand them." Johnston brought Connors and Dooley to the front parlour of Christie's hotel. They readily accepted Christie's invitation to sit down and have a drink.

On Christie's instructions, Senior-Constable Johnston went away to let it be known that Christie was busy reviewing the evidence with the two informers. He ran into the solicitors, and they accepted his invitation to join him in the front parlour for a drink. When they came in, Christie was sitting at a table with his brief in front of him, talking to Connors and Dooley, who did not know what he was up to. Johnston pretended to apologise for intruding, and took the solicitors somewhere else. One of the solicitors called out to Christie as he was leaving: "I see I was right about the informers."

Christie gave the men five shillings each and told them he would give them the same if they called on him at nine o'clock sharp in the morning. They stepped outside into an angry crowd waiting for them, and there was a stand-up fight. "I ran out and found Connors and Dooley knocking their opponents down like ninepins," Christie said, "but being good men with their fists, next morning Connors and Dooley rolled up to time none the worse for their fight and told me they were suspected of being the informers, which they thought was a good joke." Christie told them that if they kept the joke up, there was another ten shillings for them.

He told them to come to court with him. "When they see the real informers giving evidence, you will have the laugh on them," he said. "Besides, I may take proceedings against the roughs that assaulted you last night." The two men replied: "Oh, let them slide. They had the worst of it." Christie seated the men prominently in the court room so that the solicitors and prisoners could see them. The three lawyers approached Christie and said their clients would plead guilty to one charge if he would withdraw the others and not prove convictions. Christie agreed.

The chairman of the bench, Mr Smallman, police magistrate, said: "As your cases will take a considerable time, Mr Christie, we propose to adjourn them all till Monday. In the meantime, we will dispose of all the other cases." Christie responded: "I think if your worship will take them now, we can finish in half-an-hour, as I understand they are all going to plead guilty."

The bench was thunderstruck, he said later; generally such cases were fought out. Each offender in turn pleaded guilty and was fined £25. Christie applied for four guineas costs in each case, but the lawyers strenuously opposed this, and the bench fixed the sum at two guineas. "The fines amounted to £350 with 28 guineas costs," Christie wrote. "Not bad, considering I had no evidence to adduce."

He continued: "Returning to Melbourne that night, the police magistrate and the solicitors had a friendly game of whist on the way down. During the journey, the solicitors chaffed me about their bluffing me and getting their men off so lightly. I said, 'If you got the costs reduced, I got all I wanted, a conviction in each case'." He told them about the informers not returning from Melbourne. "They were staggered, saying, 'What! Were not Connors and Dooley the informers?' I said, 'No. When you said last night you knew they were the men, I jumped at the idea and used them as a bluff'. A chorus of, 'Well I'm dam'd! We could have got costs against you.' I said, 'Yes, but you didn't'."

Not long after this, Christie went to Yarrawonga on the Murray River to prosecute Jimmy Ah Fook for selling liquor without a licence at his home. Ah Fook had faced similar charges several times, but had always escaped conviction. Before Christie left Melbourne, he was told that Ah Fook could speak good English, so Christie did not go to the expense of taking the government's Chinese interpreter, Mr Hodges, with him.

Christie put up at Ted Prevot's Yarrawonga Hotel, and early next day, met Sergeant Lyons, who told him that the two prosecution witnesses, John Thrift and Christina Robinson *alias* Mrs Lem Ken, could be relied upon to give straight evidence, although an attempt had been made to square them. When that failed, Ah Fook had concocted a defence that would be difficult to break down.

Ah Fook had engaged a solicitor, Mr Stewart, and would call two Chinese to swear they were at his house on the day in question, and saw John Thrift give Ah Fook two shillings to go out and buy whisky. These two Chinese would say that they accompanied Ah Fook to a hotel about 400 yards away, saw him buy the whisky, then return home and take the bottle and two glasses into a room where John Thrift and Christina Robinson were sitting. "So you see," said Sergeant Lyons, "you won't have the ghost of a chance to win the case, more especially as they will give their evidence in Chinese. As you have no interpreter, you won't be able to cross-examine them."

Christie said: "Why, you told me in your report that Ah Fook could speak good English, or I would have brought Hodges up." Lyons replied: "Oh, Ah Fook can speak good English, but the other two will 'no savee English' and they know they can't well be fitted for perjury if they stick to their own language. And there is no local interpreter. Besides, they have brought Jimmy Young, the Chinese interpreter from Beechworth to interpret for them and assist Mr Stewart. They think they will win easily."

Christie said to the sergeant: "You know the saying, 'desperate cases require etc.' Where does Jimmy Young put up?" Christie went to Jimmy Young's boarding-house and found him at breakfast. The two were old acquaintances, and talked of old times, until Christie said: "I want you, Jimmy, to act as government interpreter today, as I know you are thoroughly honest. I will give you two guineas and your train fare." Young replied: "Ah Fook's no good, bring me here and growl about paying me one guinea. Besides, I will like to act as government interpreter."

Once this was settled, Christie said: "The sergeant tells me you have been getting two of your countrymen to swear lies. I told him you were honest and would not do such a thing." Jimmy Young said:

"Ah Fook make them swear lies, not me." Christie said: "Now, as a matter of fact, were the two Chinamen at Ah Fook's house on the day in question?" Jimmy Young replied: "No, they were at Si Goon's garden down the river on the New South Wales side, miles from here. If they get Ah Fook off, they are to get £2 each."

Christie told Jimmy Young: "You go to the court, but don't tell anyone you have seen me about the case, and when it is called on, I will have you sworn in as interpreter for the government." Jimmy was delighted, wrote Christie. When the case came on, Ah Fook's lawyer, Mr Stewart, had Jimmy Young sitting beside him and the two Chinese witnesses close by. Christie asked Mr Stewart: "Does the defendant plead guilty?" The solicitor became indignant, and said: "Certainly not! I can prove my client's innocence by two disinterested witnesses, two Chinamen who happened to be with Ah Fook when the liquor was purchased by him at a neighbouring hotel."

Christie asked: "Do the two Chinese you intend to call for the defence speak English?" Stewart replied: "Oh no, they will give their evidence in their own language, as will the defendant." Addressing the bench, Christie said: "Your worships, I did not bring Mr Hodges up because I was informed the defendant speaks good English, a fact your worships are no doubt aware of, as I am informed the same magistrates now sitting tried Mary Ah How." Mary Ah How, who lived with Ah Fook, had been committed for trial on a charge of robbery from the person of Fung You the previous October.

The magistrates remembered this case, and told Mr Stewart that Ah Fook would have to give evidence in English. Christie went on: "With reference to the two Chinese witnesses to be called for the defence, I will be unable to cross-examine them, having no interpreter." Christie said to Mr Stewart: "How do you propose to examine them yourself?" He said: "Oh, we have gone to the expense of bringing an interpreter to act for us," pointing to Jimmy Young. Christie said: "Your worships, the difficulty is solved, as Mr Young can be sworn in and act as interpreter for the government at the usual fee."

Stewart protested, but Christie had Jimmy Young sworn in, and told the bench: "When I have to go into the enemy's camp and use their interpreter, they need not grumble, as if anyone will be at a disadvantage, it will be my side." Christie asked for depositions to be taken. He had good reason to know, he said, that the defence evidence was a pure fabrication; he would call Si Goon, the employer of the two Chinese, to show they were not at Ah Fook's place on the day of the offence, but working for Si Goon at his place in New South Wales, miles from Yarrawonga.

Christie then asked that all witnesses be ordered out of court. As they were going out, he said to one of the constables so that the two Chinese could hear: "Si Goon is in the clerk's room at the back. When I call him, go round and bring him into court." The Chinese understood this. Fearing that Si Goon would be called to contradict their evidence, "they cleared off as fast as their legs could carry them in the direction of the Murray bridge," Christie wrote.

When the prosecution case closed, Mr Stewart called the two Chinese witnesses, but they could not be found. Christie won the case, and paid the interpreter in full although his services had not been needed. Ah Fook was given the option of a £25 fine or three months in gaol. Christie won costs of five guineas. He always pressed for costs, which were important in defraying his department's outlays.

Unexpectedly, Christie soon found himself back in the Western District, in the township of Mortlake. Two years earlier, at Nirranda, when Long Wilson went to gaol for making illicit spirit, the worm of his still had disappeared. Christie had never lost interest in finding it. Just before daybreak on a Saturday morning, Christie and two constables raided the house of a long-time Mortlake resident, Thomas Tholburn. They searched in vain, and were about to give up, until Christie noticed that Mrs Tholburn glanced at the ceiling.

When he tried to reach the ceiling, Mrs Tholburn began fighting him. She was a strong woman who held her own against him in a fierce rough-and-tumble. They fought under different rules, however; Mrs Tholburn was a biter. There was no doubt, wrote *The Terang Express* at the time, that when Christie encountered this powerful woman "he met a tartar". Christie's bitten hand had to be bandaged.

While the fight went on, the two constables found a worm in the ceiling. They then hurried with Christie to a house which Tholburn owned two miles away, and they uncovered a furnace, vat, casks and other equipment needed for a still. It had all been bought in the Heytesbury Forest a few days earlier. This attempt to resurrect the Western District's illicit distilling was stopped before it began.

Returning to Melbourne, Christie received word that two men were about to arrive from Sydney by the *SS Peregrine* under suspicious circumstances. Christie met the ship, picked out the men and kept them under surveillance. One was Bernard Goldsmith *alias* John Schwartz, and the other was Charles Tomlinson. They lived for a fortnight at Man's Hotel, La Trobe Street, then moved to an isolated cottage surrounded by a large garden, on the high banks of the Yarra at Kew. Night after night Christie watched the house, but could not discover what the men were up to.

One night, while reconnoitring at the back, he was lying beside a bush. "It was a pitch dark stormy night when I saw Tomlinson emerge from the back door and come down the path towards me," Christie wrote, "I lay perfectly still, and drew my revolver in case of accidents. He passed within a foot of me on the way to the closet. In case he might return on my side of the bush, I determined to beat a retreat and started, as I thought, by the same way as I came in, but miscalculating my route, I crawled under the fence at the side instead of the end, and fell down the rocks about ten feet, where I lay stunned for some little time."

If he had gone under the fence a little further up, he would have fallen over a precipice into the Yarra. Even the spot where he landed put him in danger of falling if he did not take care in getting out. He visited the house soon after this, and found a notice in the window saying it was to let. He got keys from the agent and searched it, without discovering what the men had been up to.

A few months later, a market gardener from North Brighton called on him and said that two men who had been renting an orchard alongside his garden were acting suspiciously. They worked all night and were seldom seen about during the day. A light generally burned in a back room at night, and he could hear strange sounds. James Smithson was the market gardener's name. Christie telephoned Sergeant Ryan of Brighton and asked if he knew Smithson and whether Christie could rely on him. Ryan said that Smithson was a straight, honest man.

When Smithson described the men, Christie recognised them as Tomlinson and Goldsmith. They had rented an orchard on Point Nepean Road, North Brighton, and on the orchard was a neat little four-roomed villa, known as 'Lee Villa'. Christie made himself up as a travelling tinker and walked to Brighton to work through some of the neighbouring gardens before approaching Lee Villa. The first place he got work was at the market garden of Young Me, who gave him sixpence for soldering on the tap of his water tank, which had been broken when a mate backed a cart into it.

Christie did odd jobs at several neighbours then, seeing Goldsmith and Tomlinson working at the side of their house, he crossed the road and asked in a Scots accent if they wanted any jobs done. They said no. During this short time, Christie noticed the men had a hose laid on from a tap in the yard. It passed through a round hole in the wooden wall of the back room, which appeared to be the kitchen. If they were distilling, the water would be necessary for the condenser.

Christie came back after dark by crawling through the orchard, He could see the men, but they did nothing unusual. He came back the next night when they were having dinner, and he noticed they were dressed to go out. When they did so, he followed them to the North Brighton railway station and watched them take a train for Melbourne. Christie returned to the house, and got in by shooting a window catch. In three of the rooms he found nothing suspicious. A fourth room, the one in which the hose entered from outside, was locked. Christie went outside, put his nose to the hole and detected the smell of brewing. He also found what seemed to be an overflow pipe.

What puzzled him was how the men could fire a still without a chimney or flue in the back room. A few days later, he revisited the house disguised as a Salvation Army man selling *The War Cry*. He knocked at the back door, and the two men came out and ordered him off the premises. During this visit, Christie noticed the hose was laid on from the tap, through the hole in the wall, and water was running through it. Early next morning, still in his Salvation Army suit, he went back to the house.

He had arranged with Mr Joyce, of customs, and Constable Kane, of Brighton, to come along the road in a cab as soon as they saw him enter the front gate. If Christie found the two men at home, he would take off his hat. Going around the back of the house, Christie met Tomlinson, who said: "I told you the other day not to come round here with your damn *War Crys*, so clear out." Goldsmith came to the door and said: "What's the row, Charlie?" Tomlinson replied: "It's this damn *War Cry* man again."

Christie wrote: "I could hear the cab just opposite the villa, so I doffed my caddey, that is took off my hat, and drawing my revolver, covered the two men, at the same time calling out who I was. Joyce and Constable Kane rushed the house, and the men threw in the sponge. A glance at the back room showed me a complete distilling plant. I soon found out what puzzled me about no flue or chimney, as they used a powerful primus or kerosene stove under the still, as it emitted no smoke." Goldsmith and Tomlinson could not pay their fines of £100 each, and went to gaol for a year.

About this time, Dr Wollaston was receiving complaints that illicit spirits were being offered for sale at various suburban hotels. "A smart-looking foreigner" with bags like a commercial traveller's was hawking the spirits in sample phials. Christie called at several hotels, and at one of them he learned that the traveller had submitted his samples to the landlady, but because her husband had been absent, he had said he would call in the coming week.

With the landlord's co-operation, Christie assigned a detective to lodge at the hotel, and, when the traveller called, to shadow him. Christie told the landlord to buy on his behalf four gallons of whisky and four of rum, to be paid for on delivery. The traveller called and the sale was arranged. In a conversation over a drink, the traveller said he could supply any quantities required once or twice weekly. The landlord said he could do with eight or ten gallons every week if the traveller could knock sixpence a gallon off the price, which he knew was possible because the spirits were illicit. Off guard, the traveller admitted this.

When the traveller went away, he was followed by the detective whom Christie had left at the hotel, but he lost him, so Christie decided to watch for the delivery of the liquor himself. One afternoon, a smartly-dressed young woman wheeled a pram into the bar with a covering over it under the hood. After drinking a glass of lemonade, she wanted to know if she could leave two tins of kerosene in the bar until her mistress called for them later on. Christie made no objection, so she took out the tins, saying they were too heavy for her to wheel home. She put them in a corner of the bar and left.

Next day the traveller called and asked how the landlord had liked the eight gallons he had sent him. When the publican said it had not arrived yet, the traveller said: "Nonsense. My wife left it here yesterday. It is in two kerosene tins, I deliver all my liquor that way to take the down off. You had better pour it into your quarter casks and let it mix with your other spirit, and then I defy the Excise to pick it out. Besides, I can get the empty tins, so if you will have them ready tomorrow afternoon, I will send for them."

Christie did not learn of this conversation until the traveller had left. He decided to be on the spot when someone called for the empties the next day. A nice-looking widow called at the side entrance, left her pram there and went to the side parlour. She had a glass of lemonade and told the publican she had come for the empties. The nursemaid and the widow were the same person. She put the empties in the pram and covered them over, leaving in view only a wax child's head with a cap on. Over this she cast netting, apparently to keep the flies off.

Christie did not know the widow was his quarry until the landlord signalled to him. Christie followed her at a distance. He in turn was followed by old Charley Longlass, a cab driver whom Christie had engaged for the purpose. The woman looked back several times, but failed to see Christie. As she got near the Hawthorn bridge, he saw that she was likely to cross it so he dropped back to Charlie Longlass's cab and jumped in. "I put on a large poncho and told Charley to drive over the bridge and go to the top of the hill," Christie wrote. "From there I could easily watch every turn she made. As I passed her, I obtained a good look at her.

"On getting to the top of the hill, I easily traced her into Fenwick Street, off Studley Park Road, and getting over a fence I got a splendid view of her movements. She wheeled her perambulator in through a gate at the bottom of the street, where there was a large villa standing back in a large garden, quite by itself, right on the bank of the Yarra. I then left and returned after dark to reconnoitre the place.

"It was very dark. I went round the outside fence noting each point. I then crept up to the house, and on looking through the window in which I saw a light, there sat the woman and the traveller having supper. I slipped down the garden and was busy examining the shed when I saw the back door open and the man come towards me. I crept under the fence, and in doing so, fell ten feet on my head on to a bank which overlooked the Yarra 100 feet below. I received a heavy shake but never moved, although the man, hearing some noise, called out, 'Who's there?' After he had returned to the house, I carefully picked my steps up the bank and went home."

Christie returned next day with two constables. As there had been several big tobacco robberies in the city, he pretended he was searching for stolen tobacco. He saw several things which convinced him the couple were making illicit spirits, but he could not see the still. Apologising for his trouble to the couple, he left. Their names were Richard and Ann Ullett. Next night he saw a van being loaded with their household effects. The couple got in the van and drove to a house in Abbotsford, where the goods were unloaded.

Watching again the next night, Christie saw Ullett leave the house in Abbotsford carrying a spade. He walked to his old house in Fenwick Street, and dug up something from the garden. It seemed heavy as he carried it down the steep bank to the Yarra and lowered it into the water. In daylight, Christie got a boat and pulled up the Yarra to the spot. He found a wire fastened to a tree root, and when he pulled it up he found a splendid copper worm, on which he scratched his initials before lowering it back.

There was still no watertight case against the Ulletts, and all that

Christie could do was watch them. In the next two months, they twice moved house in the darkness. He eventually located them in Buckingham Street, Richmond, and he rented a house opposite their own. One night, the couple kept up a heavy fire all night, and a good flow of water had run down their side drain. Christie and two policemen kept watch on a Sunday night when the couple were absent. When Richard Ullett came home, Christie knocked gently on the front door. Ullett opened it slightly, saying: "Who's there? Is that you, Annie?" Putting his foot in the door, Christie said: "No, I am Detective Christie of the customs."

Christie succeeded in opening the door. He grabbed Ullett, and they wrestled. "I was done, but thinking he must be worse, I held on and he gave in," Christie wrote. He drew his revolver and bailed Ullett up in a corner. "I opened the front door and the police came in answer to my call, at which I was not sorry," he said. Christie was aged 50 by now. Ullett later told him the reason he fought so hard was to get hold of a heavy life-preserver behind the door to use as a weapon. "If he had, he would have settled me," Christie said.

When he searched the house, he found a distillery at work. Mash tubs were full of liquor in various stages of preparation, the worm bore his initials, and there were large quantities of essences of rum, whisky and brandy used for flavouring the distilled spirit. Christie arrested Ullett under the name of Laxton. Charged with having possession of an unlicensed still, Laxton was fined £200 in default a year in gaol. He forfeited the entire contents of the house, including furniture.

CHAPTER 15

Swindlers beware!

Of all the ships which Christie searched for contraband, none caused more public excitement than the Norwegian freighter, *Phos*, which entered Melbourne for the first time on 27 July 1897. Christie's tip-off must have been remarkable, for he went to her berth with his usual posse of customs men, and boldly declared that he intended to find uncustomed and unreported goods. On a surprise visit to the captain, J.B.Johnsen, he demanded to have access to all parts of the ship in the name of the Queen.

Then, as if he were wielding some kind of divining rod, he began to lay bare a series of hiding places near the captain's cabin. One find followed another so quickly that the aft part of the ship became blocked with merchandise, mainly spirits and cigars. Six wagon loads were taken to the Queen's warehouse.

Detecting a false bulkhead in the captain's cabin, Christie removed a panel and found packages of revolvers and ammunition, and boxes of shirts and handkerchiefs. A clothes press had a false bottom fitted with shelves holding bottles of brandy, whisky and schnapps. In the chief officer's cabin, a bulkhead held two cases of spirits.

Recesses in the saloon walls held a few packets of matches, but beyond these there were boxes of cigars and canisters of cut tobacco. In an office next to the captain's cabin, a mirror hid a secret opening to a bulkhead crammed with spirits and tobacco. Below a chest of drawers, Christie found a big haul of cigars. Customs men went to the galley, and looked in the tea, rice and sugar bins. The bins held whisky, brandy, gin and tobacco under shallow coatings. In a cabin which had been set aside for a hospital, a water tank unscrewed to reveal liquor and tobacco.

Christie then made Melbourne sit up in astonishment. At the end of the day, he superseded the captain and took possession of the ship. This was within the law, but such an action was exceedingly rare. It came to light that Captain Johnsen, a part owner of *Phos*, had supervised her construction five years earlier in Stettin, which is now the Polish city of Szczecin. It also became obvious that she had been fitted with all sorts of hiding places. Christie justified seizing *Phos* on the ground that this gave customs authorities a substantial surety for any fine.

Captain Johnsen was taken to a police court, where his lawyer, Mr.W.H. Croker, pleaded successfully that a magistrate had no jurisdiction in such a case involving a sum exceeding £100; Supreme Court proceedings were necessary, he said. Captain Johnsen then exercised his option to settle the matter with the Minister for Customs. He was fined £300 and made to forfeit all the goods.

By now, Christie was even more of a Melbourne identity, and the Press used such words about him as 'famous'. He was a familiar sight on the Yarra of an evening, a lone rower, mature, well-built, and silver-haired, pulling the oars powerfully. When he tackled a customs case in ordinary clothes, the newspapers sometimes thought that this was noteworthy, for his skill at disguising himself had become well-known. More and more, he appeared in court as the customs prosecutor.

One case he was mixed up with concerned a Melbourne Club steward named W. H. Burgess, who had come back from England and had been charged with illegally landing four suits of clothing and three pairs of riding breeches without paying duty. It was not a big case, but the newspapers liked it; Christie and the Melbourne Club were two magic names. The steward claimed that the clothing was for his own use. But a club member was found wearing one of the suits.

There were dozens of such small but important cases. Moss Aarons, a pawnbroker in Lygon Street, Carlton, was prosecuted for selling cigars bearing a false trade description. The box lid carried the trademark and the name of a well-known German brand, 'Florida

Monaco', but the cigars were described as colonial rubbish. Aarons had bought the cigars from A.D.Solomon, of Cardigan Street, Carlton. Generously, Christie described Solomon as a decent, hard-working family man who was hard up; Solomon was about the best cigar-maker in Melbourne, Christie said. Solomon and Aarons were fined £10 each.

In the straightforward Melbourne society of the 1890s, a city tobacconist's shop which daily attracted sailors did not go unno-ticed. Suspecting why the sailors were there, Christie put the shop under surveillance. The result was that E.B.Beck, tobacconist and hairdresser, was fined £10 for possessing smuggled tobacco.

A different case concerned protected game birds which were shot out of season. Customs men were told that the birds were brought into Melbourne in baskets under thin layers of dead birds that were not protected, and were lodged in various cool chambers. Christie and his men raided some of the chambers and seized 200 baskets containing wild duck, goose, teal, widgeon and plover quail, and then they searched some cafes and seized more.

At some cafes, the birds were actually on the menus. Seeking to establish a court case beyond challenge, the customs department gave one of its officers money to buy a quail dinner. He ate the dinner and kept the birds' claws as evidence, and put bones in his pocket so that an ornithologist could identify them. It was all in vain. The lawyers said it was not an offence to keep game killed before the closed season began; and who was to say that this game had been killed later?

Christie's biggest case in 1897 made headlines, on and off, for almost seven months. It was known as the Weenen Conspiracy, and it was important for revealing fraud by a manufacturer betraying the protectionist system which had been designed as his safeguard. It also showed Christie at his best as a detective, and it gave him two opportunities to wear disguise.

"In the beginning of 1897," he wrote, "there was great talk and excitement amongst a number of leading gentlemen and some of the principal officers in the customs department concerning the alleged discovery of a very rich gold mine, the 'Cedric', at Bright, which most of them were interested in. A small crushing had taken place which showed 30 ozs to the ton, and as the report from the mine showed that the reef was getting richer as they went down, Mr Harry Weenen had purchased the mine on behalf of a syndicate (many of whom were officers of the customs).

"Weenen had suddenly budded out from being a cap manufacturer in a small way in Lygon Street, Carlton, to a warehouseman and manufacturer in a large way in Gipps Street, Collingwood. He moved in the best commercial circles and was looked up to as an energetic and successful merchant. He attended all the principal race meetings, and it was in everyone's mouth his wonderful success as a backer of horses, never less than £500 a meeting. He was the talk of the city."

Weenen's "first fatal step", said Christie, was to arrange for someone to introduce them. This intermediary was Archibald Smart, the customs department's senior landing surveyor, responsible among other things for examining imports and assessing duty. Smart claimed to be one of the first people in Victoria to ride a bicycle, at Warrnambool in 1870. The meeting he arranged took place in Christie's office in the Customs House, where Weenen said: "I have heard so much about your skill as a detective that I have been most anxious to make your acquaintance." After some talk about his turf successes, Weenen spoke of the Cedric mine. He was going to have about 3 cwt of quartz crushed, he said, but as there was so much swindling in mining and crushing, he would be glad of Christie's advice about how to protect his interest.

Christie told him to go to Fluff-Ums, the tent and sail makers in Flinders Street, and get them to make three canvas bags of the strongest material; Weenen should take the bags to the mine, and stand by to see the stone to be crushed taken out; then he should put it into the bags with his own hands, so that no loose gold could be dropped into any of the bags. As each bag was filled, Weenen should tie the opening securely and seal it. Then he should lock the bags in his hotel room until a train took the ore to be crushed in South Melbourne at the Otis engineering works.

Delighted at this advice, Weenen got Fluff-Ums' address from Christie, boasting still about his turf winnings. After Weenen had gone, Archibald Smart asked Christie: "Well, what do you think of Weenen?" Christie replied: "I am not at all favourably impressed with him. He cannot look you in the face, and I am sure he is lying about his winnings at the races." Smart left in a huff, and he reported Christie's comments to two others, one of whom was a customs officer.

This officer said: "Those detectives would suspect their own mothers. I think Weenen is one of the straightest and most genuine men I ever met." He recounted how Weenen had once come into the Customs House to say he had received £3/10/0 too much on a drawback claim, which was a kind of subsidy.

These three men called on Christie a few days later, and one of them told him Weenen had done as Christie had said about the canvas bags, and intended to take them to the mill to be crushed. "He has a great opinion of you, Christie," the man said. Christie replied: "Well, I have very grave doubts about him. I would advise you three gentlemen to be very careful of him. As to his heavy winning at every race meeting, my honest opinion is that it is a cloak for something we cannot fathom at present."

The fact was that Christie had already caught Weenen out as a liar. Weenan had called on him two days earlier and said Fluff-Ums had made the bags, and they were a good job. By coincidence, Christie had to visit Fluff-Ums about a pair of sea boots for his son, young John, who was an apprentice at sea. While there, Christie said to the Fluff-Ums manager: "By the by, I hope you made a good strong job of those three canvas bags for the gentleman I recommended." The manager said: "We have not made a canvas bag for over a month."

To make sure of his ground, Christie went to every sailmaker in Flinders Street, and none knew anything of the bags or Weenen. "Now, why did he take the trouble to call and tell me a lie about the bags?" Christie asked his three visitors. "As you are all concerned in the mine, be careful." The visitors left, annoyed. A few days later, Archibald Smart came in and said Weenen was taking his three bags of quartz to the Otis mill that morning. Christie said: "Let's jump into a tram and run over to see the crushing."

When they arrived, they were met at the gate by a mining agent named Evans, "one of the biggest scoundrels in Melbourne at that time". As they were talking, Weenen came up, obviously annoyed that Christie and Smart were present. Weenen had three old wheat sacks full of quartz. Christie said: "I thought you said you got three bags made at Fluff-Ums to bring the quartz down in." Weenen hesitated and mumbled something. Christie continued: "You might at least have got three new corn sacks for safety. Look at the quartz sticking out of some of those holes. You could put your hand through." Weenan said: "That must have been the friction in the van."

Christie pulled out a large piece of quartz, saying: "I will take this with me. Goodbye", and in an undertone to Evans, ("the scoundrel"), he said: "You are trying a daring attempt at a swindle. Be careful what you allege is the result of the crushing. Otherwise, there will be trouble. I won't have my friends taken down. You might as well crush the metal off the road as this stuff."

When they were out of hearing, Smart said: "I am now satisfied there is a screw loose somewhere. Weenen was staggered at our turning up at the mill. Your appearance has spoiled the crushings." The next thing Christie heard about it was that the stone had yielded not 30 ounces to the ton, but a miserable few pennyweights. He determined now to make some inquiries about Weenan's allegedly successful betting. In disguise, he went to the next race meeting, and watched the arrival of "a dashing turn-out with three up-to-date swells". They were Harry Weenen; Arthur J. Whightman, his traveller, and William Hyndman, a customs drawback officer. The three made their way to the saddling paddock and began to bet on the first race.

Christie noticed that Hyndman did the betting, taking £3 to £10, which they won. On every race, Hyndman invested from £3 to £5. Between races they drank champagne. At the end of the day, they were walking to their trap and Christie heard Weenen say to Hyndman: "How do we stand?" Hyndman said: "We are £12 to the bad." Next day Christie was surprised to be told that Weenen had had the devil's luck at the races; he had won £475. "How do you know?" Christie asked his informant, who said: "He showed me his book."

Christie was well acquainted with Mr and Mrs McKellar, who kept the Glasshouse Hotel in Gipps Street, right opposite Weenen's factory, so he called on them, and they were discussing old times, when Weenen, Whightman and Hyndman walked in. They went into an adjoining room and did not see Christie. As Mr McKellar went to serve them, Christie put his hand to his mouth and said: "Mum's the word." Christie heard Weenen say: "Bring in our usual bottle of Monopole right off the ice." The men then drank a toast to the Queen. Mrs McKellar told Christie the men had their bottle every morning at eleven, and were also splendid customers all through the day.

Weenen and the other two returned to the warehouse, and McKellar came back to Christie and told him Weenen had won £475 at the races. Christie led the McKellars to believe he was after some coiners, and told them not to mention his visit to anyone. The same night, he disguised himself as a swagman and went back to Gipps Street. Sitting down on a doorstep of a house next to the McKellars' hotel, he observed the hands as they left Weenen's factory for the night. He repeated this for several nights until he discovered where some of the leading hands met, a hotel in Smith Street.

He disguised himself as a steward from an intercolonial steamer, met them several times at the hotel and finally asked one of them: "Could you do with some good cigars?" The man replied: "Rather. Where are they?" Christie said: "I can bring any quantity on the next trip from Sydney and send them ashore amongst the washing to the laundry, where you can get them from me the night we arrive." The man said: "My boss, Mr Weenen, is nearly out of smokes. I am sure he would jump at the chance to get a couple of thousand. Besides, he can square any of the customs officers. There would be no trouble about getting them ashore," and turning to one of his mates, he said: "Would there, Minty?"

Minty replied: "My boss could smuggle a ton if he liked." After the other men had left, Christie walked down the road with Minty, who seemed dissatisfied about something Weenen had done. "If I like to speak, he and some of the customs would have a bad time," Minty said. As they walked on together, Minty unfolded a complex story of how Weenen was defrauding the customs department of enormous sums.

Weenen's firm would import serge or woollen material ostensibly to be made into caps. The material was subject to 30 per cent duty, but this was remitted if it were meant for caps. In due course, to gain this remittance—known as a drawback—Weenen would ask the customs department to send a drawback officer to watch the material being cut up for caps and to sign a certificate saying that this had been done. But Weenen had certain drawback officers in his pay. Hardly any dutiable material was cut up, although the amount of cap-cutting which the officers certified to was prodigious. The few caps which did come out of the factory were made from colonial cloth.

This was only a small part of the swindle. The larger part was much more lucrative. Material which had thus escaped duty was made into suits and sent to other colonies for sale. Through the intricacies of customs law, these were entitled to a drawback on exports. So Weenen would pocket the amount of duty a second time. He then worked a third swindle by submitting fraudulent invoices claiming a drawback on double the number of suits which he shipped. It later came to light that Weenen's drawback on one particular export worth £1100 was £277. In one year, he was said to have received spurious drawbacks of £5000.

When Christie reported the fraud to Dr Wollaston, customs investigators moved into Weenen's factory and spent months trying to unravel his affairs. They included Christie, but were under the control of Archibald Smart, who was responsible for the whole of the landing and drawback staff in Melbourne. It was not until February the following year, 1898, that Christie could issue summonses against Weenen, five of his employees and three customs officers, alleging conspiracy to defraud the revenue. After a wait of two months, the men came before Magistrate Panton, who committed them for trial. During the magistrate's hearing, Christie caused a sensation by alleging that Weenen had tried to bribe him to get the prosecution stopped.

Weenen had first asked Christie at the factory: "What do you want out of this?". On a subsequent occasion, Weenen had told him: "If you can get the commissioner to settle this case, I will fix you up all right." Finally, while they were drinking in the bar of the Exchange Hotel, Weenen took Christie into the smoking room to talk to him privately, and offered him £200 — "100 sovereigns down on the nail, and the remainder when the case is settled".

Christie told Weenen to come to his office next day. Here he accepted the 100 sovereigns from Weenen, and by arrangement, was called to the telephone in another part of the building. He invited Weenen to go with him, and on the way, took him to Dr Wollaston's office and reported what had happened. He entrusted the gold to the the customs department, which continued to hold it.

When the case came to to the Supreme Court, Minty, the man who had first alerted Christie to the swindles, gave evidence as an informer. Minty's evidence, said Mr Justice Hodges, had been "most eloquently supported by an ominous silence" from the men in the dock. Weenen put up a ragged defence, hindered by his failure to produce some of his books or explain some of his figures. At the end of a 16-day trial, the jury found Weenen and four others guilty. Weenan went to gaol for a year and was fined £500. His traveller, Arthur Whightman, went to gaol for four months, and a cutter, John Brodigan, was fined £50. Two customs officers, William Hyndman and Thomas Nelan, went to gaol for three months.

Mr Justice Hodges said: "How many thousands of pounds you may have robbed the country of I don't know, but I know it is a considerable amount." He called the swindle "lying, low-born deceit with no redeeming features of any sort in it". It had been a gripping case for the public, unnerved to realise that customs men could be bribed and that other firms might be as guilty as Harry Weenen's. At least one newspaper cartoon reflected this view. It depicted a circle of soft-goods importers hiding their faces with their hats as they knelt in prayer and intoned: "Oh! Lord we thank Thee that we are not where Weenen is, and beseech Thee to give us strength to drawback from our ancient customs."

The Public Service Board quickly inquired into charges of negligence against several junior customs officers. Some of these officers were earning only about £3 week, and the temptation to accept bribes must have been strong. Classified as non-clerical, they had few skills, and had been transferred to customs from government institutions such as the lunatic asylum or the gaols. To the relief of Dr Wollaston, the board acquitted all of them of doing anything wrong.

Despite being deeply involved in the Weenen case, Christie attended to other customs duties. In one case, he sent a Chinese informer named Ah Shing into various shops in Little Bourke Street to buy two kinds of Chinese spirits made from rice. The phonetic names of this sly grog were noo-my and we-shang, and apparently the sales were more widespread than anybody had imagined, for when the cases were called in the District Court, "seemingly half the population of Little Bourke Street" turned up, packing the benches and spilling into the upstairs gallery, which was seldom used.

The magistrate was Christie's old boss in the detective force, Charles Hope Nicolson, who had been forced to resign as Acting Chief Commissioner of Police after the Kelly hunt. Nicolson had suffered this blow in a manly and dignified silence, and had become respected as a police magistrate. He had some trouble with these sly-grog cases, however, not merely because of the bewildering variety of Chinese names, but because the customs department informer, Ah Shing, turned out to belong to the same Chinese secret society, the Ghee Hin, as one of the defence witnesses, Koon You.

The names *were* bewildering. Koon You was a cook for Koong Cheong, who was licensed to sell liquor, but was charged with selling less than a statutory quantity. Chew Ghee, his accountant, was charged with him. Then there were charges against Ho Eye, Soong Kwong, Ah Kee and Hing Man. Ah Shing gave evidence about buying noo-my and we-shang from Sim Kwong Shing's shop, Sun Goon Loong's shop and Hing Kee's shop. It must have been a hell of a morning for Nicolson. In the end, he dismissed Koong Cheong's case and two others. The remaining Chinese were fined £25 each, and paid it on the spot.

These cases were among the last that Nicolson heard. On a Saturday afternoon at the beginning of August 1898, he died at the age of 68, having worked until a few days earlier. Twice in his life he had suffered deep disappointment at moments when he was close to

Christie unleashes his powerful left at the end of the 31st round of his fight with Abe Hicken on 17 October, 1876 in the Princess Theatre.
(J.B. Castieau)

Also using his left, Sherlock Holmes trounces a ruffian in The Adventure of the Solitary Cyclist (The Strand Magazine, 1904)

*Holmes as a 'simple minded
clergyman' in* A Scandal in
Bohemia. (The Strand
Magazine, 1891)

*Christie as a swagman, a
disguise he used in both
city and country.*
(J.B. Castieau)

*Holmes as 'a common
loafer' in* The Beryl
Coronet.(The Strand
Magazine, 1892)

Holmes matches a slipper to a bloodmark on a window sill in The Valley of Fear.
Compare this to the way Christie matched boots to the head wounds of a prostitute found
on the Yarra bank. (Page 70). (The Strand Magazine, September 1914–August 1915)

Christie in his Christy Minstrel outfit. In such a disguise he sang and played the banjo to pub crowds as he hunted a thief.
(J.B. Castieau)

As a tinker, Christie infiltrated the close-knit Nirranda district as he searched for illicit distillers.
(J.B. Castieau)

As a labourer he keeps watch on a suspect house. (J.B. Castieau)

Late in life, Christie retained his compelling face. His hair turned white early. (Victoria Police Historical Unit)

Christie's grave in the Box Hill cemetery, Melbourne.
(John Lamb)

Christie in 1912. He gave the copy of this photograph to Tom O'Callaghan and his wife as a Christmas card. (Victoria Police Historical Unit)

achieving great honour; and twice—at least in public—he had borne his disappointment as if nothing had happened. The first occasion was his removal from the Kelly hunt in 1880; the second was his removal from the top post in the police force in the same year.

In a sense, Nicolson was irreplaceable. He was one of the last remainders of the Victorian police who had been on the goldfields in the 1850s. He had joined the force as a mounted cadet in 1852 and, long before the Kellys, had seen adventurous service against bushrangers. He had then reformed the detective force, and he had risen to the rank of inspecting superintendent. Many people in the colony had cause to remember Nicolson's efficiency and sense of honour. He was "one of the most honourable, brave and conscientious officers who ever served Victoria". He probably would have made a good chief commissioner.

A big crowd attended the funeral at the St Kilda cemetery. The Administrator of the Government sent his carriage; the senior magistrate, Joseph Panton, and his colleagues turned up, and so did the Chief Commissioner of Police, Hussey Malone Chomley; the retired Kelly hunter John Sadleir, and the great civic administrator, E.G.FitzGibbon.

Christie himself thought he was courting death the following November. Dr Wollaston called him in and told him to hurry to the town of Macarthur, near Warrnambool, to seize bacilli of the bubonic plague which an English doctor had brought with him from India. Wollaston passed on a message from the Minister for Health: "If, on this special service for your country, you should catch the plague, you will be buried with all due ceremony, your relatives will be provided for and a fitting monument will be erected to your memory." Christie was almost overcome by emotion when he heard this, Wollaston said later.

The doctor who had imported the germs, six months earlier, was Leonard Haydon, who wanted to experiment with them. When he refused a request by the Ministry of Health to give them up, the board of public health sent its health officer, Dr Gray, to Macarthur. He reported back that Dr Haydon would not relinquish the germs unless he received £300 compensation.

Customs had no legal power to interfere with the importation, for there was no duty on microbes. But the board of public health learned that the microbes had been imported in gelatine, on which the duty was threepence a lb. As Haydon had not paid this, customs was entitled to seize the gelatine.

This was the stage at which Christie was brought in and told he would be buried with ceremony. He was put on a train and told to seize the microbes despite all hazards. The health officer, Dr Gray, was on his way back to Melbourne when he was stopped by a telegraph message and told to join Christie at Macarthur. Gray met Christie at Warrnambool, and the two of them travelled on to Port Fairy, arriving at midnight. They were up at daybreak, and by 11 a.m. they had driven to Macarthur. Dr Haydon and his brother, Gerald, who was also a doctor, met them in the main street and said they had heard Christie and Gray were coming.

The four of them went inside the house, while a constable patrolled outside, ready to help. Leonard Haydon told Christie he had done twelve months' work on the microbes, and he repeated his request for £300 compensation. What Christie said is not known, but Haydon eventually went into his brother's surgery and brought out a tin box which contained 30 glass tubes filled with gelatine. This, he said, contained the bacilli of the bubonic plague.

Christie quickly closed the box and put seals on it. Haydon admitted he had two more tubes, and he promised to hand them over. It seems to have been a casual sort of arrangement, because he did not do this until after the party had eaten lunch. Then Dr Gray lit a kerosene fire and boiled all the tubes.

Leonard Haydon may have been hardly done by. He maintained he was a public benefactor who had brought the bacilli from India solely in the interest of protecting the Victorian public if plague broke out; he would have had the only known antidote ready for immediate use. He said the public health department knew he imported the bacilli, and had actually inspected the tubes soon after he arrived. There had been no secrecy. His brother had written to the premier about it.

Haydon was an eminent bacteriologist whom the English government had sent to India specifically to deal with the plague at a time it was raging there. He said the only known antidote was dead germs and their products, and he had at great trouble kept pure cultures for this purpose. "Similar deadly germs are kept in every bacteriological laboratory in the world worthy of the name," he said. The health department later confirmed it had known about the bacilli, but said it nevertheless supported the seizure.

CHAPTER 16

The Sherlock Holmes connection

Even today, when Christie's name has faded from the public memory, some people still know that George Robertson, the legendary bookseller, was prosecuted long ago for selling dirty books. The year was 1901, and the books were Boccaccio's *Droll Stories* and Paul de Kock's *Monsieur Dupont*. On Christie's information, George Robertson and Co. Pty Ltd, of Little Collins Street, was charged with having "imported into the State by the steamer *Wilcannia* certain prohibited books to wit . . . ", and so on.

"I feel defiled in my mind by reading them. I felt as if I needed a bath after it," said the star witness, Professor Edward Morris, of the University of Melbourne. (Laughter in the District Court, said a newspaper). Both books were "thoroughly indecent", he said, and *Droll Stories* should be destroyed.

The prosecutor, W. H. Croker, reversing his usual role as a defence lawyer, had set the tone for this case by describing the books as literary garbage of the worst kind. They had no literary qualities to redeem them, he said; the importers had tried to make money by catering for the tastes of a certain depraved class.

In this prosecution, Christie also abandoned his usual role; he was a mere witness, who announced that he had read the books and considered them indecent. When cross-examined, he was fair enough to say he would not contradict George Robertson and Co. if it stated it had been importing the books with impunity for years. This seems to have been the cornerstone of the firm's defence; it had sold the books for years, and it did not understand why it was now in this court.

The answer probably was that a wowser had complained to customs, and Christie had dutifully responded. Whatever the explanation, the bench, led by Panton, fined the firm the high amount of £100. For some reason, it then reduced this immediately to £25. Nobody realised at the time that this was a significant case in the brand-new Commonwealth of Australia. Customs was to seize many more books, and remain a censor for a continent for more than half a century.

When the Australian colonies federated in 1901, the move had brought more fame to Dr Harry Wollaston, who was later knighted. He had already been chairman of a committee to advise Sir George Turner, Victoria's first Australian-born premier, on financial aspects of the Commonwealth of Australia Constitution Bill. Turner was a protectionist who enjoyed the support of Alfred Deakin, Isaac Isaacs and *The Age*. He became the Commonwealth's first treasurer.

At federation, Wollaston took charge of trade and customs on a national scale, holding the title of comptroller-general and permanent head of the department. Working with the first federal customs minister, who was the strong protectionist Charles Kingston, Wollaston drafted legislation and the first commonwealth customs tariff.

Christie, too, found more fame. For the second time, he was chosen as a royal bodyguard. This time, his charges were the Duke and Duchess of Cornwall and York, later to become King George V and Queen Mary, who came to Australia for the opening in Melbourne in 1901 of the first federal parliament. Anyone looking for scandal found none here. Unlike his uncle, the gadabout Duke of Edinburgh who had collected women, the Duke of Cornwall and York was a quiet husband who collected stamps. The two men were completely different.

As early as November 1900, Dr Wollaston, fearing that European anarchists might try to disrupt the royal tour, had instructed Christie to keep all incoming ships under surveillance. With help from the police, Christie began boarding ships night and day, armed with his wide powers of search. It was arduous work, he confessed in a letter to Wollaston. A new State government, headed by Sir George Turner, ordered the surveillance to continue.

In January 1901, Christie received an anonymous tip that W.J.Beck, 'anarchist and chemical mechanic', would arrive on

SS Oroya. Certainly a W.J.Beck arrived in Fremantle soon afterwards, and transferred to *SS Cuzco* which was sailing to Melbourne via Adelaide. Christie made one of his famous train dashes to Spencer Street Station to meet the boat train from *Cuzco*, but he could find nobody on the platform tallying with Beck's description. The matter was handed to the South Australian police.

Incognito, Christie began visiting several 'foreign rendezvous' in Melbourne, which, he suggested, should be carefully searched about a fortnight before the Duke arrived.

Wollaston sent all of this information to the Premier, adding a note explaining Christie's surveillance role. This suggests that Sir George, new in office, was not completely in the know. And here we find the only clue as to why it was Christie, not a policeman, who became the Duke's shadow. Wollaston wrote: "It was also determined (but he did not say by whom) that he should attend on the Duke when he arrived."

The correspondence duly found its way to Hussey Malone Chomley, Chief Commissioner of Police, who was uneasy about this arrangement. He wrote back: "I beg to state that arrangements are completed for detective service in connection with the visit of His Royal Highness. Mr.Christie cannot be recognised by the Police Department." It seems apparent that the government overruled him.

The choice of Christie as the couple's bodyguard was an enormous tribute to his character, reputation and the strict discretion he had exercised for more than 30 years in speaking (or not speaking) about his first royal tour. In 1901, never moving away from the Duke and Duchess, he toured Australia and New Zealand with them on the royal yacht *Ophir*. If there were secrets about this second tour, we shall never know, for he said nothing. He was proud, however, of a letter he subsequently received from the department of external affairs thanking him for the way he had discharged his duties, and assuring him that the royal couple's appreciation of his services could not fail to gratify him.

An indication of Christie's high standing in Melbourne came in 1902, when one of his brothers died in Scotland. Many people knew that Christie had a brother who was manager of the Bank of Australasia in Perth, but few could have known of this Scottish brother, the military one; they had no reason to. Yet now they read in *The Herald* a long obituary about his army exploits at Cawnpore and Lucknow, his work as a governor of Edinburgh prison, his "indefatigable zeal" as a pioneer of prisoner aid, and his many positions in the community.

There were descriptions of the funeral pipers, the gun-carriage horses, the ceremony, the crowd of mourners, the 120 soldiers of the Black Watch marching with arms reversed, and the firing party of 80. You would have thought that here was an heroic son of Melbourne lying dead. Finally, there was the text of a letter which Christie had received that morning from the Governor-General of Australia, Lord Hopetoun, who had known his brother. Hopetoun begged Christie to accept his sincere sympathy.

Christie was 57 now, and although he was remarkably hale, he spent less of his time on the road and more of it preparing briefs or prosecuting. Some of the cases are amusing at this distance. In May 1904, Christie brought Edward T. Gay to court, charged with having imported indecent pictures on watches. The pictures were set into the backs of the watches and revolved with the clockwork. Christie said Gay told him the first lot of watches he imported depicted the king and queen. They were unsaleable. Then he received "a decolette", and wrote back to the exporter asking for fancy samples. These were "in the altogether".

The magistrate, Mr Dwyer, and the justices of the peace inspected the pictures through a magnifying glass. Mr Dwyer said: "There's nothing indecent in this one—a boy with his finger up his nose." Richard Moorehead, a customs officer, replied: "Perhaps something is coming later." Mr Dwyer: "Here's one of a woman at a bal masque. She certainly seems to have on less clothing than they wear at these places." Edward T. Gay's pictures were obviously considered less corrupting than George Robertson's books; the fine was £10.

One by one, the men who had been part of Christie's early life were dropping away. William Henry Manwaring, the old Crimean warrior, died in 1905, aged 80. Otto Berliner had died in 1894, aged

58. At various times, Berliner sent out information about his General Mercantile Agency and Private Inquiry Office, at 78 Elizabeth Street, Melbourne, and in it he claimed a number of flattering things about himself. He said he had been principal officer in the detective office, an inspector of police, the first person in Australia to open a private detective office, and the first person in the British dominions to secure the conviction of a coiner of gold.

In the space of a year, said Berliner, his private office had handled 4,000 inquiries "to the entire satisfaction of those who saw fit to employ me". He must have done reasonably well, for he could show testimonials, and he maintained a branch office in Bond Street, Sydney.

Berliner's version of why he left the detective force in 1866 was that he had spoken plainly about his belief that an innocent man was hanged for the Margaret Graham murder at Daylesford two years earlier. This plain talk "was not relished in certain quarters", he said; stung by "unmerited slights", he had resigned.

Berliner had been concerned in a sensation at the Opera House just before the International Exhibition of 1880. John James McGregor Greer, an Ulsterman who had been in the colony for only a week, was sitting with his French-born wife, Anice, who had been guilty of a shipboard affair with Louis Soudry, a French Government official. The Opera House was packed. At the fourth interval of *Gli Ugonotti*, Soudry walked up to the couple and began speaking to Mrs Greer. Her husband pulled out a revolver and shot each of them in the head. Amid pandemonium, Greer then shot himself. He died, but the other two lived.

Otto Berliner was part of this case because Greer had hired him a few days earlier. Berliner had gone to Mrs Greer and told her that if she did not come to her senses and continued to say that she would rather be a mistress than a wife, he would take her before two doctors who would commit her to the asylum. Mrs Greer had spurned him. The grossness of Berliner's tactic says much about him.

Another who had died was Prince Alfred, Duke of Edinburgh. In 1874, he married Grand Duchess Marie of Russia, and in 1893 he became Admiral of the Fleet. In the same year, he succeeded to the

Duchy of Saxe-Coburg and Gotha and went to live in Germany, where he died of heart disease in 1900. One of his four daughters became Queen of Rumania. Alfred's only son was already dead.

Christie was still going strong. One night in August 1910, at the age of 65, he disturbed opium smugglers at Victoria Dock, and they attacked him. This time, his great strength and skill were not enough to save him from a murderous assault in which he was stabbed and left for dead. That powerful old heart refused to stop beating. He was found in time, and while he lay ill in bed, inquiries about his progress came in almost daily from Government House, Parliament House, the bureaucracy and the public. When he recovered, his hearing was faulty. Believing that this would hamper his court work, Christie retired at the end of the year without pension or compensation, although the customs department did pay his medical bills.

The Lord Mayor of Melbourne held a public presentation to Christie to recognise his services as a customs officer and acknowledge his esteem as a citizen. Perhaps the accolade which Christie cherished most came in a letter to him from the acting Prime Minister: "I feel that after a lifetime spent in the service of the state, your retirement, rendered necessary through injuries received while carrying out the responsible duties of your office, calls for some brief reference from the Government of the day to your many and great services to this country.

"And will you let me say too for myself how very much I admire those qualities of courage, tact, tenacity of purpose, unswerving devotion to duty, and unimpeachable integrity which have characterised you throughout the whole of your career. I hope you may long be spared, and that the effects of the recent cowardly attack upon you may not prove permanent. The loss to the department through your retirement will be felt keenly. Wishing you the happiest of New Years, I am, dear Inspector Christie, Yours truly..."

It was signed by William Morris Hughes. Even criminals wrote to Christie thanking him for his gentlemanly behaviour. Some poor folk wrote to the Lord Mayor from Little Bourke Street, enclosing one pound (known as a quid) for Christie's testimonial. The spelling was quaint. "The sugar (money) aint mush has times his werry bad or we would give another quid," the letter said, "has he was always respektd and liberal with is sugar."

Punch in Melbourne published a long and unusually passionate tribute. Part of it said: "For years and years, John Mitchell Christie, detective, pugilist, oarsman and gentleman, was the idol of the Victorian public. His many astounding feats of athletics, his hair-breadth escapes, his extraordinary ruses and tricks as a detective, all lifted him out of the common round of mere ordinary detectives and gave him a standing among the great, romantic heroes of the profession, Lecoq, Sherlock Holmes (who came later). And Christie was real. His feats were genuine. His mysteries and his stratagems, and his wonderful acumen were cold living facts which could be, and were, proven in the light of day in the courts and in the Press. Criminals feared and hated him. Several vowed his death. Christie never blanched, but went about his work as fearlessly as ever."

Punch went on: "The employment of mouchards, spies and in-formers was of course part of the business; but Christie went one better. He was his own informer. He used to disguise himself and lurch about among the criminals, living with them, drinking with them, quarrelling with them, but all the time following up his clue, seeking the information, obtaining it, and then, at the revolver's point, laying the criminals by the heels. The Christie methods were dramatic, they were romantic, but they were effective."

The paper claimed that Christie refused to touch a penny of the purses and the proceeds from his fights. "He declared that he did not fight to make money, but because he liked it. Besides, he was a gentleman and not a professional pug. The amateur pugilist had not then come into existence. In any case, Christie was outside that class altogether. So he handed over all the money realised in the ring to charity."

Christie practically drove smugglers, crimpers and illicit distillers out of business. In detecting customs frauds, he recovered fines and penalties for his country amounting to £35,000, enough at that time to buy more than 35 houses. His own house, 'Kilmany', in Northcote Road, Armadale, was valued at £960. Here, he seems to have lived happily in his last years, apparently alone. According to one of his

Melbourne relatives in 1991, Christie's son disappeared from his life after going to sea. The two had had a blazing row.

For a few years, Sir Harry Wollaston stayed around. He retired in 1911, and was succeeded in trade and customs by his son-in-law, (Sir) Richard Lockyer. Between 1917 and 1919, Wollaston chaired the Commonwealth Film Censorship Board. He died in 1921.

Joseph Panton, the magistrate who had heard so many of Christie's court cases, died in 1913, aged 82. Like some other public men during his time, Panton was a British achiever: he had been senior commissioner for gold at Bendigo in 1854, and it was on his recommendation that Governor Hotham established the Chinese protectorate. Panton had also mapped the Yarra Valley. The hamlet, Panton Hills, was named after him. He had declined a knighthood.

Tom O'Callaghan became Chief Commissioner of Police in 1902, and retired in 1913. He had led a charmed life, surviving the 1880s royal commission censure, opposition from within his own force, and a separate royal commission censure in 1905. This censure said that his administration had many blemishes and that he held an improper interest in licensed premises at Carlton. It also said that he caused opposition within the force by postponing his retirement. O'Callaghan did not die until 1931. In the meantime, he had served as a councillor with the (Royal) Historical Society of Victoria, and had written, among other things, a useful *List of chief constables, district constables, police cadets and police officers.*

Christie and O'Callaghan seem to have remained friends. Christie gave him his photograph in 1912 as a Christmas present. Whether old friends regularly kept Christie company in his retirement may not have mattered, for he was a self-sufficient man as well as a gregarious one. And there were other things to occupy him, for he was disciplined. One discipline he undertook was the book of his reminiscences, put together by J.B.Castieau, and published in 1913.

This must have been immense fun. For the first time, Christie had the leisure to sit down without interruption, review his adventures and summon up such figures as Chinaman Jack, Tommy the Dancer, Isabella Hartigan, Buenaventura Quiroga, Copper Johnson and Jimmy Ah Fook. He proved to be amazingly accurate in setting down dates, names and the details of crimes and sentences spread over a career of 43 years. This book ensured that later generations would know Christie's name.

Occasionally his name got in the newspapers. In Swanston Street once, frailer now, he saw a cabbie insulting a woman, and shaped up to him. When the cabbie turned his abuse on Christie, not knowing who he was, Christie hit him, and threatened to hit him again. The man got in his cab and drove away.

In Melbourne on 11 January 1927, the heat was so fierce that it became torture for policemen on point duty, wearing heavy uniforms and standing for eight hours in the sun. The City Council was remaking roads. Each time a policeman needed to shift his position to a new line of traffic, he had to free his feet from sticky puddles of tar and bitumen, which were oozing all around him. The policemen came off duty with painful feet and ruined boots.

Twice that day, the temperature reached a century. The coolest the weather became was 72 degrees at 6 a.m. This was the day on which Christie died. He was 81, and was at his Armadale home, a weatherboard cottage of four rooms and conveniences. He died from heart failure, associated with senile decay. The newspapers made a big thing of his death. Ironically, a new Duke and Duchess of York had arrived that day in the Canary Islands, on their way to Australia to open the first parliament house in Canberra. One likes to think that had he lived, they would have invited Christie to some function or other so that they could meet the man who had served their family so well.

Christie left an estate valued at £10,000, which was a large amount for many others, but neither large nor small for a man who had mixed with the great, earned big rewards, owned hotel businesses and never been unemployed. The house in Armadale accounted for one-tenth of his legacy, the bulk of which was a share portfolio. The biggest assets here were 1575 shares in The Herald and Weekly Times Ltd (£5591) and 844 shares in Goldsborough Mort and Co. Ltd (£2152). He had Commonwealth bonds (£558), and stock (£499). He also held 100 shares in Combined Victorian Theatres (£100).

The will was dated 1908. To his seaman son, Christie left £500. A codicil of 1911 left £105 to a Melbourne theatrical manager, Frederick Aylon. After paying debts, the balance of his estate, almost 95 percent of it, was left on trust absolutely to his solicitor, Frederick Thomas Krerouse, of Toorak Road, Toorak.

Christie's biggest legacy was his writing. Unpolished, and giving the impression that it flowed from his hand as soon as his thoughts took hold, it provides a strong, vivid, rare description of urban crime in the 19th century. The background is so much in focus at times that we can forget Christie's existence if we wish, and simply look at the way people behaved, what slang they used, where they lived and how they entertained themselves.

Then, when we shift our gaze to look more closely at Christie, who is the central figure, we remember with surprise that Sherlock Holmes, who made his debut in 1886, had not been invented when Christie was a police detective, yet certain parallels between them are unmistakable. The disguises, the intuition, the derring-do, the ever-present horse cab and the sudden twists of fortune could fit with equal ease into a Holmes story or a Christie story. The one big difference is that Christie relied less on deduction and more on his knowledge of the distinctive way each criminal worked.

Many such contrasts are available. When Christie began investigating the theft of jewellery from the burlesque actresses, the Zavitowski sisters, he found that the burglars had climbed a verandah post and shot the bolt of a window with a knife. He concluded that the same burglars had used this technique in robbing Spann the jeweller. Furthermore, he could at once name them as William Williams and William Smith *alias* Smart, and after watching Smart he concluded that the loot had ended up with the fence David Scott, a jeweller in Stephen Street. This successful piece of detection was typically Christie. Let us not deride it for its simplicity, for no matter how primitive Christie's methods seem today, they worked, and they required an agile brain and a good memory to fit techniques to names and faces.

Now let us watch Sherlock Holmes as he begins to solve a murder in the case named *A Study in Scarlet.* A man's body without any apparent wound has been found in a locked room, in which the walls are spattered with blood. Scrawled in blood on one wall are the letters 'Rache', which Inspector Lestrade of Scotland Yard believes to represent 'Rachel'. Find the woman, he thinks, and you solve the murder.

Holmes examines the corpse minutely, 'feeling, pressing, unbuttoning', even sniffing it. Like Christie, Holmes is relying on observation. But he goes further in his conclusions. "There has been a murder done, and the murderer is a man," he announces, "He was more than six feet high, was in the prime of life, had small feet for his height, wore coarse, square-toed boots and smoked a Trichinopoly cigar. He came here with his victim in a four-wheeled cab, which was drawn by a horse with three old shoes and a new one on his off fore-leg. In all probability the murderer had a florid face, and the fingernails of his right hand were remarkably long." The murder weapon was poison, says Holmes, and he adds: "One other thing, Lestrade. Rache is German for revenge."

Such thrilling perception was beyond Christie, or at least he did not lay claim to anything approaching it. Perhaps he did not need to. But his intuition was actute, as he demonstrated when he saw the old lag Briely carrying a ladder down Elizabeth Street one evening, and knew he was up to no good. Christie stuck with this case for what must have been several hours, first by swapping clothes with his cab driver and getting boldly close to the crime scene, then disguising himself as a drunken sailor and then dropping through the roof of Heymanson's store to confront Briely and do battle with him in the dark. Christie did as well here as Holmes could have done. In a later incident, he was to perform that masterpiece of observation of recognising a wanted man whom he had never seen and who had been charged under a different name. Holmes could not have done better.

At the root of the different methods used by the two detectives was Holmes's awesome erudition. Holmes was a graduate of Oxford or Cambridge or both; Christie was a drop-out from a military school. It is significant that Holmes's first meeting with his biographer, Dr John H. Watson, in 1881, was in the laboratory of St Bartholemew's Hospital, London. Holmes was bent over a table absorbed in his work, when he suddenly cried with pleasure, "I've found it! I've found it!", and carrying a test-tube, he ran towards Watson and his companion to announce, "I have found a reagent which is precipitated by haemoglobin, and by nothing else." This was an immense discovery, which meant that even the smallest drop of blood could now be detected.

Then, when Watson was introduced, Holmes said: "You have been in Afghanistan, I perceive," demonstrating at once his remarkable deductive talents. Holmes was a great scholar. He read Thoreau, Darwin, Winwood Reade, Thomas Carlyle, Petrarch, Meredith, Flaubert , Goethe, George Sand and Catullus, among others. At the other end of his reading were the newspaper agony columns, which advertised such dramas as articles lost and found, wills to be read, rewards on offer, information beneficial to certain parties, and missing friends. Holmes's knowledge of past and present crimes and criminals was huge.

Like Christie, he drew constantly on this knowledge. Christie, who did not tell us what he read, neverthless read gainfully, for it was only by knowing the *Police Gazette* that he was able to recognise the man he identified under another name. Christie gained his knowledge of crime and criminals by wearing down his shoes as he walked the Melbourne footpaths. Unlike Holmes, he did not have much leisure to read, for he worked all the time and Holmes did not. Holmes had many spells of indolence. But he did walk. Like Christie, he walked all over his city and he knew the myriad alleys and blind turns. Like Christie, he was tall and strong (he could effortlessly straighten a bent poker) and he boxed. Both men had a strong left hand. Christie relaxed as well by sculling. Holmes relaxed by fencing, Japanese wrestling and hypodermically injecting himself with cocaine or morphine.

Homes could discuss the possibilities of Chaldean roots in the ancient Cornish language, or the cause of the change in the obliquity of the ecliptic; and if this tired him he could switch to the topic of atavism and hereditary aptitudes. He wrote a monograph on the Polyphonic Motets of Lassus, a monograph on 160 separate cyphers, a treatise on tobacco, and a study of bee-keeping. He played the violin. He could identify forty-two different impressions left by the tyres of bicycles, and distinguish seventy-five different perfumes.

Christie knew none of this. He lacked scientific and classical training, and even if he had possessed it, he had scant means of putting it to use. The closest Christie came to a scientific solution to a case was to remove a suspect's boots and match them with the marks of violence on the head of Susan Egan, murdered on the Yarra. Twenty years later, Holmes used this technique in *The Boscombe Valley Mystery*, except that he was handling a rock, not a pair of boots. The rock was the murder weapon, Holmes said; it corresponded to the victim's head injuries. Holmes had similar success in matching a slipper to a blood mark on a window–sill in *The Valley of Fear*.

So you can see it was not merely the use of disguise which made people link Christie and Holmes as similar detectives; they had much in common despite the barrier of Holmes's superior education. Both men were loners, even though Christie had the backing of a department, and Holmes was in touch with Scotland Yard. Holmes's one friend was Watson. Did Christie have friends? We can only guess that three people played an unusually friendly part in his police life: Tom O'Callaghan, Levi Walker's wife (if in fact she was his mistress) and the Duke of Edinburgh. We may include O'Callaghan because we know that as late as 1912, long after the two men had gone their separate ways, Christie gave Mr and Mrs O'Callaghan his photograph as a Christmas card. We may include Mrs Walker (whatever her given name was) on the assumption that Christie was willing to risk his career on a relationship laden with peril and disgrace.

The Duke we may include with more confidence. Certainly he admired Christie and sought his company, and Christie served him well. No matter how brief their association was, and no matter how scandalous anyone's activities were, a clear picture is established of two young men drawn to each other in an easy-going mateship. It was undoubtedly proper, formal and at times stilted. They would not have called each other John and Alfred. But they seem to have had a relaxed and happy time locked in each other's company night and day over longish periods. Men who are not friends cannot do this. The Duke sought Christie four times, first as a bodyguard for

Victoria, then for New South Wales, then for New Zealand and finally for service as a detective at the royal household in London. On the second and third occasions, the Duke did not merely ask for Christie; he insisted.

No matter how good Christie was as a bodyguard, the Duke would have balked at having a shipboard companion who got on his nerves and could not be congenial in his circle. One suspects that Christie was not just the bodyguard but the happy companion in play.

Holmes, who had a prim side, would not have liked the Duke. Holmes nevertheless behaved admirably when he accepted a case involving the Duke's scandal-ridden elder brother, Edward, Prince of Wales, heir to the throne. In this case, *The Adventure of the Beryl Coronet*, a distressed bank manager calls on Holmes and says that on the previous day he has been visited in his office by a man whose name is so exalted, "a name which is a household word all over the earth – one of the highest, noblest, most exalted names in England." – so exalted that he cannot reveal it.

This exalted man is thus not named, but many Holmes scholars identify him as Edward, Prince of Wales. Prince Edward wants to borrow £50,000 over the weekend. The banker lends it to him on the security of 'one of the most precious public possessions in the Empire', the Beryl Coronet, which he takes home for safe-keeping. During the night some of its precious stones are stolen, and Holmes's job is to get them back quickly.

In real life, Edward was fair game. He had already been involved in two court cases, one about gambling and the other about adultery. In the gambling case (1891), Lieutenant-Colonel Sir William Cumming brought a libel action to counter an allegation that he had cheated in the illegal game of baccarat. Edward, who had been present at the game, went into the witness box on his behalf. Later he had to apologise to Parliament for having failed to report dishonourable conduct by a fellow officer.

In the other court case (1871), Sir Charles Mourdant sought a divorce from his wife on the grounds of her adultery, and he named two members of Edward's circle as co-respondents. The wife claimed that the child she had borne was the result of adultery with others, including Edward, Prince of Wales. Edward went briefly into the witness box, denied the allegation and was free to go. He was not cross-examined.

It is not surprising therefore to find Edward turning up in a bank manager's office asking for a weekend loan of £50,000. But it is noteworthy that both Christie and Holmes had these encounters with British royalty. Holmes, of course, went further. He declined a knighthood later in life, but he did accept a present from a certain gracious lady – we all know who she was – at Windsor Castle. Christie's career did not take him so far as that, but he did have dealings with Australian governors and with the governor-general, the gracious lady's Australian representative.

Between Christie's Prince Alfred and Holmes's Prince Edward, there were some startling parallels. For example, they both liked to kill things. Edward's record of game shot at his home in Sandringham in the season 1896-1897 includes nearly 14,000 pheasants and more than 6000 rabbits. Alfred went to the Austin home, Corio, during his Victorian tour, and in a couple of days his party shot more than 1000 rabbits, before moving on to Robertson's at Colac. Here they shot snipe and cockatoo. What on earth could they do with them all?

Nicknames, too, were interesting. Edward's intimates called him Tum-Tum. One of Alfred's intimates called him Darling Matilda. Both led lives of scandal. Then there was Edward's son, the Duke of Clarence, who was suspected at one time of being Jack the Ripper. Queen Victoria produced some astonishing descendants.

His Royal Highness Darling Matilda slips easily into the trio of possible Christie friends. In one way or another all were outside the separate laws that were supposed to govern them. But so were Christie and Holmes when it suited them.

When Christie was struck by stones while sculling on the Yarra, he did not prosecute his assailant, John Sharp; he thrashed him. When Christie disarmed the smuggler, Buenaventura Quiroga, who was trying to kill him, he did not march him to a lock-up; he roughed him up and let him go, for reasons which he did not deign to explain. Christie was his own judge and jury sometimes. And remember, when prize-fighting was outlawed, Christie indulged his love of it.

Holmes was even readier to be his own law. When he had deduced who had stolen the jewels from Edward Tum-Tum's Beryl Coronet. he recovered them – disguised as a 'common loafer' – and he let the culprit and his lover-accomplice go free. "I saw that a prosecution must be avoided to avert scandal," Holmes said, "and I knew that so astute a villain would see that our hands were tied in the matter." Besides, Holmes reasoned, the villain's lover was being punished enough simply by remaining with the villain.

In various cases, Watson accepted such reasoning, but he balked when Holmes disguised himself as a plumber and wooed and became engaged to a housemaid of the 'king of all blackmailers', Charles Augustus Milverton, whose mansion he was planning to burgle. Watson expostulates, "Surely you have gone too far?" Holmes replies that he has walked out with the maid each evening and talked with her and has got all he wanted; now he knows Milverton's house like the palm of his hand.

"But the girl, Holmes!" cries Watson. Holmes shrugs. "You can't help it, my dear Watson. You play your cards the best you can when such a stake is on the table." In his defence, Holmes adds that he has a rival who will cut him out the instant his back is turned.

Holmes and Watson burgle the mansion to crack a safe and retrieve imprudent letters written by a woman about to be married. Now Holmes is outside both the ethical and criminal laws. Interrupted, the pair hide in the curtains, and watch an unnamed woman confront Milverton and tell him his blackmail has ruined her life and caused the death of her husband, 'the noblest gentleman that ever lived.' She draws a revolver and empties round after round into Milverton. Holmes restrains Watson from leaping out of hiding, and they escape. Later they look in a shop window displaying photographs of the celebrities and beauties of the day. The photograph of one woman arrests them. "My eyes met those of Holmes," Watson tells us, "and he put his finger to his lips as we turned away from the window." Once again Holmes has been judge and jury.

Then there is the *Boscombe Valley Mystery* in which Holmes finds the rock which fits a murdered man's head injuries. Unmasked by

Holmes's other deductions, the murderer, suffering from a fatal disease, tells a pitiful tale of having been blackmailed. Holmes responds with compassion. "Well," he says, "it is not for me to judge you. You are yourself aware that you will soon have to answer to a higher court than the Assizes." To ensure that an innocent man does not hang, Holmes keeps the murderer's confession in case it is needed.

One could continue giving such examples. "Get out!" Holmes orders a thief at the end of *The Adventure of the Blue Carbuncle*. As the man flees, Holmes says: "After all, Watson, I am not retained by the police to supply their deficiences." And he goes on, "I suppose that I am commuting a felony, but it is just possible I am saving a soul. This fellow will not go wrong again. He is too frightened. Send him to gaol now, and you will make him a gaolbird for life."

Unlike Christie, who did not try to explain his actions, Holmes had a philosophy about them: "I think there are certain crimes which the law cannot touch, and which therefore, to some extent, justify private revenge." (*Charles Augustus Milverton*). He might have added, "There is also a place for private compassion." Here the two men differed. One cannot imagine Holmes interrupting wedding celebrations to inquire about smuggled wedding presents. Holmes would have obtained a result, but in a more devious way.

One point, however, on which the two detectives might have agreed is Holmes's statement, "It has long been a maxim of mine that the little things are infinitely the most important." It was a little thing that led Christie to Chinaman Jack's loot after he had arrested him on the night of black-face singing in the bars of Little Bourke Street. Having locked Jack up, Christie turned up at the watchhouse next morning to see if Jack's pals would bring him breakfast. One did – Kate Laurence, Jack's paramour. Christie shadowed her home, searched the house and found loot hidden under the hearth stone. The idea about breakfast was only a little thing. Some detectives may not have bothered.

With more certainty we can accept that Christie would have applauded Holmes's statement, "You play your cards the best you can." So far as we know, Christie did not falsely woo a housemaid in order to burgle a blackmailer's mansion, as Holmes did, but he had reason on many occasions to play his cards the best way he could. In fact, when the deal went against him, he was at his best. One example is the customs case at Korumburra when, without stepping outside the law, he hoodwinked the opposition lawyers into believing he could produce witnesses to sly-grogging. Ruses were a Christie specialty.

"You play your cards the best you can." This attitude may have led Christie into his relationship with Mrs Walker (assuming it existed). It seems a reasonable thing to happen to a detective already consorting with criminals; a felon's wife, with her head on the pillow, could have been a rich source of unexpected information. Then again, she may have been just a strumpet, and Christie no more than an ordinary male. But the testimony was that he 'lived with her', implying (in those days) something almost permanent and quite shocking. 'Dressed her like any lady.' It is possible that he loved her. Either that, or he was snooping.

Whatever the truth, Mrs Walker is the only romantic attachment mentioned in the Christie papers, and then, not by him but others. (He did not once mention his wife, but this is a usual safety precaution with policemen even today. Christie had not married at this stage). Holmes too had only one woman in his life, Irene Adler, who teased and outwitted him in *A Scandal in Bohemia*. On his watch chain for the rest of his life, Holmes kept a sovereign she had given him. "To Sherlock Holmes she was always *the* woman," wrote Watson. Otherwise, Holmes scorned romance, and he thought marriage might bias his judgment.

Just as there was only one woman for each of these two detectives, so for each there was one outstanding brother. Holmes's brother was Mycroft, seven years his senior. Holmes claimed that Mycroft had the superior powers of observation, but had no ambition and no energy to follow anything up. Mycroft spent his life walking from his lodgings to the government offices where he audited the books in some of the departments and acted as inter-departmental adviser. In the evenings he went to the eccentric Diogenes Club in which members, who could not belong unless they were unsociable, were forbidden to converse.

It is worthwhile reproducing a conversation between Sherlock and Mycroft as they study an approaching man and use their talent at deduction:

"An old soldier, I perceive," said Sherlock.

"And very recently discharged," said Mycroft.

"Served in India, I see."

"And a non-commissioned officer."

"Royal Artillery, I fancy," said Sherlock.

"And a widower."

"But with a child."

"Children, my dear boy, children."

This is very clever. Could Christie have done it? The answer is probably no, but not because he lacked good observation. The answer is that Christie and Holmes dealt with different human material. Holmes, for example, looking at a man's calloused hands, might type him as a labourer, a reasonable assumption in class-structured England. Christie would have been more cautious because, living in Melbourne in the 19th century, he was part of the most topsy-turvy city in the Empire.

Who was master and who was man? This could be a genuine dilemma. A millionaire contemplating his rose garden at Toorak might have the hands of a navvy and the manners of a goat. A young man down on his luck might turn out to be the third son of an earl. So in assessing men at a glance, Christie had the harder task of the two. He could not look on a man and say dogmatically that here was someone who worked in stables because he had chaff on his collar. Despite this, his judgments were swift and accurate. Harry Weenan, the drawback cheat, went to gaol because Christie knew from the instant they met that something was amiss. Weenan was a crook. Christie knew it deep down. He did not need to explain his misgivings as Holmes would have done. He simply knew. Christie's instincts were as sharp as anyone's.

One magnificent thing which did unite Christie and Holmes – and indeed, united most of Melbourne with most of London – was their knowledge of where they stood in the world. They knew with absolute certainty where they stood, just as they knew their names and the course of the sun. They were British subjects. To be British was to be everything to which a person could aspire. To be British and members of their class meant that the entire pattern of their lives was laid out for them in the smallest detail, and they followed this pattern as if it had come from God.

To be British meant an absence of doubt. Trains ran on time to the minute, cheating was an abomination, the Empire was the greatest force for good which mankind had known, Sunday was sacred, cruelty to dogs was inexpressibly bad, the Ten Commandments were immutable, men opened doors for women, the strong helped the weak, men (not women) worked because God had ordained it, a man's home was his castle which he ruled with total authority, and military heroes (especially dead ones) were idolised.

General Gordon, killed at Khartoum while fighting the unspeakable barbarians, is a case in point. Holmes and Watson kept Gordon's photograph on their wall. Melbourne erected Gordon's statue near Parliament House, and Christie would have seen it often. Perhaps he raised his hat as he passed, as some men did. Gordon was the Empire's ideal hero, a general of modest demeanour who had been outnumbered by the enemy and gone bravely to his death carrying not a gun, it was said, but a swagger stick. Gordon had not flinched from that powerful obligation called duty. If there was one quality of the British Empire which Queen Victoria's subjects admired above all others, this was it.

A man must do his duty, be he a general, a train driver, a postman, an explorer, an inventor or someone far lower, someone at the very base of the pyramid whose apex was the Throne itself. If anyone were challenged in duty beyond his capacity, he must scorn ridicule, risk injury, be a man, even die. "Be a little soldier!" was something said to infants to stop them crying when they skinned a knee. "Be a man!" was said to cheats, snivellers and cowards, and by 'man' Victoria's subjects meant 'Englishman'. He had no peer.

When members of the 1880s Royal Commission on the police heard stories of how detectives used paid informers in an institutionalised way to trap criminals, they could think of no greater condemnation than to say that this was not the action of an Englishman. These words said everything. Alas, the English themselves had already discovered that detectives were imperfect. Their own Detective Branch had been found corrupt and been disbanded in 1878, replaced by a Criminal Investigation Department, on the lines of that which later came to Melbourne.

Sherlock Holmes embodied everything which the Victorian era admired: bravery, fair play, duty, decency, patriotism, a desire to right wrongs and protect the weak from the predatory, and an intellect which functioned with the same order and logic as a railways timetable, the telegraph system, the civil service, an electric light globe, the bicycle, and indeed the monarchy and Empire itself. There was a place for everything and everything was in its place.

But this was not always true for Melbourne. The framework was there, but people kept bending it out of shape. To the Irish at Eureka, fair play meant something else. To the protesters who stoned Parliament House in August 1860, shouting 'A vote, a rifle and a farm!' fair play meant unlocking the rich men's land. To the stonemasons who built the great Victorian-style buildings, fair play in the heat of the Australian sun meant a shorter working day, and they won it; the eight-hour day surprised England. To the early legislators, fair play was the secret ballot; the 'Victorian ballot' the world called it, for it was the first. Melbourne was a restless place.

Living in different environments, Christie and Holmes could not fail to be different in the way they worked. Holmes could remain a gentleman. Christie – although everyone said he was a gentleman – was actually a bit of a knockabout. He was equally at home in the drawing room of Government House or the stinking bar of a low pub in an alley behind Little Lonsdale Street. True, he was not alone in this, for Holmes could wander through his own city in the same way; but Holmes did not impart the feeling, as Christie did, that he was enjoying himself. Holmes was doing a job. Christie was having fun. The surprising thing is that both men were so successful.

It was valid of *Punch* in 1910 to imply that Christie was Australia's Sherlock Holmes. It recognised that here was a man who stepped outside the accepted notion of detective work in Melbourne, who

237

was brilliant at disguise and the use of ruses; whose bravery was unquestioned, whose success rate was high and whose instincts had the pinpoint timing of a thunderbolt.

It would be fun to play with time and move Holmes back to 1869, and watch him standing in the Little Collins Street muster room, brushing against the Melbourne detectives as they heard evidence given at the inquiry into whether Secretan had played favourites. Holmes would have borne this politely, weighing each statement and deducing who was lying, who suffered from a weak chest, who was on bad terms with his wife and who was prone to sleep in stables. But he would have become abruptly alert when someone was sent to fetch the arrest records of these strange men. Manwaring 12, Eason 1, Fook Shing 14, O'Callaghan 28– and suddenly, Christie 56, a figure which no other detective could approach.

Fook Shing would have interested Holmes because he would have deduced that he smoked opium. Here was a like spirit. Perhaps Fook Shing would know where to get some good stuff? Holmes injected it (as he did cocaine) and it is ironic that Christie spent time in customs halting its illegal import.

But Fook Shing would have been just a diversion, tolerated for a few seconds until Holmes turned his full attention to Christie and began to ask about his cases. This information would rivet Holmes, who would say as he did later in his career: "It is a mistake to confound strangeness with mystery. The most commonplace crime is often the most mysterious because it presents no new or special features from which deductions may be drawn." (*A Study in Scarlet*).

The two men would eventually have other things in common. Holmes suffered Professor Moriarty, in whom he believed there was a criminal strain of blood. (Manwaring would be all ears). Christie suffered Otto Berliner. Each detective was brought down by his own special enemy, and each then spent time in the wilderness before re-establishing his career. Each suffered bad beatings, Christie in particular. Each had a strong connection with India, but then, so did half the Empire. Again and again, India or Indian veterans (including Watson) occur in Holmes's adventures.

At the end of their meeting, perhaps Holmes would add: "Those stories of the ruses. I enjoyed them so much, Mr Christie, that I made a mental note of some. Goodbye. You have had some acquaintance-ship with royalty, I perceive!"

It is important that Christie left a body of writing, because it makes him real. We know that Holmes is not. But we still need to ask whether Holmes and Christie influenced each other. The evidence that Christie influenced Holmes cannot exist, for Sir Arthur Conan Doyle, Holmes's creator, began writing his series long before Christie published his own. Sherlock made his debut in 1887. Christie did not publish his recollections until 1913. Sir Arthur had probably never heard of Christie, and there is no primary evidence that the two men met when Sir Arthur visited Australia in 1920-1921.

But it seems probable that Holmes influenced Christie; that is to say, influenced the way Christie wrote. This is because the Holmes stories not only preceded Christie's by 26 years; they created some-thing novel: they gave the world the notion of a well-mannered, intelligent, dare-devil detective; and the world liked it so much that the notion spread quickly to other crime literature. This new sort of detective was a cut above other men.

Christie did not always have this image. His early reports to his police superiors – in the late 60s, early 70s – do not show him as a likeable dare-devil. It is only when he wrote his recollections 30 or 40 years later that he became the invincible hero, because the recollec-tions coincided with the rise of the literary detective.

Like all police detectives in Melbourne, Christie was required to write a prompt report of his cases and submit them to his department chief, either Nicolson, Ryall or Secretan. Sometimes, when you study these reports after reading his memoirs, you wonder if you are looking at the correct document. Not once in his entire police career, does Christie mention his disguises. Not always is he the central figure. Sometimes the reports of his cases are not written by Christie, but a colleague who was with him and held a higher rank.

Christie's marvellous story (in his memoirs) of how he busted the Halliburton warehouse gang is an extraordinary contrast to the scant and pedestrian account he wrote of the same exploit in his detective report on 12 August 1870. In the detective report, he mentioned none of the preliminaries such as visiting Coyle's hotel, shadowing Ben Long, or disguising himself as a swagman and talking to the hotel landlady and the woman down the lane. Nor did he write of overpowering the gang in a fight. This report begins with the information that Christie:

> "was keeping the six criminals (named in the margin) under surveillance, until a favourable opportunity should offer, which would lead to their arrest and conviction; at 4.30 p.m. on the 23rd July while watching their house, he (Christie) saw them busily engaged measuring a quantity of cloth; and as he had that morning received information that a warehouse had been broken into and a quantity of cloth carried away, he immediately came to the conclusion that they were the guilty persons: he immediately went to the Detective office, saw Mr Secretan and informed him of his suspicions, who instantly started for the men's house with him, but meeting Dets Harrington and Brown, he instructed them to accompany him"

One other example that contrasts Christie's report-style and memoir-style concerns the case of Tommy the Dancer, in which Christie disguised himself as a parson to catch the men who were robbing houses in Carlton. Christie had been a detective only nine months, and held the most junior rank, that of third-class. The detective report was written by Detective second-class Hannan, and Christie co-signed it without additions.

Hannan's account was that, acting on information received, the detectives succeeded in arresting a man named Robinson. They searched his house and found stolen property and new boots. They arrested a second man in whose house they found boots identical to those found at Robinson's. Christie's memoir embellished the case, using such terms as "modus operandi" and "the coast was clear", and it also gave Christie prominence over Hannan: "I and a couple of detectives divided Carlton in Sections and laid ourselves out to watch about . . . I soon set on a plan . . . "

In his parson's garb, Christie followed the criminals to a lane off Madeline Street, discovered their house by a ruse, and went off to fetch Detectives Hannan and Harrington. Subsequently, they secured the men "after a desperate struggle". There is none of this in the detective report.

Christie's memoirs unfailingly give him the role of the clever, risk-taking detective found in popular literature. This is not to say that he invented some of his adventures, although it is possible that he did, and it is possible that elsewhere he slipped up on some of the details. He certainly did not invent the cases, the dates, the characters or the outcomes. What Christie did was present each case in a style to which the public had become accustomed.

He gave us a hero (himself). He gave us a narrative: "Jumping on the evening train, I proceeded direct to the Detective Office where I met Inspector Secretan who seemed very pleased to see me." He gave us certain words such as crack (burglary) and graft (work), demonstrating that he was familiar with the criminal world, and creating an atmosphere which signalled danger. He gave us many accounts of the way criminals operated (they hit the Halliburton lock with a brick and made the works fall out). He gave us suspense (none of his cases is solved until the end). And he gave us dialogue.

None of these props was needed—or indeed, was possible—in a two-page detective report to a superior in the 1870s. Because Christie did not include them, we should not assume that they are spurious. He did not mention his disguises, either, and there could be several reasons for this. One that springs to mind is a need to guard his secrecy, even among some of his brother detectives. Another reason could be a departmental policy requiring him to stay quiet about the practice. A third could be his superiors' exasperation at receiving reports which contained more than the essential facts of an investigation. A fourth could be his concern about not being mocked for his cleverness.

Certainly, Christie did not invent his disguises in the customs department. The newspapers knew of them. It is significant, too, that *Punch* in 1910, recording Christie's police career, spoke of his disguises as if they were by now common knowledge; and this was in 1910, before his revelations had been published.

As well as imitating Sherlock Holmes, Christie could have drawn on an established genre of popular Australian detective fiction.

James Skip Borlase and Mary Fortune wrote stories about detectives who dressed in disguise and who made arrests through using informants, observation and deduction. Borlase wrote one of the earliest Australian detective stories, *The Night Fossickers of Moonlight Flat*, set in 1852 on the Victorian goldfields. It is told by a detective in the first person. He disguised himself "to all appearances as true a devotee of pick, shovel and cradle as any of the heterogeneous mass around me . . . "

At the end of the story, Borlase relates that three murders can be attributed to Spider Ned, "or, as he was called on his indictment, Edward Barton *alias* Edward Brunton *alias* Thomas Dunn *alias* Michael Dunealy." This was exactly the way Christie wrote. One example of many is Christie's Christopher Johnson *alias* Joe Brown *alias* Tom Wilson *alias* Copper Johnson.

Mary Fortune wrote *The Detective Album* under the pen name 'W.W.' in *The Australian Journal* from 1867 to 1909. She married Percy Brett, a goldfields policeman, and used his sources for some of her stories. After her marriage broke up, she continued to associate with policemen and detectives to gather ideas. As with Borlase, Christie is likely to have been aware of Mary Fortune, whose stories were widely read. Some of Mary Fortune's detectives dressed in disguise, as Christie did. Her Detective Harper dressed as Puggins the peddler to solve a murder in 1891. He was:

> " a funny-looking little man, carrying an oilcloth-covered box in one hand. He looked like a peddler of some kind . . He was dressed in an old-fashioned brown suit, and wore nice little drab gaiters . . ."

In *Blairs Secret*, dated 1884, Detective Henry Bateman is disguised as a gardener on a farm "close to the You Yangs, and within sight of Hobson's Bay." Mary Fortune wrote a story about a character who bears an uncanny resemblance to Christie. It is possible that Mary Fortune and Christie could have been acquainted; both lived in Melbourne over the same period, and were successful in their separate careers, which were related through crime and detection. *A Government House Romance* was written in 1892, by which time Christie had left the detective force and was prominent in customs.

Mary Fortune introduces the story by writing that she:

> "was favoured with particulars of the following case from a
> once well-known detective, who is now superannuated, and
> special interest attaches to the narrative because of its
> intimate connection with the household of a colonial
> Government House of bygone days."

The story began with the Governor General requesting that a
"reliable detective" be sent to investigate robberies at Government
House.

"Will you go?" the Inspector asked of Dunn.

"Of course," Dunn replied, "but I must have carte blanche."

Dunn subsequently arrived at Government House disguised "in
so queer a rig that one of his own mates would hardly have recognised him." Compare this to the words of Christie's landlord when
Christie dresses as a swagman in the Halliburton case: "If I had not
seen you rigged-out like it before, I would have collared you for a
thief"; or of Christie's farmer friend in the Nirranda illicit-still case:
"Your own mother would not know you."

Christie was familiar with Government House through his connection with Prince Alfred's visits of 1867-1869, and the Duke of
York's visit of 1901. When he was with Prince Alfred, Christie dressed
as a sailor or a gentleman according to need.

Christie's memoirs dealt exclusively with his successes, for it was
vital when writing in the popular detective style to present himself as
somebody whose career had been spotless. We learn of his setbacks
in the police department only by reading the detective files at the
Public Record Office. This is the one place, for example, that we find
the full story of Thomas Moore, assaulted while wearing handcuffs.
It would be unfair to say Christie was cheating in his memoirs by
ignoring such incidents; he was not writing an autobiography; he was
not writing of his personal life either; he was writing a series of
almost-unrelated exploits to please himself and his public.

Nevertheless, it is difficult to avoid the thought that he may have
gone a bit too far. While it is true that dates, names, outcomes and
so on can be verified, the evidence for his disguises in the detective
force rests on flimsy corroboration; and he certainly was not the

243

leader in many of the cases he investigated. Some of his other activities described in the manuscripts may be fiction.

No matter what you learn about him, Christie remains a contradictory figure. Of his career, we can say that the latter part, in the customs, was brilliant, and that the first part, in the detective force, was probably both good and bad—bad because it is difficult to overlook evidence to the 1880s royal commission that he was on the take, or to overlook the fact that former colleagues spurned him when he applied to rejoin them in a cleansed force. It is easy from this evidence alone to infer that Christie was part of the infamous nursery of crime.

It is also possible that he was a brash and objectionable young man, whose head became swollen by early successes, which included the Duke of Edinburgh's tour. In the cramped muster room of Little Collins Street, this would have been intolerable to colleagues, willing to cut him down, as they tried to do when they claimed that Secretan was playing favourites. And then Christie changed. Having left the police department and its fairly rigid disciplines, and having become wiser, he found a role in customs that allowed him almost total freedom to be a detective in his own way. His promotion to detective-inspector completed this process. He was the boss. And it was then that he bloomed.

Of Christie's private life, we know almost nothing. This was the way he structured it. Even in his grave at the Box Hill cemetery he guards his privacy. On his tombstone, his family motto, 'Pro Rege', meaning (loosely) for the monarchy (or the state), reminds us of his long public service. But there is no hint of the private Christie; the rest of the inscription mentions no wife, no children, no parents; nothing but "John Mitchell Christie, Inspector of Police and Customs." Even here, somebody got it wrong.

Appendix

**Editorial, *The Leader*,
Melbourne, Saturday, June 10, 1876**

THE POLICE FORCE

The reports which the Chief Commissioner, Captain Standish, and Sub-Inspector Secretan, in charge of the detectives, have made to the Chief Secretary in reply to the allegations recently advanced of favoritism. disorganisation, and inefficiency existing in the general body of the police, and the detective branch of the service, are not by any means satisfactory. They leave the impression that, though there is an apparent answer forthcoming to the several imputations put forward, the force is nevertheless far from being the effective agency for the prevention, detection, or suppression of crime which it ought to be, which undoubtedly it once was, but which there is too much reason to fear it no longer is at the present time. The charges in question were made by ex-Detective CHRISTIE on his recent retirement, and likewise by Mr OTTO BERLINER, who was for so long a period admittedly a most efficient detective officer. The charges advanced by the former are, in effect, that the detective body is disorganised and inefficient by reason of some of its members being persons without either fitness for their peculiar duties, or respectability of character, to associate with whom is a degradation, and that the few effective officers still remaining would soon quit the force in disgust if it were not better managed and their position improved. To this is added a statement that if a Government inquiry were instituted some very strange revelations would be brought to light. Captain STANDISH meets these charges first by endeavoring to disparage the testimony of CHRISTIE. In doing this he adopts a supercilious and exceedingly personal tone towards the accuser, which detracts from the worth of his defence. The assumption of lofty disdain at the imputations, as if, coming from such a quarter, they must necessarily be groundless, betrays in reality a consciousness that they are far otherwise. He says: - "I am not aware that the position ex-Detective Christie recently held in the force was such as to entitle his opinion as to its management to the consideration which it has received." This adoption of the Who-are-you style is mere subterfuge. If a recent member of the force is not a competent witness on the subject of its alleged mismanagement or inefficiency, who is? Next it is sought by Sub-Inspector SECRETAN to discredit CHRISTIE by asserting that there was a charge of untruthfulness hanging over him when he resigned. Now CHRISTIE challenges inquiry; and it is plain therefore that he believes himself to be provided with proofs, and that he has no reason to fear any imputations on his truthfulness being established. The objections so contemptuously advanced on these grounds against his averments or his credibility must consequently be dismissed as of no value. Indeed this is shown both by Captain STANDISH'S own admissions, and the conflicting assertions of Mr SECRETAN, whom he has called to his support. Captain STANDISH says:- "I should think that the detective force has of late years lost some of the prestige it formerly possessed." He attributes this to the difficulty of obtaining the services of able men; and this difficulty he accounts for by pointing out that "owing to the insufficient pay of the members of the detective force many eligible persons possessed of the necessary qualifications refrained from joining that branch of the service." And he adds, "vacancies in the detective force have thus been filled up by members of the general police of comparative inexperience. "On the other hand, Mr SECRETAN declares in his report that the detective branch "is as well organised at present as it ever has been"; that "at present the characters of the members of the force, both individually and collectively, will bear favorable comparison with those of any previous period", and that "its efficiency will also compare favorably with the detective forces of the other colonies or of the old country." As the evidence of the two authorities is thus seen to be so contradictory, it is plain there is room for attaching credibility enough to Mr CHRISTIE'S allegations to entitle them to the enquiry he seeks for.

Captain STANDISH declares that he has no fears of strange revelations being brought to light; that such an inquiry might perhaps do some good, but that on the other hand it would unquestionably do harm, would injure discipline and produce ill-feeling. He winds up by asserting that it is only a slander to assert that the police have ever held back from arresting great offenders until the issue of a reward for their apprehension stimulated their activity. Now all this merely skims the surface of the dissatisfaction existing in the public mind with respect to the police force. This dissatisfaction arises from the general sense of insecurity produced by seeing how frequently perpetrators of the worst outrages against person and property, and the peace and safety of society generally, escape without detection, or that if they are ultimately apprehended, it is merely a matter of accident, and is not due either to the vigilance or skill of the police. The Burrumbeet atrocity, for example, is a recent instance in point. The allegations of Mr BERLINER throw some light on this particular part of the subject. He cites instances by name of such experienced and meritorious officers, such as Detectives BLACK and EASON, being purposely slighted and kept back, whilst inferior, and in fact worthless members of the force, have, through favoritism, been promoted over them.

It is said the Goverrnment are satisfied with the report of Captain STANDISH, and do not mean to institute any inquiry into the condition and management of either the detective or general police force. This is what might have been expected from the members of the present Administration, who, we fear, are not the men with the moral courage and rectitude to probe the festering source of the unsoundness of a great State institution such as that which, there is reason to believe, afflicts the police force. But the culpable apathy of the Government affords no ground why the public should be indifferent; and as a matter of fact the community at large feels strongly the necessity both of inquiry and reform in this department of the public service. It is a matter of notoriety that the police have often no eyes for the haunts of debauchery and gambling frequented by the depraved of both sexes, whose pecuniary means, style of living and appearance invest them with an air of exterior respectability; whilst

247

the miserable dens in which poverty-stricken vice and crime take refuge are pounced upon and swept off with a vigor that would be most wholesome if it were but impartially applied to the high and the low alike. It is not these obscure and repulsive sinks of squalid infamy which bring ruin on the promising youth of the better classes, and overwhelm with shame many a respectable family. It is the elegantly appointed and gaily decorated rendezvous, where vice assumes its most attractive guise, amidst the intoxicating influences of dice and champagne, that lures on the thoughtless and the young to that ruin from which too late they find there is no redemption. But where or when has any one focus of debauchery of this gilded and seductive kind ever been exploded by the police? Is it to be supposed that they are ignorant of the whereabouts or character of such social plague spots? The idea is absurd. There is not one of them on which they could not lay the finger, and their habitués are no strangers to the force. Whence then comes the immunity of such establishments, their owners and frequenters from any notice or interference from the police? Are there any amongst the higher officers of the force who are observed by their subordinates to look with favoring countenance on, and even at times participate in, the infractions of law and morals practised in these dainty resorts of criminal indulgence? If such there are it is sufficient to account for the inability of either constable or detective to see what all, who care to look, so plainly notice. It is considerations of this kind which weigh with the public in looking beyond the thin veil with which Captain STANDISH seeks to screen the aspect of unsoundness in the force which, with all his adroitness, he cannot conceal. It is felt that the mystery must sooner or later be fathomed, that doubt and suspicion must be removed, and that the general feeling of confidence in the integrity and efficiency of the police, which once existed, must be restored. The fact is, those who have the responsibility of dealing promptly and adequately with it are afraid to touch the subject.

CONVERSION TABLE

MONEY: One pound (£1) or one sovereign equals twenty shillings (20s).
One shilling (1s) equals 12 pence (12d).
One guinea equals twenty-one shillings.
In 1966 when Australia adopted decimal currency, one pound equalled two dollars.

DISTANCE: One mile equals 1.61 kilometres.
One yard equals 0.91 metres.
One foot equals 30.48 centimetres.
One inch equals 25.40 millimetres.

WEIGHT: One pound (lb) equals 454 grams.
One stone equals 6.36 kilograms.
One ton equals 1.01 tonne.
One hundredweight (cwt) equals 112 lbs.

AREA: One acre equals 0.40 hectares.

TEMPERATURE: 100 degrees Fahrenheit (100°F) equals 37.77 degrees Celsius (37.77°C)

Notes

Abbreviations: ADB (Australian Dictionary of Biography)
CRS (Commonwealth Archives)
PROV and VPRS (Public Record Office Victoria)
RHSV (Royal Historical Society of Victoria)
SLV (State Library of Victoria)
VPA (Victoria Police Archives)

Chapter 1

Tom Delaney's descendants in the Western District of Victoria regard Christie as a romancer. In 1991, one of them, Mary O'Callaghan, of Warrnambool, scorned Christie's claim that he obtained information about Sparks's illicit still when he was left in the Delaney kitchen with the two small girls; they would have been too young, she said. Nor was there a person called Deasy, "a name unknown and unrecorded in the district". Mary O'Callaghan also said that when Christie's men raided Pat Delaney's home, her mother and aunt were there as teenagers. The raiders accepted a bacon-and-eggs breakfast, but turned the contents of the house upside down. (Letter by Mary O'Callaghan in author's possession).

In J.B.Castieau's version of this raid, Delaney is called Denis O'Brien, and Deasy is called Murphy. The account published here is from Christie's manuscript 'Capture of the Celebrated Nirranda Still.' The story of firing shots when raiding Delaney and Love in the later encounter is from the *Warrnambool Standard* 22 and 24 May 1894; police in armour is from *Warrnambool Echo* 24 May 1894; James Love fined £250 is from *Standard* and *Echo* 29 May 1894; capture of still is from *Terang Express* 8 May 1894. Descriptions of 'Mountain Dew' and Delaney's flight from police at Allansford are from family information printed for a Delaney/Dunne descendants' reunion in 1978. Tanning the murderer's hide: letter to the editor, *The Age*, from J.M.Allan, son of cricketer Frank Allan, 6 May 1961.

£20 reward: CRS 3853/2, Vol 1 (customs officers' register of appointments and salaries).

Chapter 2

Detective William Manwaring seems to have been an intelligent, observant and diligent man who could feel scorn for high and low alike. In his diary-notes, he left an unflattering impression of Prince Alfred's tour: "As time went on the Prince mania spread widely through the colony causing many absurdities. His personality expanded into magnitude filling the public mind with abasement by his awful majesty which was nothing to be impressed by, but people who are thus troubled suffer by their own delusions."

Manwaring wrote his diary-notes in 1897. His son gave them to the Public Library (now the State Library of Victoria) in 1933 (SLV 1515 Ms 114). It is tragic that the son first censored them, sometimes deleting pages at a time, to save embarrassing the descendants of some of his father's targets. It is impossible to say if Christie's name once appeared here.

Manwaring scorned the way the police handled the murder of a boy during the Orange-Catholic clash on the night Prince Alfred attended a ball at the old Exhibition Building on the corner of La Trobe and William Streets (later the site of the Royal Mint). "The news of the terrible event reached the Prince's ballroom quickly," he wrote, "but was treated by the Police authorities as a mere item of news and the Commissioner of Police and the Chief of Detectives kept on with the festive dance, giving no orders to send the best officers to promptly investigate the case, and so valuable opportunities to secure evidence were lost, for no subordinate could leave the ballroom without orders, for myself and the other detectives were on duty there attired in dress suits."

Manwaring also scorned the detectives who later handled the case: "On the following morning, two of the leading detectives Black and Williams, and myself, were told off to take charge of the case but I soon found that my colleagues who were mere thief-takers saw nothing in the enquiry but a deal of hard work and no profit, so after a few days they backed out and by falsely pretending they were losing the chance of capturing dangerous thieves, got out of the case altogether, and the burden of its management fell on me."

Manwaring left an ultimately flattering assessment of Nicolson who, he said, was a Scot who arrived in Victoria in 1852 and after joining the police force received rapid promotion because his uncle, Colonel Joseph Anderson, was adjutant-general of imperial troops in Australia. "Quite ignorant of police business", Nicolson nevertheless distinguished himself as a goldfields mounted officer by capturing several bushranger gangs. Manwaring said Nicolson grew up in a rural district, 'an arcadia compared with the pandemonium of crime then prevailing in Australia'. Like many other policemen, Nicolson used agents to obtain information. "These men were outside the service and unknown to us, and he deluded himself to believe that the work of detecting crime was a romance that could be managed easily, but experience taught him wisdom, and he became a most sagacious head of the department," Manwaring wrote

It would be fascinating to know what Manwaring thought of Christie, who may have seemed to him a bit of a showman. Beyond doubt Christie was a striking figure. Many newspaper accounts testify to his 'gentlemanly bearing', his charm, his flow of conversation and his excellent grooming. His height of nearly 6 feet, his other physical details, and his enlistment date and progress in the force are documented on his record sheet (VPA Melbourne). However, surprisingly little information is known about the Little Collins Street detective office, which was between Stephen (Exhibition) and Russell Streets behind the Eastern Market. The premises were rented, and we know from a note left by Nicolson that he considered them unsatisfactory, particularly during heavy rain, which came through a window and flooded the cellar.

As for Christie's early life, which includes his schooling, boxing lessons, work in Gippsland and arrival in Melbourne, almost our only source of information is J.B.Castieau's book. This account is so *Boys' Own Annual* that one would hesitate to accept it if it were not so neatly in keeping with the other melodramas in Christie's life. Christie's arrest of the Chinese boot thief at the Eastern Market comes from Castieau. Reading this, you must ask yourself how Christie could have so easily lost his bearings and strayed with his prisoner to the Carlton Gardens, when the detective office was just around the corner. Several Christie stories seem implausible. Those which can be checked turn out to be correct.

The shenanigans of other detectives such as Hudson (who got

drunk and slept in the stables) and Potts (who manhandled the mariner) are documented in the police files, VPRS 937/181/1 and VPRS 937/182/2. In these same files, however, the Chinese detective, Fook Shing, remains a bland figure. He pops in and out of files, making short reports on crimes that do not seem to encompass much more than Chinese gambling offences. His arrest rate was middling. Fook Shing did have a brief moment of glory in the Kelly hunt, in July 1878. Detective Eason, one of the few Melbourne detectives assigned to the hunt, sent a telegram from Bechworth requesting Fook Shing's services after it became known that Ned Kelly's lieutenant, Joe Byrne, an opium addict, bought opium from a Chinese at Woolshed.

Of all the eccentricities evident among the detectives, none was more outlandish that Fook Shing's opium habit, which came to light during the 1880-1883 Royal Commission on the Police in Victoria. Detective Charles Forster, one of the department's more upright members, said in reply to a question: " . . .there is the Chinese detective, Fook Shing, who does nothing but take opium and go to sleep. The whole system is rotten." (31 May 1882. Question No. 1119).

A different question at the royal commission disclosed the police view that Collins Street was the preserve of better-class prostitutes, who dressed demurely so as to minimise the attention which their businessmen clients might attract. (Sergeant James Dalton, 9 May 1882, Question No. 934).

The police report grading prostitutes into three classes was from Secretan to Standish on 9 February 1870, and its detail indicates that the police had a thorough knowledge of prostitution and the locations of four work environments (assignation houses, brothels, private houses, hotels). Many references exist about Sarah Fraser's brothel in Stephen Street. The Duke's visit there with Standish is from Standish's private diary and Curtis Candler's addendum to it (both SLV Ms 9502). The story of naked women on black velvet at Standish's dinner party is from Candler.

Prince Alfred's promiscuity was no real secret. John Norton, eccentric owner of Truth, described him as 'one of the most prurient-minded, lecherous-living, brothel-bilking, tradesmen-tricking rascals that ever ran amok.' The historian J.M.Forde wrote that when the Duke was in Sydney, a detective followed him with a notebook, recording details of his philandering. Alfred was also seen to be greedy. He ran out on a Melbourne washerwoman, owing her £26 for laundry, and she followed him to New Zealand to collect it. At Ballarat, when shown some gold nuggets, he dismayed his hosts by pocketing them. "If our thrifty young Duke took a fancy to anything nice," wrote *The Age*, "he forthwith made himself a present of it."

The names of 48 *Galatea* deserters (or stragglers) are listed in the Victoria Police Gazette of 12 and 19 December 1867. Rewards of £1 and £3 were offered for the arrest of each. In the end, only nine remained missing. More details are in VPRS 937/201/3.

Other References

The kerfuffle over Fenians: VPRS 937/5/5.

Christie's fight with O'Leary: Christie scrapbook, SLV Ms 12720.

Theft of St Francis Church poorbox: VPRS 937/182/1.

'Please look for a boy named Matheson': VPRS 937/183/1.

Forensic tests on Chinaman's stomach: VPRS 937/183/3.

Chapter 3

During David Young's long wait for trial on a charge of having murdered Margaret Graham at Daylesford, a police agent was placed in jail with him. The agent's letters to Nicolson have survived in the police files at the Public Record Office, Melbourne. They do nothing to show that Young was innocent or guilty. (References to the murder, the verdict and controversy are contained in VPRS 937/181/1, and also in *The Herald* 2 August 1865 and The Age 31 July 1865).

It says much for Otto Berliner's manner that he could ruffle the sophisticated Captain Standish, who, accustomed to governing an unpredictable and wayward group of men, had become adept at diplomacy and staying calm. His fury on this occasion adds weight to Detective Manwaring's diary-note that Berliner was 'not fit to mix with cultured people'. (SLV Manwaring diary-notes 1515 MS114).

The strange thing is that Standish later treated Berliner with great politeness. When the Varieties music hall burned down in July 1870, a criminal act was suspected, and Berliner was retained as a private detective by the Sydney Insurance Company and others. Berliner called on Standish and said he was anxious that Detective Williams be assigned to the case.

Standish's attitude seems to have been one of compliance. Despite his distaste for Berliner, Standish told Secretan that Williams should be given the case unless he was otherwise engaged, and added: "Mr Berliner will call at the Detective Office at 6 p.m. and Mr Secrtetan will be good enough to inform him if Detective Williams is available." (VPRS 937/184/1). An inquest found that the fire started in the neighbouring shop of Frank Marton, but it could not say how.

In the Heymanson warehouse case, the constable's 'dark lantern' which Christie took with him in his pursuit of Briely was the 19th century equivalent of a modern flashlight. By moving a knob the user could dim the light or switch it off without extinguishing the flame.

Other references

Christie and Brown confirmed in force 6 January 1868: VPRS 937/182/1.

J.D.Scott's drinking: Manwaring diary notes SLV 1515 Ms114.

Carlton housebreakings: Christie manuscript 'Belzie, Johnston and Tommy the Dancer', also Detective report VPRS 937/182/5. The manuscript differs considerably from the official report (see Chapter 16).

Christie promoted to 2nd class: VPRS 937/182/4.

Secretan arrives from Dunolly 28 April 1868: VPRS 937/182/4.

Esther Green's lavender water: VPRS 937/183/2.

Revolt against Secretan: VPRS 937/183/2.

Silk robberies: Narrative from Manwaring's diary notes SLV 1515 Ms114; Griffiths's escape and capture VPRS 937/183/2; Manwaring's indecision VPRS 937/183/2; Manwaring's explanation diary notes SLV 1515 Ms114; Nicolson's anger VPRS 937/183/6 and 183/2; Barnfield dismissed VPRS 937/183/2.

Nicolson transferred to Kyneton 8 March 1869: VPRS 937/183/3.

Chapter 4

Having declined the Duke of Edinburgh's request to join the detective branch of the royal household in London, Christie returned to Melbourne alone from the New Zealand tour. J.B.Castieau wrote that he carried many handsome presents from the duke and members of his suite. The duke's gifts included a gold watch and chain.

On Christie's first visit to the detective office after this, he wore a frock coat, silk hat, patent leather boots and white spats. He did not go to the muster room but to the public inquiry room, where he rapped on the counter with a gold-headed cane and said in a posh English drawl:"I want you to send a couple of detectives down to my hotel where there has been a robbery." The joke failed. Robert Moore, who was chief clerk at the time, recognised Christie, looked him up and down and said: "By Jove, I think there certainly has been a robbery or a fire and you have been in it."

Christie had been with the duke day and night on an arduous tour, but there was no suggestion that he take time off. He resumed work next day.

Other references

Christie appointed NZ bodyguard VPRS 937/135, also VPRS 93/ 183/3-4; "Miss Cleveland is the star" and HRH declines goldfields visit VPRS 937/182/4; royal japes - Castieau, pp 73-85;"those interesting little stories about the Duke" - *Herald* ND scrapbook SLV Ms12720; "peccadiloes of princes" - *Punch* ND scrapbook; Christie's financial arrangements 937/183/3-4-6.

Prize-fight guidelines: VPRS 937/183/4.

Melbourne Club invitation: VPRS 937/183/4.

Conviction of Turner, Moore, Weekes: VPRS 937/183/6.

Standish questions Dobbin report, Christie replies: VPRS 937/ 183.

Joseph Brooks the coiner: VPRS 937/183/3 and Castieau pp 41-46, whose account differs from the official one.

Whittlesea rape: VPRS 937/183/3.

Chapter 5

The case of Detective John Carter, who was fatally injured by a horse cab, illustrates the relaxed standards under which some applicants joined the police department last century. Originally Carter was rejected for police service as physically unfit because of 'a weakness in the chest'. Today it seems surprising that he was neverthless later allowed to enlist after he signed a document acknowledging his weak chest and agreeing that if this disability made him unfit or incapable as a detective, he waived any right to benefits and privileges of the Police Reward Fund (Carter document, VPA).

Another valuable document is Christie's manuscript account of the Halliburton robbery (SLV 'Halliburton Robbery 1870'). This document is crammed with information about the way burglars operated and how they might have lived. Christie excels himself here in his portrait of an urban environment centred on the lane and the cottages behind the North Melbourne hotel at which he posed as a swagman. However, his official report of this case (VPRS 937/184/6), as opposed to this recollection of it, is starkly different, a fact which is discussed in Chapter 16. A reference is also in *The Age* of 23 July 1870.

The Mannix case (VPRS 937/184/2) is a puzzle. Why did Secretan hasten to Pentridge to see to see a prisoner wanting to give information about a robbery? There was no reason for Secretan to bestir himself. Secretan was later to be castigated by the 1880-1883 Royal Commission on the police for his improper association with criminals (See Chapter 11). In view of this, his action in the Mannix case arouses suspicion.

Other references

Superintendent Bookey's hostility at Geelong: File of correspondence Christie-Bookey, Bookey-Standish, Standish-Bookey, Standish-Secretan VPRS 937/218/2.
Susan Egan murder: VPRS 937/189/3-4.
Notorious garrotters Moore and Bourke: VPRS 937/184/1.
Detective Murray absconds: VPRS 937/184/2.
Joe Brown gives prisoner tobacco: VPRS 937/184/1.
Detective Crooke allowed to resign: VPRS 937/184/1.
Lomax and O'Callaghan squabble: VPRS 937/184/2.
Captain Wilson the 'unfortunate' drunk: VPRS 937/184/2.

Chapter 6

Probably nobody will ever get to the bottom of the Thomas Moore case, but it is hard to ignore the presence of skullduggery. Here was detective clawing at detective for motives unknown. Two things are clear, however. The first is that Christie gave a shifty answer in court when he was asked if he slept with Levi Walker's wife. The second is that Detective Joe Brown wanted to see Christie destroyed.

Happily, the transcript of the police inquiry (VPRS 937/184/4) is preserved intact, and this too is valuable for the glimpse it gives of the Police Department behaving fairly and thoroughly while keeping a loose control of the questions and evidence it permitted. The transcript of the second inquiry by the government cannot be found.

Thomas Scott, the man whom Christie was initially seeking about the skeleton keys, managed to escape but was arrested in November by Detective Potter at Clunes and returned to Melbourne on a remand warrant. His fate is not known.

The allegations about Constable Flood at Beechworth are contained in VPRS 937/515.

Other references

Harry Power: Montford's plan to entrap him VPRS 937/184/2; McCulloch's threat to sack officers at Beechworth and Benalla, and Standish's letter to them VPRS 937/135; Power gives away his pipe VPRS 937/184/2. See bibliography for other Kelly details.

Rate collector defaults: VPRS 937/184/3.

Chapter 7

Sergeant James Dalton, of the general police, who was favourably known all over Melbourne for many years, is among the people credited with inventing the word 'larrikin' as a synonym for street ruffians. After bringing some of them to court, Dalton is supposed to have told the bench in his Irish accent: 'Plaze, your worships, Oi found the prisoner a-larrakin (larking) about the strates.' Christie is quoted in J.B.Castieau (P.23) as saying a magistrate asked Dalton how he had managed to capture so many prisoners by himself, and Dalton replied: 'Plaze, yer worship, it was surrounded them moiself Oi did, Sorr!' The fact that Mrs Spann, the jeweller's wife, under the influence of a spiritualist medium, grabbed Sergeant Dalton as a crook when the clock struck midnight would have seemed hilarious in old Melbourne.

Other references

Daly, Mackay and Jackson in put-up robbery: *Age* 3 February 1877.

Mayor and magistrate's court praise Christie over Nat Dwyer, William Turner and William Robinson: VPRS 937/185/2.

"Something must be wrong" *Age* 29 June 1871 referring to Police Gazette; see also VPRS 937/185/2.

Christie fights Jack Thompson in athletic hall: Castieau pp 99-101.

Zavitowski sisters: Christie manuscript 'Zavitowski and Spann Robberies 1871'.

Five charged over prize fight: VPRS 937/185/4.

Madame de Beaumont's missing diamonds: VPRS 937/185/4.

O'Callaghan supplies liquor to prisoner: VPRS 937/185/4 and O'Callaghan record sheet VPA.

Chapter 8

Constable William Considine, who nursed the dying Ah Suey on the horse trip from Sebastopol to Beechworth, later became a celebrated detective-sergeant in Melbourne. Drinking in Young & Jackson's bar one day in 1892, he heard a man tell some friends about an interesting travelling companion he had met on board ship on the way to Western Australia a few weeks previously. This traveller had shown the man a pair of scissors which he had made from two knitting needles.

Considine was instantly alert. This trick with knitting needles was an accomplishment which Frederick Deeming, mass murderer, in the guise of Baron Swanston, was known to have boasted of in Melbourne. Suddenly Considine had a clue to Deeming's whereabouts. "Did he give you his card?" he asked the man, who said yes and showed it to him. Considine identified the murderer's handwriting by the way he made the initial letter of his name.

Considine found out what hotel Deeming stayed at when his ship reached Perth, and within a few hours one of the greatest criminals of the century was under lock and key. Considine had picked up perhaps the most valuable piece of information which had ever fallen a Victorian detective's way.

Melbourne's cheapest prostitutes worked from Charlie Wright's Coliseum music hall in Bourke Street, according to Christie (SLV manuscript 'Roberry with Violence 1872'). Sergeant James Dalton of the general police was later to confirm this at the 1880-1883 Royal Commission on the police. Dalton was asked if many prostitutes were at the Coliseum, and he replied: "They are the principal supporters. It was only for that that the place existed at all."

He was next asked: "The lower orders?", and he said: "Yes, not the ones that go to the stalls of the Theatre Royal, but a lower type of woman." Dalton was asked: "Sailors' prostitutes?" He replied: "Yes, and lower than them, the dirty old things along Elizabeth Street and other places." (Royal Commission on the Police in Victoria, Evidence 1880-1883, Questions 926-928, 9 May 1882).

Other references

Wooragee murder: VPRS 937/415.

Ovens district: Apart from the Wooragee murder (see above) Christie's activities in the Ovens District, plus activities of contemporaries, VPRS 937/414.

Manwaring becomes resident clerk: Record sheet VPA.

Brooks the coiner caught again: VPRS 937/186/2.

Nine shillings for cabbie Thomas Carrol: VPRS 937/186/1.

Pietro Zala fleeced by prostitutes: Christie manuscript 'Robbery with Violence 1872'.

Superintendent Bookey dies: VPRS 937/186/5.

Mayor's gold chain: VPRS 937/186/3; *Herald* 24 December 1872.

Chapter 9

Dublin-born William Saurin Lyster, whose wife's stolen jewels Christie recovered, was the father of opera in Melbourne, a much-respected figure who first brought his company to the Theatre Royal on 25 March 1861. Lyster's admired position in Melbourne society may explain why Standish and the detective force moved with urgency to recover the loot. The fact that Lyster could introduce Wagner to Melbourne in 1877 with a performance of *Lohengrin* indicates how comfortable the city felt with its new-found sophistication. Wagner himself heard about this performance in a letter he received in Germany. He seems to have been surprised that this could happen at the other end of the world. In 1867 Lyster bought land near Monbulk in the Dandenong Ranges near Melbourne. The area is still Lysterfield.

Christie's previous account of the Lyster robberry (in J.B.Castieau) claimed that Lyster became fed up with the lack of progress other detectives made in the case despite the incentive of a £50 reward. In desperation he called in Christie, offered him £10 and told him to spare no expense. "No thanks, Mr Lyster," Christie replied, "You have already generously offered £50. If I succeed, that will recompense me."

In the course of hunting up all the professional cracksters, Christie met Dick Jones the tailor, newly discharged from Pentridge. Suspecting that Jones was the thief, Christie laid a plot by letting drop the false information that an honest pawnbroker, William James, was a fence who could handle any quantity of loot and melt it down at once. Christie offered Jones £25 for information about the robbery, but Jones refused it. Christie then told the pawnbroker what he had done and asked him to report if Jones brought anything suspicious to his shop. The plan worked. Next day James brought Christie some of the loot and described the seller in a way that fitted Jones.

Christie and Detective Hartney turned Jones's house over on the excuse of looking for skeleton keys made by Levi Walker in the Pentridge blacksmith forge, but they found nothing and went away. A cabbie alerted by Christie reported subsequently that he had taken Jones to a second pawn shop. Hurrying there, Christie and Hartney found Jones with the loot. Christie claimed that Lyster gave him £50 and a complimentary ticket to admit two to any theatre under his control for as long as he was in the business. Who knows where the truth lies? The detective report at the Public Record Office (VPRS 937/189/3) is specific that the reward was only £20 and that it was split in the way described in this chapter.

Other references

Christie's rewards: record sheet VPA.

Nigger minstrel disguise: Christie manuscript 'Chinaman Jack Robbery 1873.'

O'Ferrall absconds with £9000: VPRS 937/191/1-3-4; Police Gazette November 1873, p 283.

William Bailey case: *Age* 20 March 1874.

Arrest by Dowden, Lomax and Lennon: VPRS 937/189/1; *Age* 29 May 1874.

Constable Boyd arrests Detective Lennon: VPRS 937/189/1-2-3.

Standish's special report to Chief Secretary: VPRS 937/189/3.

Otto Berliner's letter criticising Standish report: VPRS 937/189/3.

Chapter 10

Although rowing became an important sport in Melbourne, information about its early days is scant. The main source used here and in later chapters is John Lang's *The Victorian Oarsman*, with a rowing register (1919 A.H.Massina and Company, 350-352 Swanston Street, Melbourne). It is from here, for example, that the description of the upper Yarra is taken. This is a curious little book with a table of results in the middle.

Other references

Christie promoted to 1st class: Record sheet VPA.

Chinaman Jack arrested: Christie manuscript SLV 'John B.Wallace alias Chinaman Jack 1875'.

Standish's memo on rowing: VPRS 937/191/2.

Christie's 'championship' challenge against Cazaly, 18 December 1875: Castieau pp 105-108.

Otto Berliner accuses Christie, Standish replies etc, Christie resigns: VPRS 937/190/2.

Christie's speech at town hall: *Daily Telegraph* 12 May 1876; VPRS 937/192/1.

Burrumbeet rape: VPRS 937A/26/2.

Standish replies to Christie's speech: VPRS 937/192/1; *Argus* 3 June 1876.

Press reaction to Standish: VPRS 937/192/1. *Age* 3 June 1870; *Argus* 5 June 1870, *Daily Telegraph* 5 June 1870, *Herald* 10 June 1870.

Christie's letter to *Argus*: 7 June 1870.

Christie and prisoner A.H.J.Bishop: VPRS 937/192/4.

Detectives' pay rise: *Daily Telegraph* 29 July 1870.

Chapter 11

One of the worst examples of detectives' corruption brought before the 1880-1883 royal commission concerned Patrick Boardman, son of a state school teacher. As a boy in 1870, Patrick was arrested for disorderly conduct and sent to an industrial school as an orphan. He was released later at his father's urging. In 1874 his father sent him to New Zealand to separate him from his associates. Patrick found a job and behaved well. Secretan, however, sent the Dunedin police particulars of Patrick and described him as a bad character. Patrick lost his job, but the chief commissioner of police in Dunedin, taking an interest in the case, got him a job up-country as a shearer.

In 1877 Patrick returned to Melbourne, fell in with bad company who included a man named Britchner, and was induced to try to rob the Commercial Bank at Hotham (North Melbourne). Arrested, he was sentenced to three years jail. On his release, he was suspected on scanty evidence of complicity in robbing a hotel. About this time, Detective Charles Forster, an honest man, saw Boardman and asked him to corroborate to the royal commission a statement he had made about the attempted robbery of the bank.

Before he did so, Boardman went to Sydney as a bookmaker. While there, he learned that the Melbourne detectives had obtained a warrant against him as a vagrant. Boardman voluntarily returned to Melbourne, made a long statement to the royal commission, surrendered himself to police, and on the evidence of detectives, was sentenced to 12 months jail. Boardman appealed. Pending the hearing of the appeal, the royal commission made its own investigations.

The following facts came to light: (a) the detectives had no grounds to tell the New Zealand police of any suspicion about Boardman, (b) Britchner was a fizzgig acting for the detectives and he deliberately entrapped Boardman into the attempted bank robbery for which he had been arrested, (c) the detectives had full knowledge of all this, (d) the detectives stationed themselves in an hotel awaiting Britchner's signal, (e) evidence supported Boardman's claim that the robbery was concocted between Britchner and Detectives Hartney and Duncan.

A different case of corruption was revealed by a criminal named James Walshe who had, in company with two men named Bird and Taylor, stolen some pictures and sold them to a Mrs Lamb, living in Franklin Street. Detectives O'Callaghan and Nixon saw the pictures while searching the premises for stolen goods, and Mrs Lamb told them she had bought them from Walshe, Bird and Taylor. O'Callaghan later ran into Walshe in Bourke Street and was about to charge him, but Walshe theatened to implicate Taylor, who was alleged to be a police fizgig. O'Callaghan told Walshe to say no more about it.

Under severe cross-examination at the royal commission, Mrs Lamb was not shaken in her evidence that Walshe, Bird and Taylor were the names she gave police; not Watson, Yates and Carter, which were the names the detectives alleged she gave them. Members of the royal commission tried to see a supplementary crime sheet which would have disclosed whether the detectives were lying, but it had been removed from the detective office. "The Commissioners were met by the same difficulty that arose at almost every stage where Detective O'Callaghan's conduct was open to question," their report said.

Other references

Christie opens athletic hall: Castieau p 89.

Fight with Sharp on Yarra bank: Castieau pp 104-105.

Victorian Rowing Association formed: Lang, John, *The Victorian Oarsman with a rowing register*, 1919, A.H. Massina & Company, Melbourne, p 47. Background to rowing - Lang, John, pp 23-28, pp 43-49, p 125.

Christie's sculling victories 1876, 1877 and defeat 1878: Lang John, *The Victorian Oarsman with a rowing register*, 1919. pp 43-44.

I Zingari Club, location: At Edwards' boat shed - Lang, John, *The Victorian Oarsman*, 1919; club secretary (Christie) at European Hotel, Swanston Street - *Sands and McDougall Melbourne and Suburban Directory* 1876. The club is not mentioned in the directory before this date or after 1879. I Zingari was a foundation member of the Victorian Rowing Association, and Christie was its secretary in 1876-78, according to Gunn, M.S., *Victorian Rowing Register*, 1878, Maxwell, Chancery Lane, Melbourne.

Yarra River: above and below Princess Bridge, typescript, nd, prepared for Quay River Cruises, RHSV, pp 7-8.

Princess Theatre fight: Castieau pp 91-97; Corris, Peter, *Lords of the Ring*, Cassell Australia Limited, [1980], pp 44-46.

The Bluff, illegal fight: Castieau pp 101-102; James, John Stanley, *The Vagabond Papers*, 1969, ed. Cannon M., Melbourne University Press pp 214-220; Corris, Peter, *Lords of the Ring*, Cassell Australia Limited, [1980].

European Hotel, Christie licensee: VPR0 1601/p1 1879-1880. Public renewals show Christie was granted a licence renewal on 10 December 1878, which presupposes that he held the licence already; Cole Collection vol 1, part 3 p 213 lists J.M.Christie as publican of European Hotel for 1877 (Mrs E.Goodwin listed for 1879).

Sir Henry Barkly Hotel, Christie a partner: Sands and McDougall, *Melbourne and Suburban Directory* 1881, 1882, 1883, 1884, 1885.

Married Emilie Ada Taylor Baker 29 November 1877: Victorian marriage certificate 2270/7978.

Toorak boxing match: Castieau p 101 coyly names the referee at the doctor's house as 'a well-known captain'. Contemporary references in Christie's scrapbook say Standish regularly attended these Toorak boxing matches.

Rourke names Christie as corrupt ("I know a man once in Carlton . "): Royal Commission on Police in Victoria, Evidence 1881-1883, former Detective David Rourke replying to Questions 2693-2695, 31 May 1883.

Detective force disbanded etc: Royal Commission on Police in Victoria, Evidence 1881-1883, Recommendations in Special Report on the Detective Branch, 9 January 1883, pp xiii-xlv.

Chapter 12

Christie recorded at least one example of his practice of using two women strangers to search suspected women smugglers. In February 1891 he received a tip-off that some valuable lace would be on board the incoming P & O steamer *Valetta* and that someone would try to smuggle it ashore at Williamstown. Incognito he strolled through the vessel and became suspicious of two stewardesses and two other women. When three of them went ashore, he caught the same train as they did to Spencer Street, where a colleague whom he had alerted was waiting.

Together they shadowed the women to a Collins Street florist, where the women immediately went into the manager's office. Before they shut the door, Christie caught a glimpse of a desk covered with Maltese lace, which he seized. Leaving his colleague to stand guard, he dashed to Williamstown and searched the stewardesses' berths, where he found a plant of lace and cigars hidden in false bottoms of their boxes. Christie recruited two women who were strangers to each other, and took them back to the florist to conduct a search. He took the women's names and addresses in case they were needed as witnesses. (SLV manuscript 'Maltese lace ex *Valetta*').

Other references

1880 International Exhibition, police telephone line: Helen Doxford Harris manuscript UP.

Birth of Christie's daughter: Ada Amelia Christie was born in South Australia in 1880. Her death certificate shows that she spent three years there.

Christie's customs salary and rank: microfilm CRS 3853/2 vol 1, Commonwealth Archives, Middle Brighton.

Christie applies to rejoin detective force: VPRS 808/6.

Daughter dies 31 March 1885: Victorian death certificate 6563/1895.

Wife dies 27 July 1885: Victorian death certificate 6563/1885. The certificate shows that she spent the previous three years in South Australia.

Wollaston's careeer: *Cyclopaedia of Victoria, 1903*, Cyclopedia Company. Melbourne; ADB 1891-1939.

Quiroga, Buenaventura: Christie manuscript, SLV 'Quiroga Customs 1888'.

Interrupting the wedding: Castieau pp 212-213.

Searching ships: Christie manuscript SLV 'Searching the Chinese Steamers'.

Chinese immigration trick: Christie manuscript SLV 'Searching the Chinese Steamers'.

Yee Jug: scrapbook SLV Ms 12720.

"Wailing like men demented": scrapbook SLV 12720.

Chinese smuggling ginger: Christie manuscript SLV 'Ah Say Smuggling 1893'.

Copper Johnson: Christie manuscript SLV' Copper Johnson Smuggler etc 1893'.

Steamers *Guthrie* and *Tsinan*: scrapbook SLV 12720.

Chapter 13

A search of newspapers and court and prison records has failed to uncover evidence that Tom Delaney or anyone else was charged with having pushed a man over a cliff at Moonlight Head. A Delaney descendant, Mary O'Callaghan, of Warrnambool, scorning Christie's reference to the 'Kelly Gang', said in 1991 that"there never was any gang". (Letter held by author).

Other references

Wreck of *Fiji*: *Age, Argus, Herald* 9-30 September 1891; *Warrnambool Standard* 9, 10, 11, 12, 14, 15, 19, 22 September 1891; *Terang Express* 30 October 1891; Christie's departure for Moonlight Head VPRS 937/487/5; Delaney fined for smuggling - register Camperdown court of petty sessions VPRO 297/8; Christie's encounter with 'Kelly Gang' - Christie manuscript SLV 'Capture of the Celebrated Nirranda Still'; Christie and Delaney talk in watchhouse - 'Capture of the Celebrated Nirranda Still'.

Crimps: Castieau pp 160-169; background - Lockwood, Rupert, *Ship to Shore: a history of Melbourne's waterfront and its union struggles,* Hale and Ironmonger, [1990], pp 14-15.

No. 2 Bosisto Street, Richmond: scrapbook SLV Ms 12720.

Grocer sells cheap whisky: *Terang Express* 18 May 1894.

Children's Hospital bazaar: scrapbook SLV Ms 12720.

Chapter 14

It is worth noting that in both the Peregrine and Ullett cases, Christie almost fell down a cliff into the Yarra in identical circumstances. One would have thought that here was too good a coincidence for him to miss. His failure to link the two incidents, even by merely referring to one in the manuscript of the other, raises doubts that he experienced this peril twice. One is forced to conclude that he tried out the story of the cliff fall in both sets of circumstances to see which suited it better. He did not know that one day both manuscripts would find their way into print. (Ullett case SLV manuscript 'Robert Laxton 1895').

Other references

Korumburra and Yarrawonga court cases: Christie manuscripts SLV 'Korumburra 1895' and 'Jimmy Ah Fook 1895'.

Mortlake raid: *Terang Express* 21 May 1895.

Men from SS *Peregrine*: Christie manuscript SLV 'Brighton Still 1895'.

Chapter 15

Birds did not need to be dead to concern the Customs Department, which was the body entrusted with preserving native fauna. Christie told of how he once seized a cockatoo and a magpie from a suburban house after two elderly women neighbours complained of their bad language. When Christie went to the women's house, one of them, who was red-haired, took him into the backyard to demonstrate how the birds next door harassed them. "Hello, carrots," said the magpie, "Where are you off to? At it again?" The cockatoo said: "What the hell are you going to do?"

Christie took the birds to the Customs House and put them in the basement, but their loud swearing attracted an audience of sailors who were in the building. The birds were then sent to the zoo with a note to the curator, Mr Le Soeuf, saying they were a gift. Mr Le Soeuf was horrified when he heard them run through their vocabulary. He asked Christie to take the birds back because of the effect they would have on visitors, particularly women and children. In the end the birds were destroyed.

Christie also described how he was once transporting a magpie in a kerosene tin under the seat of a railway carriage. Several women were among the passengers. Suddenly the magpie said: "What the hell's that?" One woman shouted: "Oh, there's a man under the seat!" and in the hubbub which followed, Christie kicked the tin to make the bird shut up, but its language became worse. In later life, Christie kept a parrot.

Other references

SS *Phos*: scrapbook SLV Ms 12720.

Three topics, (1) Moss Aarons, (2) E.B.Beck, (3) game birds out of season: Christie scrapbook SLV Ms 12720.

Weenan case: Christie manuscript SLV 'Weenan & Others Conspiracy 1898'; report of bribery attempt and court case - scrapbook SLV Ms 12720.

Liquor in Chinatown: scrapbook SLV Ms 12720.

Nicolson dies: scrapbook; *Weekly Times, The Leader* 8 September 1898.

Bubonic plague bacillus: scrapbook SLV Ms 12720.

Chapter 16

J.B.Castieau's account of how Christie became bodyguard to the Duke and Duchess of York says only that the Governor-General, the Earl of Hopetoun, sent for him one day in April 1901 and asked him to hold himself ready to attend personally on the couple throughout their Australasian tour. "It was generally understood that this step was taken upon a suggestion from the imperial authorities in appreciation of Christie's services when in attendance upon HRH the Duke of Edinburgh."

For the 1901 tour, Christie organised police surveillance in every State, but only he was in evidence, 'tall, straight, silver-haired', and few onlookers knew who and what he was. Photos of the day show him as a haughty figure, who could have been mistaken for any person of high importance.

Other references

Shooting at Opera House: *Argus* 26 July to 3 August 1880, *Australasian Sketcher* and *Illustrated Australian News*, 31 July 1880

George Robertson prosecuted: scrapbook SLV Ms 12720.

Christie's appointment to Duke of York tour: VPRS 1163/465.

Duke and Duchess of York 1901: scrapbook SLV Ms 12720, Castieau pp 84-85.

Brother dies: *Herald* 24 April 1904.

Indecent pictures on watches: scrapbook SLV Ms 12720.

Otto Berliner: *Australasian* p 525 SLV, death notice 22 September 1894, repeated in *Age* and *Argus*; Ferguson, J.A., *Bibliography of Australasia* 1894 item 6949 SLV; 1897 pamphlet SLV 824 V 66 headed '*Report respecting the working order and management of the Private Detective Office by Mr Otto Berliner*', printed by Wilson and McKinnon, Collins Street East; Biographical notes '*Men of Our Time*' SLV 920-045 H88 pp x-xii; '*Men of the Time in Australia*' Victorian series 2nd edition 1882 compiled by Captain H. Morin Humphries, Melbourne 1882.

Christie attacked at Victoria Dock, scrapbook SLV Ms 12720;

Castieau p 233; *Punch* 29 December 1910.

Policemen stuck in tar: *Age* 12 January 1927.

Christie dies: *Age, Argus* death notices and obituaries 12 January 1927; Victorian death certificate 47/1927.

Will: dated 21 March 1908, codicil 23 May 1911 PROV.

Official version of Halliburton robbery: Detective report Christie to Secretan VPRS 937/184/2.

Official version of Carlton robberies: Detective report Hannan to Nicolson 937/182/5.

Early Australian detective fiction: Borlase, James Skipp, 'The Night Fossickers of Moonlight Flat', in Knight, Stephen, *The Best Australian Mystery Stories*, Penguin, Australia, [1989], pp 12, 18, 36.

Mary Fortune's marriage etc: Sussex, Lucy, *The Fortunes of Mary Fortune*, Penguin, Australia, [1989], introduction.

Link between Christie's writing and other detective literature of the time established by Joanne Gourley in essay for University of Melbourne, UP, [1991].

Mary Fortune's fiction in *The Australian Journal*: "A funny-looking little man . . ." - WW, '*Little Puggins the Pedlar*', 1891, pp 219-225. "Close to the You Yangs, and within sight of Hobson's Bay" - WW, 'Blairs Secret', 1889, p 276. "A once well-known detective" - WW, 'A Government House Romance', 1892, p 453.

Christie buried: Box Hill cemetery, Melbourne, grave site Presbyterian 1033, row 153, No 19. Interestingly, Christie's police record sheet (VPA) describes him as Church of England.

Bibliography

PRIMARY SOURCES

Box Hill Cemetery ledgers.

Cole Collection, vol 1, part 3.

1879-1880 Publican renewals. PRO 160, p1.

Police Record Sheets. VPA (Christie, Thomas O'Callaghan, William Henry Manwaring, John Carter, Otto Berliner).

Christie manuscripts, SLV.

Scrapbook of Detective Inspector Christie. Police and customs cases. SLV Ms 12720.

Customs officers' appointments and salaries. Commonwealth Archives, Middle Brighton, microfilm CRS 3853/2 vol 1.

All detective reports, correspondence and notices in VPRO series 937 between 1863 - 1883.

Christie marriage certificate 2270/1877; death certificate; 47/1927; daughter's death certificate 6563/1885; wife's death certificate 9953/1885.

Will, dated 21 March 1908, VPRO Melbourne.

Application to rejoin detective force. Correspondence VPRS 808/6.

Letters to Standish during royal tour of NZ. VPRS 937/182/4.

Oral history: Christie in-law.

DIARIES

Candler, Curtis. Addendum to diary. SLV 9502.

Manwaring, William Henry. Diary notes 1897. SLV 1515 Ms 114.

Standish private diary, transcribed by Candler or unknown. SLV 9502.

NEWSPAPERS AND PERIODICALS

Age.
Argus.
Australasian.
Ballarat Star.
Australian Customs Historical Journal.
Daily Telegraph.
Government Gazette.
Herald.
Leader.
Ovens and Murray Advertiser.
Punch.
Terang Express.
Victoria Police Gazette.
Warrnambool Echo.
Warrnambool Standard.
Weekly Times.

GOVERNMENT REPORTS

Victorian Government. *1881-83 Reports and Minutes of evidence of the Royal Commission into the Circumstances of the Kelly Outbreak, the Present State and Organisation of the Police Force etc.* Government Printer, Melbourne.

Victorian Government. *Police Commission Proceedings, 1883.*

Victorian Government. *Special Report on Detective Branch, 1883.*

Victorian Government. *General Report of the Royal Commission on Present State and Organisation of the Police Force,* Government Printer, Melbourne, [1883].

Victorian Government. *Report of the Royal Commission on the Victorian Police Force,* Government Printer, Melbourne, [1906].

SECONDARY SOURCES

Australian Dictionary of Biography 1891-1976. Melbourne University Press, Carlton,[1966-90].

Baggot, Alex. *Coppin the Great: Father of the Australian Theatre,* Melbourne University Press, Carlton, [1965].

Baring-Gould, William S. *The Annotated Sherlock Holmes.* (2 vols). John Murray, London, [1968].

Berliner, Otto. Pamphlet headed 'Report respecting the working order and management of the Private Detective Office by Mr Otto Berliner, 1897', printed by Wilson and McKinnon, Collins Street East, Melbourne.

Blakeney, Thomas S. *Sherlock Holmes: Fact or Fiction?* John Murray, London, [1932].

Borlase, James Skipp. 'The Night Fossickers of Moonlight Flat', in Knight, Stephen, *Dead Witness: the Best Australian Mystery Stories,* Penguin Australia, [1989].

Brown, Max. *Ned Kelly, Australian Son.* Angus and Robertson, NSW, [1948, 1980].

Buckley, Jerome Hamilton. *The Turning Key. Autobiography and subjective impulse since 1880.* Harvard University Press, Massachusetts, [1984], chapter 3.

Cannon, Michael. *Life in the Cities. Australia in the Victorian age: 3.* Nelson, Melbourne, [1975].

Castieau, J.B. *Reminiscences of Detective Inspector Christie.* George Robertson & Company Propty Limited, [1913].

Cave, Colin (ed). *Ned Kelly. Man and Myth.* Cassell Australia Ltd,[1968]

Campbell, Ruth. *Mallesons. A history 1852-1986.* Printed by Brown Prior Anderson Pty Ltd for Mallesons Stephen Jaques, solicitors and notaries, Melbourne, [1990].

Clyne, Robert. *Colonial Blue. A history of the South Australian Police Force, 1836-1916.* Wakefield Press, SA, [1987].

Coffey, Bill. *The Brackens.* Bill Coffey, South Melbourne, [1990].

Corris, Peter. *Lords of the Ring.* Cassell Australia Limited, [1980].

Cyclopaedia of Victoria. vols 1-3, Cyclopaedia Company, Melbourne, [1903].

Davison, Graeme. *The Rise and Fall of Marvellous Melbourne.* Melbourne University Press, Carlton, [1978].

Delaney/Dunne Reunion 1978. Family history compiled by descendants of John Delaney (1794-1876) and Bridget Dunne (1812-1884) and Edmund Dunne and Mary Russell, in the Western District of Victoria.

Ferguson, J.A. *Bibliography of Australasia.* Angus & Robertson, Sydney, [1941-1969].

Gunn, M.S. *Victorian Rowing Register.* Maxwell, Chancery Lane, Melbourne, [1878].

Greig, A.W. *Theatres of Old Melbourne. Argus,* 2 December 1911.

Haldane, Robert. *The People's Force. A History of the Victorian Police.* Melbourne University Press, Carlton,[1986].

Hardwick, Michael and Mollie. *The Sherlock Holmes Companion.*John Murray, London, [1962].

Hare, F.A. *The Last of the Bushrangers. An account of the capture of the Kelly Gang.* Hurst & Blackett, London, [1892].

Harris, Helen Doxford; and Presland, Gary. *Cops and Robbers: a guide to researching 19th century police and criminal records in Victoria.* Harriland Press, Forest Hill, Victoria,[1990]

Keating, H.R.F. *Sherlock Holmes:The Man and His World.* Thames and Hudson, London, [1979]

Knight, J. *Narrative of the Visit of HRH The Duke of Edinburgh to Victoria.* Melbourne,[1860].

Knight, Stephen. *Form and Ideology in Crime Fiction.* Indiana University Press, Bloomington,[1980].

Lang, John. *The Victorian Oarsman with a Rowing Register.* A.H.Massina & Company, Melbourne, [1919].

Lockwood, Rupert. *Ship to Shore. A history of Melbourne's waterfront and its union struggles.* Hale & Ironmonger, Sydney, [1990].

Loney, Jack. *Wreckers, Smugglers and Pirates. In South Eastern Australian waters.* Marine History, Portarlington, Victoria, [1989].

Love, Harold. *The Golden Age of Australian Opera: W.S.Lyster and his companies, 1861-1890.* Currency Press, Sydney, [1981].

MacKenzie, Margaret. *Shipwrecks.* 3rd edition, National Press Pty Ltd, Melbourne, [1964].

McLaughlin, Noel. *Waiting for the Revolution: a history of Australian nationalism.* Penguin Books Australia Ltd, [1989].

McKinlay, Brian. *The First Royal Tour 1867-1868.* Rigby Limited, Australia, [1970].

McMenomy, Keith. *Ned Kelly: The Authentic Illustrated Story.* Currey O'Neil Ross Pty Ltd, Victoria, [1984].

McQuilton, John. *The Kelly Outbreak 1878-1880.* Melbourne University Press, [1979].

Napier, Valantyne. *Act as Known.* Globe Press, Victoria, [1986].

Neale, Ralph P. *Jolly Dogs are We: the History of Yachting in Victoria 1838-1894.* Landscape Publications, Victoria, [1984].

Norman, Charles. *When Vaudeville was King.* Spectrum Publications, Melbourne, [1984].

O'Callaghan, T. *List of Chief Constables, District Constables, Police Cadets and Police Officers in Victoria 1836-1907.* Government Printer, Melbourne, [1907].

Pearl, Cyril. *Always Morning. The Life of Henry Orion Horne*, Cheshire, Melbourne, [1960]

Prout, Denton; and Feeley, Fred. *50 years hard: the story of Pentridge Gaol from 1850 to 1900.* Rigby Limited, Adelaide, [1967].

"Richmond". *Scenes in the Life of a Bow Street Runner by "Richmond" drawn up from his private memoranda.* Dover Publishing Company Inc, Toronto, [1827, republished 1976].

Sadleir, J. *Recollections of a Victorian Police Officer.* George Robertson, Melbourne, [1913].

Sands and McDougall. *Melbourne and Suburban Directory.* Melbourne, [1866-1885]

Sturma, Michael. *Policing the criminal frontier in mid-nineteenth century Australia, Britain and America*, in Finnane, Mark, *Policing in Australia.* New South Wales University Press, Kensington, [1987].

Sussex, Lucy. *The Fortunes of Mary Fortune.* Penguin Books, Australia Ltd., [1989].

Twopeny, Richard. *Town Life in Australia.* ed. Cannon, M., facsimile edition of 1883, Penguin Books, Australia, [1973].

"Vagabond", (James, John Stanley), *The Vagabond Papers - sketches of Melbourne life , in light and shade.* (5 vols), George Robertson,

Melbourne [1877-78].*The Vagabond Papers*, ed. Cannon, M., Melbourne University Press, [1969].

Victoria Police Force. *Manual of Police Regulations for the Guidance of the Constabulary in Victoria.* Government Printer, Melbourne, [1856].

Victoria Police Force. *Regulations for the Guidance of the Constabulary of Victoria.* Government Printer, Melbourne, [1877].

Victoria Police. *Police in Victoria 1836-1980,* Government Printer, Melbourne, [1980].

W.W. (Mary Fortune). 'Little Puggins the Pedlar', in *The Australian Journal,* December 1891, pp 219-225.

W.W. (Mary Fortune). 'A Government House Romance', in *The Australian Journal,* April 1892, pp 453-458.

WW (Mary Fortune). 'Blair's Secret', in *The Australian Journal,* January 1884, pp 276-283.

West, John. *Theatre in Australia.* Cassell Australia, Sydney, [1978].

Wilkes, John. *London Police in the 19th Century.* Cambridge University Press, [1977].

Yarra River from above and below Princes Bridge, typescript, nd, RHSV, Melbourne.

INDEX

Aarons, Moss
  pawnbroker   196
Abbotsford   193
Adler, Irene   234
Admiral Hotel
  cnr Collins & King Sts   145
Adventure of the Beryl Coronet, The
  230
Adventure of the Blue Carbuncle,
  The   233
Age, The   80, 87, 93, 95, 120,
    122, 137, 143, 148, 173, 218
Ah Fook   185
Ah Moke   166
Albion Hotel, Geelong   62
alderman jemmy   31
Alexander, Detective
  of Heathcote   31, 115
Alfred, Prince
  see: Duke of Edinburgh
Allansford Bridge   9
Allen, Frank   9
Allen, R.
  pawnbroker   133
Amess, Samuel L.
  Mayor of Melbourne   114
Argus, The   143, 173
Arnott, George
  nigger minstral   117
Arthur, Mounted Constable
  4, 5, 7
Ashe, James   141
Auckland   42
Audit, Inspector G.
  Acting Police Commissioner,
  Noumea   121
Australasian, The   164

Australian Journal, The   242

Baber, Sergeant   110
  praised by Supt. Barclay   111
Babington, Sergeant
  of Kyneton   90
Bailey, Detective   94
Baker, Charles
  alias Young   75
Baker, Emilie Ada Taylor
  (Christie's wife)   150
Ballarat   22
Barclay, Superintendent Hugh
    Ross   104
  rebuffs by Standish   105
  recommends reward for
    Christie   107
Barnfield, Detective   32, 36
  lies about Griffiths   37
  sacked from police   38
Barry, Sir Redmond   20, 133
Barry Street, Carlton   27
Bateman, Detective Henry   242
Baths corner   136
Bayley, Constable William   120
Beaumont, Madame Diane de   99
Beck, E.B.
  tobacconist   197
Beck, W.J.
  'anarchist & chemical mechanic'
    218
Beechworth   48, 89, 103, 105,
    186
Bell, Alexander Graeme   157
Bell, Fanny
  prostitute   69

Belvoir   48
Benalla   88, 89, 103, 151
Bendigo
   see: Sandhurst   31
Berliner, Otto   25, 26, 115, 124,
      137, 221
   adverse comments by Nicolson   26
   at royal commission   154
   death 1894 aged 58,   220
   joined detective force 1859,   25
   left force   26
   opens private detective office   26
   reprimanded by Standish   26
Berry Government   151
Bishop, A.H.J.
   forger   143
Bitten, Ned   147
'Black Albert'   178
Black, Detective   32, 135
Black Johnson   47
Blairs Secret   242
'Blueskin'
   publican & crimp   177, 178
Bolger, Constable   180
Bookey, Superintendent Power
      LePoer,   61
   complains to chief
      commissioner   63
   death   114
Borlase, James Skip   242
Boscombe Valley Mystery, The   229,
      232
Bosisto Street, Richmond   179
Bourke Street, Melbourne   13, 69
Bourke, Thomas   66
Bowen, Sir George
   Governor of Victoria   121
Box Hill cemetery   244
Boyd, Constable   122
Brady, Peter   109
Brady, Thomas   109
Brett, Percy   242
Briely
   burglar   29, 227

Bright   48, 103, 106, 197
Brodigan, John   203
Brooks, Harry   72, 75
Brooks, Joseph
   coiner   46, 65, 108
brothels
   Isabella Hartigan's
      lowest in Melbourne   112
   see: Sarah Fraser's   20
   surveillance by Standish   21
Brown, Detective Joe   27, 67, 74,
      80, 122
   gives evidence against Christie
      80
Brown, Tom   162
Brusher, Emily   114
   alias Sayers
      prostitute   112
bubonic plague bacilli   213
Buckingham Street, Richmond
      194
Buncle, Mr
   Carlton resident   28
Burgess, W.H.
   Melbourne Club steward   196
Burke and Wills monument   93
Burke, Robert O'Hara
   policeman   11
Burrumbeet   141
Butchers Arms Hotel, Melbourne
      16
Byrne, Joe
   Kelly's henchman   107
   of Woolshed   104

Callinan, Thomas   155
Cambridge   227
Camperdown   4, 174, 175
Canberra   225
Candler, Curtis
   coroner   20, 21
Cape Otway   2
Carisbrooke   100

Carrol, Thomas
  cabbie   109
Carter, Detective John   68
Carter, P.J.   146
Castieau, J.B. 224
Castieau, Mr
  governor of Pentridge   67
Castlemaine   11, 100, 124, 143
Castro, Thomas
  alias Sir Roger Tichborne   11
Caulfield   99
Cawnpore   220
Cazaly, James   136, 146
Cazaly, John   146
'Cedric' gold mine, Bright   197
Chadwick, Sergeant   109
Changsha (ship)   167
Chapman, G.F.   23
Cheong, Koong   204
Chiltern   103, 109, 111
Chilwell   62
Chinaman Jack   135
Chinese smugglers 167
Chinese protectorate, the   224
Chinese Restriction Act   165
Chinese secret society   204
Chomley, Hussey Malone
  Chief Commissioner of Police
  31, 152, 155, 158, 213, 219
Christen, Detective H.J. 39
Christey, Mr A   174
Christie, Ada
 (daughter)
  born 1880,   157
  died aged 5 years, 1885,   158
Christie, Captain James
 (brother) 14
  Black Watch   41
  died Scotland 1902,   220
Christie, Captain James
 (father) 14
Christie, Emilie
 (wife)
  death aged 28 in 1885,   158

Christie, John Mitchell   27, 41,
  61, 79, 103, 135, 145, 166,
  179, 190, 201
arrival in Australia 1863,   16
at college   14
becomes hotel licensee   150
born Clackmannan, Scotland,
  30 December, 1845,   14
boxing in Gippsland   16
bush training   16
career boxing   15
charity money raiser   148
Customs career:
advancement in customs
 department   159
and the Chinese   166
appointed Detective Inspector
 & Senior Inspector   181
appointed Inspector of Customs
 & Excise 1893,   179
appointed Inspector of
distilleries 1893,   179
appointed Inspector of liquor &
Excise 1893,   179
attacked & stabbed 1910,   222
joins customs department 1884,
  158
retired 1910,   222
royal bodyguard 1901,   218,
died 1927 aged 81,   225
disguises (police & customs)
 axeman   16
 cab driver   180
 Christy minstral   117
 council labourer   179
 criminal   14
 parson   27
 drunken ship's steward   30
 negro minstral   1
 porter   113
 sailor   1
 Salvation Army officer   1,
  179, 190
 ship's steward   201

sundowner   4
surveyor   179
swagman 179, 201
tinker   1, 190
various   1
disinherited   16
friendship with the Duke   229
influenced by Sherlock Holmes
   239
learning rowing   16
learns boxing   15
leaves Gippsland for Melbourne
   16
marries 1877,   150
opens gymnasium in Lt. Collins
   St   145
parallels with Sherlock Holmes
   226
Police career:
  and Mrs Levi Walker   79
  apprehends coiners   47
  arrests Thomas James for rape
    46
  becomes Duke's bodyguard 41
  boxes for the Duke   43
  confirmed as Detective Third-
    class 1868,   17, 27
  conspiring with criminals   155
  complaint against by Berliner
    137
  declines to go to England with
    the Duke   44
  departs force December 1875
    140
  exonerated of charges   88
  first assignment   14
  first rural posting   61
  high arrest rate   33
  joins force 1867,   11, 17
  Mayoral testimonial to his
    service 140
  meets Standish at Melbourne
    club   44
  monetary rewards   77

physical description   14
praised by chief magistrate   94
praised by Supt Barclay   111
promoted to Detective First-
    class 1875,   135
promoted to Detective Second-
    class   29
raids Griffiths the Silk burglar
    36
refutes Secretan's aspertions 143
resigns 17 Nov 1875.   139
to Sydney with the Duke   42
transferred to Beechworth   103
reason for coming to Australia
    16
recognition from acting Prime
    Minister   222
school fights   15
similarities to Sherlock Holmes
    228
style of writing of memoirs   241
success as a sculler   136
Superintendent Sadlier
    disapproves of   158
Christie, John Mitchell
  (son)
    born 1878,   150, 224
City of Adelaide, (steamer)   42
Clarke and Adams   35
Clarke, W.J. (M.L.A.)   141
Cleveland, Miss   43
Clontarf   22
Cockbill, William   99
Cody, Jack   146
Colac   4, 231
Coliseum music hall
    Bourke Street   112
Collins Street
    prostitutes   13
Colonial Bank   99
Connors, Joe   184
Considine, Mounted Constable
    William   105
Contagious Diseases Act (1878),   21

Corio   231
Corryong   103
Costello, P.
 thief   82
Coyle, Harry
 publican   72
 allegations against Christie   79
Coyne, Senior Constable   108
Crilly, Constable   105
Criminal Investigation Branch 155
crimping 176
Croker, W.H.
 lawyer 196,   217
Crooke, Detective James   32, 67
Crown Hotel, (Molloy's)
 Queen Street, Melbourne 122
Cumming, Lieutenant-Colonel
   Sir William   230
Curran, Tom
 boxing teacher   16, 146
Curtis Candler   21
Customs
 as censor   218
Customs Consolidation Act
 draft for Western Australia   176
Cuzco, SS   219

Dalton, Sergeant   98
Daly, Detective Henry 32, 65, 66,
   90, 93, 117
 high arrest rate   33
Dandenong, (steamship)   146, 148
Darling Matilda
 nickname of Prince Alfred   231
Davidson's clothing store   45
Davis, Thomas   141
Daylesford   25, 221
Deakin, Alfred   218
Deasy   6
Delaney, Tom   2, 7, 8, 175, 179
 daughters   3
 house   8
 John (Jack) (brother)   7, 175

last of the moonshine men   9
 Mrs   3, 7
 Pat (brother)   6
Delbridge, Councillor   91
Detective Album, The   242
Detective office   12
Diogenes Club
 Mycroft Holmes's club   234
distillery   191, 194
 hidden in Richmond   180
Dobbin, Samuel
 of Kensington   45
Doherty, Detective Martin   22
Doherty, Henry   123
 bootmaker and criminal   122
Doig, Morris & Co.   107
Donald, (blacktracker)   90
Donaldson's Pier   168
Dooley, Pat   184
Dowden, Detective   121
Doyle, Sir Arthur Conan
 visits Australia 1920-21,   239
Duke and Duchess of Cornwall
 and York   218
 open first parliament house
   1927,   225
Duke of Clarence
 son of Prince Edward   231
 Jack the Ripper suspect   231
Duke of Edinburgh, H.R.H. Prince
   Alfred   14, 19, 41, 218,
   221
 and the 'Psyche'   21
 anti-royalist sentiments against
   43
 arduous schedule   19
 becomes Admiral-of-the-Fleet
   1893,   221
 coarse behaviour   19
 dies of heart disease 1900,   221
 fornicating in New Zealand   42
 marries Grand Duchess Marie
   of Russia   221
 sexual hedonist   20

succeeds to Duchy of Saxe-
Coburg and Gotha 1893,
221
Duke, the
see: Duke of Edinburgh,
H.R.H. Prince Alfred
Duncan, Detective   24, 154
Dunedin   42
Dunne, Joseph
Crown prosecutor   77
Dwyer, Mr
magistrate   220
Dwyer, Nat
shopbreaker   94

Eastern Hill   122
Eastern Market   14
Echuca   148
Eckroyd family   36
Edgar, Captain   123
Edinburgh prison
Governor Christie   220
Edwards, George
alias Brown   75
Edwards, Harry butcher   69
Edwards's, James
boatshed   136
Egan, Susan
prostitute
alias Louey Brown   68
Eldorado   103, 109
Elizabeth Street   29
Davidson's clothing store   45
Empire Family Hotel
Swanston street   150
European Family Hotel
Christie licensee   157
Exchange Hotel   203
Exhibition Street   157
Eye, Ho   204
Falls-bridge   94
Fenians   22
Fenwick Street   193

Fiji (barque)   2, 9, 171
aground off Cape Otway   171
looting of cargo   173
FitzGibbon, E.G.
civic administrator   213
Fitzroy Gardens   43
fizgig   12, 17, 66, 117, 144, 154
Flinders Lane   69
Flinders Lane West,   29
Flinders Street   69
Flood, Constable Ernest   88, 104
Fluff-Ums
tent & sail makers   198
Foley, Larry
boxer   148
Fook, Jimmy Ah   185
arrest of Ned Kelly   108
Fook Shing,
see: Shing   18
Forster, Detective First-class
Charles   115, 119, 152, 155
Fortune, Mary   242
Fox, Dr.   106
Franklin Street   29
Fraser, Sarah   157
Fraser's, Sarah
see: Sarah Fraser's   20
Friar, The
criminal informant   154
Frost, Mr
wife deserter   12

Galatea H.M S.   19, 21, 22, 41,
42, 43
Galatea Hotel
Christie's lodgings   118
Gaunt's the jeweller   114
Gay, Edward T.
indecent pictures on watches
220
Gebauhr, Julius   171
Gee, Wong Ah   166
Geelong   8, 12, 61

Gem ferry   180
General Mercantile Agency and
      Private Inquiry Office
   Otto Berliner's   137, 221
Ghee, Chew   204
Ghee Hin
   Chinese secret society   204
Gibson, Richard   16, 27
   gives Christie reference   17
Gilliano, Mr
   Quiroga's false name   162
Glasshouse Hotel   47
Glenrowan   103, 104, 151
Gli Ugonotti (opera)   221
Gold Diggers Arms Hotel,
      Chilwell   62
Golden Age Hotel, Maryborough
   24
Golden Fleece Hotel, Melbourne
   117
Golden Gate Hotel   168
Goldsmith, Bernard
   alias John Schwartz   189
Goon, Si   187, 188
Gordon, General   236
Government House Romance. A   242
Gow, Ah
   alias Sun Goon   181
Graham, Constable Robert   104
Graham, Margaret   25, 221
Grant, Miss   99
Gray, Dr   213
Green, Esther   32
Greenwood, Thomas   83, 86, 88
Greer, Anice   221
Greer, John James McGregor   221
Greta   88, 104
Griffiths, Thomas
   capture by police   38
   dies in lunatic asylum   38
   family of criminals   35
   the Great Silk robber   34
   transported to Van Diemen's
      Land   34

Griffiths, Thomas, Mrs
   becomes a nurse   38
   disposer of stolen goods   35
Gunn, Annie   104, 108
   Ned Kelly's sister   88
Guthrie SS   166, 169, 171

Hackett, Judge   103
Hall, Thomas burglar
   alias Belzie   28
Halliburton & Co   70
Halliburton warehouse gang   239
Halliday, James   141
Hanging Rock   22
Hanlon, Mary   114
Hannan, Detective Second-class
      28, 30, 240
Hardy, Frank   155
Hare, Superintendent Frank   89,
      151
Harper, Detective   242
Harrington, Detective   74
Hartigan, Detective   28
Hartigan, Isabella (Bella)
   thief   112
Hartney, Detective   97, 118, 124
Harvey, Emma
   publican's wife   107
Harvie, Arthur   66
Hawthorn   65
Hawthorn bridge   192
Haydon, Dr Leonard   213
Hayward, John   91
Hennessy, Marrianne   108
Heppenstein, William   109
Herald, The   114, 220
Heymanson's warehouse   29, 227
Heytesbury Forest   5, 189
Hicken, Abe
   Australian heavyweight boxing
      champion   95, 146, 148
Hill, Superintendent Henry
   of Ballarat   141

Hodges, Mr
  government Chinese interpreter
    185
Hodges, Mr Justice   203
Holden, George
  alias Eyre
    criminal   98
Holmes, Mycroft
  Sherlock's brother   234
Holmes, Sherlock   226
  activities outside the law   232
  debut 1886,   226
  disguises   232
  Victorian England   237
Hopetoun, Lord
  Governor-General of Australia
    letter of sympathy to Christie
      220
Hotham (North Melbourne)   28
Hotham, Governor   224
How, Mary Ah
  de facto wife of Ah Fook   187
Howard Street, North Melbourne
    73
Hudson, Detective John   17, 32
  apprehends coiners   47
  arrests Thomas James for rape
    46
Hughes, William Morris
  acting Prime Minister   222
Humbug Reach   137
Hyndman, Mr
  bank manager   115
Hyndman, William
  customs officer   200, 203

I Zingari
  Christie's rowing club   136
indecent pictures on watches   220
International Exhibition, 1880
    157
Irving, Captain   18
Isaacs, Isaac   218

Islington Street, Collingwood   135

Jack the Ripper   231
Jackson, Henry
  thief   93, 117
James, Captain   18
James, Thomas   46
Jennings, Detective Peter   23, 33,
    99
Jerilderie   151
Jervis Bay   146
"John"
  slang word for Chinese   166
Johnsen, Captain J.B.   195
Johnson, Arthur
  alias Charles Robinson,
    burglar   29
Johnson, Christopher
  smuggler - *alias* Joe Brown *alias*
    Tom Wilson *alias* Copper Johnson
      167, 169, 180, 181
Johnson, Robert
  customs officer   175
Johnston, Senior Constable   183
Johnstone, Henry
  thief   95
Jones, Dick   133
Jordan, William
  accomplice to coiner   109
Joyce, Mr
  of customs   191
Judas criminals
  fizgigs
    informants   12
Jug, Yee
  Chinese seaman   166

Kane, Constable   191
Katlien, Daniel   171
Kee, Ah   204
Kee, Hing   204
Kelly, Edward (Ned) 24, 103, 108

letter from   90
Kelly gang
   (Tom Delaney's)   175
Kelly gang   150
Kelly royal commission   151
Kelly's, Mrs, shanty   104
Kennedy, Detective   22
Kenny's baths   112
Kensington   45
Kew   189
Khartoum   236
Kidney, Detective Thomas   47,
   155
'Kilmany'
   name of Christie's house   223
Kilmartin, Police Inspector   4
King, Harry   83
King River   90
Kingston, Charles   218
Koroit   2
Korumburra   183
Krerouse, Frederick Thomas   226
Kwong, Soon   204
Kyneton   44, 90

Lady Darling (schooner)   121
Lake Wallace   23
Langham, Nat
   London pugilist   15
larrikin pushes (gangs)   15
Laurence Bros, grocers   74
Laurence, Kate   119
Laxton, Richard
   alias Ullet   194
Leader, The   143
'Lee Villa'   190
Lennon, Detective   121, 122
Leong, Ah
   merciful gambler   106
Lestrade, Inspector   227
Lewis, Jack
   alias Black Jack   110
Lin, Ah   106

Little Bourke Street   13, 15, 66
   frequented by criminals   14
   O'Leary's push   15
Little Collins Street
   detective office   11
Little River   48
Lloyd, John
   police informer   89
Lockyer, Sir Richard   224
Lomax, Detective Alfred   67, 121
London Hotel   180
Long, Benjamin   72, 75, 82, 83
Longlass, old Charley
   cabdriver   192
Lonsdale Street   95
Loong, Sun Goon   204
Lord Newry   20
Lorrie, (Annie)   62
Love, Billy   89
Love, James   7, 8
Lowry, Billy   89
Lucknow   220
Lusitania SS   159
Lynch, Mickey   82
Lyons, Sergeant   186
Lyster, William   124

Macarthur   213
Mace, Jem   148, 149
   English champion boxer   15
Mackay, Detective Patrick   66, 81,
   85, 93, 120
Madeline Street, Carlton   28, 38,
   65
Man, Hing   204
Manchester Martyrs   22
Mannix, John
   receiver   65
Man's Hotel, La Trobe Street   189
Mansfield   103
Manwaring, Detective William
   Henry   33, 47, 97, 135, 220
   blames Nicolson   37

bungles search warrant   36
detective   11, 18
dies 1905 aged 80,   220
evidence against Secretan   33
expenses claim   48
made resident clerk   108
reprimanded   38
retrenched from force   153
Marshall, Detective James   32,
      81, 85
Maryborough   24, 100
McBean, Robert
   squatter   104
McCormick, Mr G.J.
   police magistrate   8
McCullough, Sir James
   Chief Secretary   89
McEwan, Henry
   alias Hugh Connor *alias* Denis
      Fogarty   76
McKellar, Mr & Mrs
   publicans, Glasshouse Hotel
      201
McKenzie, Fidler
   quarry worker   9
McLean, Councillor   91
Me, Young   190
Melbourne Club   14, 20, 41, 43,
      150, 156, 196
Melbourne Regatta   136, 146
Menmuir SS   168
Meredith, George   124
Milverton, Charles Augustus   232
Minty
   informer   203
missing persons   23
Moke, Ah   166
Molesworth, Mr Justice   98, 114
Molloy's Crown Hotel
   Queen Street, Melbourne   122
Monckton, Sergeant   169
Monsieur Dupont
 Paul de Koch   217
Montford, Sergeant   88

Moonlight Head   2, 174
Moonshiners   1, 2, 8, 10
Moore, Anne   45
Moore, Detective   32
Moore, John   66
Moore, Mrs
   boarding house   118
Moore, Thomas   79, 84
Morgan, Mad Dog   11
Moriarty, Professor James   238
Morning Star Hotel, Melbourne
      15, 117
Morris Doig & Co.   107
Mortlake   188
'Mountain Dew' (whisky)   2
Mourdant, Sir Charles   230
Murray, Detective Louis   67
Murray River   91, 105, 185
Musgrove, Mr.
   Collector of Customs   159, 162
Myrtleford   48

naked women on black velvet
      chairs   20
Nat Langham,   15
National Hotel, Geelong   61
Nelan, Thomas
   customs officer   203
New Caledonia   120
New Hebrides   121
New Zealand   70
Nichol, Captain   177
Nicholson Street   97
Nicolson, Superintendent Charles
      Hope   17, 18, 33, 37, 80,
      86, 89, 95, 100, 124, 137,
      213
   and Otto Berliner   25
   appointed acting chief
   commissioner of police   151
   Inspecting Superintendent   213
   magistrate   204
   moves to Kyneton   44

Night Fossickers of Moonlight Flat,
   The   242
Nirranda   1, 2, 6, 10, 175, 179
Nixon, Detective   154
North Brighton   189
North Melbourne   29
Northcote Road, Armadale
   Christie's address   223
Noumea   120
nursery of crime   155

O'Brien, Frank   121
O'Callaghan, Detective Tom   8,
      22, 67, 100, 121, 154
   becomes Chief Commissioner
      of Police 1902,   155, 224
   died 1931,   224
   reduced in rank   100
   reprimanded   155
   retired 1913,   224
O'Farrell, Henry James   22
O'Ferrall, Hugh James Vincent
   public servant & embezzler 119
O'Grady, Michael   65
O'Leary, Detective   31
O'Leary's push   15
On, Te
   Chinese storekeeper   105
O'Neil, James
   alias Jack the Bushranger 113
   sentenced to 3 years gaol   114
opening first federal parliament
      218
Ophir, royal yacht   219
Orient line   160
Oroya SS   160, 219
O'Sullivan, Rev John   95
Otis engineering works
   South Melbourne   198
Otway, Cape
   light   171
Ovens police district   103
Oxford   227

Paddington Hotel
   Little Collins St   122
Palmer, Inspector   67, 77
Panton, Joseph 202
   died 1913 aged 82,   224
   magistrate   88
   senior magistrate   213
Parker, Detective   91
Peechelba   11
Pentridge   24, 66, 67, 89, 90
Peregrine SS   189
Phar Lap
   champion racehorse   179
Phillips, Mr
   Bourke St pawnbroker   124
Phos (Norwegian freighter)   195
Pigdon, John   117
Pohlman, Judge   77
Point Nepean Road   190
Police Gazette   95
Police Reward Fund   17, 65
'Port Wine Mary Anne'
   a crimp   177
Port Campbell   172
Port Fairy   214
Port Melbourne
   see: Sandridge   19
Portland   22
Potts, Detective   18
Power, Harry   24, 47, 88
   his apprentice, E.Kelly   24
Power Without Glory   155
Prevot's, Ted
   Yarrawonga Hotel   186
Price, John
   penal superintendent   11
Prince Alfred, H.R.H.
   see: Duke of Edinburgh
Prince of Wales Hotel
   Williamstown   113
Prince of Wales, Price Edward
   brother of Duke of Edinburgh,
      Prince Alfred   230
   alleged adultery   231

Princes Bridge   136
Princess Theatre, Melbourne   146
Princetown   174
'Pro Rege'   244
prostitutes
    grading by detectives   13
    in Collins Street   13
    legal status   21
    low priced 157
    Theatre Royal   13
    Coliseum music hall   112
    removal from Stephen Street
        157
protected game birds   197
'Psyche', The
    Duke's prostitute   21
Public Record Office   243
Public Service Board   203
Puk, Chin   166
Punch   223, 237, 241
    publishes tribute to Christie 223
Punken, John   172

Queen Street   85
Queen Victoria   231, 236
Quinn, Constable Michael   175
Quinton, Detective Richard 36, 37
Quiroga, Buenaventura   159, 231

Red Bluff, Sandringham   149
Red Waterhole   2, 4, 5
Regatta
    see Melbourne Regatta   136
Renown (ship)   177
Reoch, Hugh
    Christie's uncle   16
        drowns in Tara River   16
        invalid will   16
Rivernook   174
Robertson, George
    bookseller   217
Robinson, Christina

    alias Mrs Lem Ken   186
Robinson the tobacconist
    Spencer Street   180
Robinson, William
    receiver   94
Rokeby Street, Collingwood.   47
Romsey   141
Rourke, David
    former detective   152, 155
Royal Commission findings into
        detective force   155
Royal visit, 1867,   19
Russell Street   69, 157
    a centre of trouble   15
Ryall, Ted, Inspector   33, 44, 66
Ryan. Sergeant   190

saddling paddock
    see: Theatre Royal   13
Sadleir, Superintendent John
        158, 213
St Bartholemew's Hospital,
        London   227
St Francis's Church   23
St Kilda Road   93
Sallars, Harry   149
Saltwater River   146
Sandfly HMS   121
Sandhurst (Bendigo)   31, 124
Sandhurst Hotel, (Queen Street)
        72, 79, 85, 88
Sandridge (Port Melbourne)
        19, 36, 41
Sarah Fraser
    known as 'Mother Fraser'   21
Sarah Fraser's (brothel)
    Duke visits   41
    prostitutes   21
    Stephen Street   20
    'under royal patronage'   21
Scandal in Bohemia, A   234
Scanlon, Mounted Constable   104
Schiller SS (ship)   139

Scotland Yard   227
Scott, David
    jeweller & fence   97, 226
Scott, J.D.
    police resident clerk
        died 1868,   27
Scott, Tommy,
    criminal   79, 82
Seaforth House
    Christie's lodgings   29
Sebastopol   103, 105
    Chinese at   106
Secretan, Frederick   27, 65, 82,
        85, 95, 115, 124, 135, 136
    confirmed as resident clerk   44
    detective's war against   32
    from Dunolly   27
    Inspector   70, 120, 136, 152
    Nicolson's protege   27
    on Christie's resignation   140
    promotion queried   124
    supplementary report from   123
    report to Chief Secretary   142
    'shanghai-ing'   176
Shannon, Jimmy   178
Sharp, Elizabeth
    prostitute   69
Sharp, John
    burglar   145, 231
Shing, Ah
    chinese informer   107, 204
Shing, Fook   238
    Chinese detective   18
Shing, Sim Kwong   204
Silk Robberies   23, 34
Sim, Chung   108
Sing, Tue
    Chinese seaman   166
Singapore   121
Sir Henry Barkly Hotel, Richmond
    Christie licensee   157
Smallman, Mr
    Police Magistrate   185
Smart, Archibald

Customs senior landing surveyor
    198, 202
Smart, Billy   82
Smith, Inspector Brooke   106
Smith, Robert   46
Smith, William
    alias Smart
    burglar   97, 226
Smithers, George
    alias Liberty Collins
    burglar   29
Smithson, James
    market gardener   190
Snowden, Mounted Constable
    2, 4
Snowy Creek   103
Solomon, A.D.   197
Soudry, Louis   221
South Melbourne court   167
Spanns the jewellers   97
Spring Creek   31
Spring Street, Melbourne   13
Stacey, Meg   114
    alias McDonald
    prostitute   112
Standish, Captain Frederick
    Chief Commissioner of Police
        17, 18, 22, 41, 61, 80,
        86, 99, 136, 141, 150
    and David Young case   25
    and Detective Hudson   32
    and Otto Berliner   25
    annual salary   20
    approves rewards   46
    as fight referee   150
    at Sarah Fraser's brothel   20
    close friends with Duke   41
    correspondence to Super-
        intendent Bookey   64
    death in 1883,   156
    demotes Christie   87
    dismisses charge against
        Secretan   34
    escorts Prince Alfred to

Government House   41
ex Royal Artillery   20
going strange   151
guidelines for fights   44
instigates inquiry into Christie
     80, 88
leading Freemason   156
Lomax & O'Callaghan affair 67
meets Christie at Melbourne
     Club   44
opposed to Christie's sports 136
personal attributes 34
recommends reward for
     Christie   107
refuses wake for Mrs Carter   68
sacked as commissioner 151
sexual hedonist   20
special report to Chief Secre-
     tary   123
tries to defend police actions
     123
trying to catch O'Ferrall   11
Stanley Street, West Melbourne 34
Star and Garter Hotel, South
     Melbourne   67
Star of the East Hotel, Melbourne
     117
Star Hotel, The, Beechworth   104
Station Pier   168
Stawell   22
Stephen Street   20, 97, 113, 157
  becomes Exhibition Street   15,
     157
Stettin, Poland
  now known as Szczecin   196
Stewart, Mr
  solicitor   186
Stills (illicit)   4
  Long Wilson's   3
  Nirranda   1
stomach in a bag
  Ah Suey's   106
Stout, W   146
Strahan, Constable Arthur

Eldorado   109
Stringers Creek (now Walhalla)
     16, 112
Stringybark Creek   103, 150
Studley Park Road   193
Study in Scarlet, A   226, 238
Sturt, Mr Evelyn
  chief magistrate   88, 94, 150
Suey, Ah
  attempted suicide   105
Supreme Court Hotel, Castlemaine
     100
Swamp, the (West Melbourne)   69
Swan Hill   141
Szczecin
  see: Stettin   196

Tanmure   5
Tanswell Hotel, Beechworth   104
Tara River   16
Telegraph, The   140
Terang   2
Terang Express   188
Theatre Royal   41, 83, 97, 122
  prostitutes rendezvous   13
  saddling paddock   13
Thistle Hotel, Geelong   63
Tholburn, Mrs Thomas   188
Tholburn, Thomas   188
Thomas Evans, burglar
  alias Tommy the Dancer   28
Thomas, John 75
  alias Young *alias* Jack theLagger
Thompson, Jack   147, 149, 150
  boxer   95
Thompson, Joe   147
Thrift, John   186
Tichborne, Sir Roger
  see: Castro
Tomlinson, Charles   189
Tommy the Dancer   240
Toohey, Sergeant Jeremiah 61
Toorak

former location of Government
House 41
Town Pier 168
Tsinan SS 168, 170, 181
Tum-Tum
Prince Edward's nickname 231
Turner, James 45
Turner, Sir George
Premier of Victoria 218
Turner, William
shopbreaker 94
Tyrrell, Police Inspector 4

Ullett, Ann 193
Ullett, Richard 193
Upper Buckley 108

Van Diemen's Land 18, 34, 35
crippling virus therefrom 13
Varieties, The 69
Venus
statue 43
Vickers, Captain 172
Victoria Dock 222
Victoria Street 74, 133
Victorian Rowing Association 146
Violet Town 103
Volunteer Arms Hotel 73
von Sanden, Baron
swindler 138
'W.W.'
pen name of Mary Fortune 242
Waddle, Elizabeth
alias Wilson 76
Wahgunya 103
Walhalla
see: Stringers Creek
Walker, Detective 70
Walker, Levi,
criminal 79, 81, 86
Walker, Mrs Levi 88, 234
Walker, Thomas 18

Wallace, Eliza 135
Wallace, John B.
alias Chinaman Jack 118, 135
Wallace, Lake 23
Wangaratta 103
War Cry, The 1, 179, 190
Ward, Constable Michael 104
Warrnambool 1, 2, 9, 174, 214
Warrnambool Standard 175
Watson, Dr John H. 227
Watt, John
Wooragee publican 109
Weekes, Elizabeth 45
Weenan, Harry 198, 235
evasion of customs duty 202
sent to gaol 203
Weenen Conspiracy, The 197
Weston, Frank 117
Whightman, Arthur J. 200, 203
White, Detective 32
Whittlesea 46
Whroo 103
Wilcannia (steamer) 217
Wilkinson, Arthur 172
Williams, Detective 115
Williams, George,
bank clerk 83
Williams, John 45
Williams, William
burglar 97, 226
Williamstown 11, 36, 113, 180
Wilson, Captain 68
Wilson, George 100
Wilson, John 148
circus proprietor & entrepeneur
Wilson, Long 3, 188
Windsor Castle 231
Wodonga 103
Wollaston, Dr Harry 159, 176,
191, 202, 204, 213, 218
Comptroller of Customs 159
joins customs 1863. 159
dies 1921. 224
Wombat Ranges 150

women searchers
  of smugglers   170
Woodend   22
Woods, Tommy   83
Woolshed   104, 107
Wooragee Outrage   109
Wooragee post office   110
worm   3, 4, 189, 193, 194
Wright's, Charley
  Coliseum music hall   112

Yackandandah   48, 103, 111
Yarra River   69
Yarrawonga   105, 185
Yarrawonga Hotel   186
Yorke, Eliot   41
  Duke's equery   42
  equerry to Prince Albert   20

You, Fung   187
You, Koon   204
Young, David   25
Young, Jimmy
  Chinese interpreter   186
Yung, Hung
  Chinese storekeeper   105

'Zala'
  scratched on door   112
Zala, Pietro   111
Zavistowski
  the three sisters   96, 226
Zingari
  see: I Zingari